The Saint Who Would Be
Santa Claus

The Saint Who Would Be Santa Claus

The True Life and Trials of Nicholas of Myra

Adam C. English

BAYLOR UNIVERSITY PRESS

Cover Design by Nicole Weaver, Zeal Design
Cover image courtesy of the St. Nicholas Center,
        www.stnicholascenter.org
Book Design by Diane Smith

Library of Congress Cataloging-in-Publication Data

English, Adam C., 1974–
    The saint who would be Santa Claus : the true life and trials of Nicholas of Myra / Adam C. English.
      242 p. cm.
    Includes bibliographical references (p. 225) and index.
    ISBN 978-1-60258-634-5 (hardcover : alk. paper)
    1. Nicholas, Saint, Bp. of Myra. 2. Santa Claus. I. Title.
    BR1720.N46E54 2012
    270.2092—dc23
    [B]
                                2012003693

Printed in the United States of America on acid-free paper with a minimum of 30% pcw recycled content.

To my siblings, Christine and David,
with whom I share so many Christmas memories

Contents

List of Illustrations

Acknowledgments

Some things can be written in solitude with little more than access to a good library. This is not one of those things. I am deeply indebted to many wonderful individuals who believed in this project and helped it see the light of day: Gerardo Cioffari for providing a place to start; Carol Myers for sharing her time and her photographs; Albert Zuurveld, The National Gallery, London, and Leo S. Olschki Publishers for the use of images; the administration of Campbell University, in particular Dwaine Greene, Mike Cogdill, Andy Wakefield, and Glenn Jonas, for funding my travel and granting a sabbatical leave to finish the writing; my colleagues in the Department of Religion and the Divinity School for their endless support; Brian Thomas for his companionship and tutelage in Latin; Campbell's interlibrary loan office for tracking down exotic sources; the Centro Studi Nicolaiani for its resources; the vigilant Carey Newman and the staff at Baylor University Press for their thorough work; Kelly Hughes for publicity; Donna Waldron for sending me to Italy; Dylan Priddy for his office assistance; Michael Smith, Gary Deddo, Jonathon Lee, and my dad, W. D. English, for reading and shaping early versions of the work—Jonathon Lee deserves special recognition for also helping me with the index; my mom for her encouragement;

xi

Acknowledgments

and of course my family, Charissa and Cassidy, who suffered through my writing frenzies. There are many other friends who helped and encouraged me along the way, and I am grateful to them all.

The feast of St. Nicholas, MMXI

Finding St. Nicholas

The image of Santa Claus appears on dolls, cookie cutters, ornaments, stamps, stickers, and T-shirts that read, "Beware of fat men bearing gifts." Coffee mugs feature the big man cruising in a hot rod, and neckties depict him relaxing in a Hawaiian shirt and sunglasses. He can be embroidered, printed, or pasted onto magnets, aprons, tote bags, lawn chairs, swim-rings, door mats, light switches, plates, napkins, pencil erasers, Pez dispensers, night lights, kick balls, piñatas, and toothbrushes. The more refined consumer might look for old-world Santas in cracked-patina oil paintings, ornately decorated figurines, or delicate Christmas ornaments. The tiny roadside town of Santa Claus, Indiana, has staked its fortunes on selling images of the man in fire-engine red—from novelty gifts to glassware, from museum displays to a Christmas theme park, the town has it all. A special post office located next to the museum receives bundles of letters each year addressed to "Santa Claus," and volunteers work like North Pole elves answering each one. The city of Toronto, Ontario, hosts the world's oldest children's parade in honor of Santa every November. The parade involves more than 1,500 volunteers and draws half a million viewers. And each year, the Macy's Thanksgiving Day Parade culminates with the arrival of Santa Claus driving a sleigh full of toys through the spectator-thronged streets of Manhattan.

Few characters have been represented more often in movies or TV shows than Santa, who has been portrayed by Ed Asner, Leslie Nielsen, Paul Giamatti, and Tim Allen, to name but a few. The bringer of holiday cheer and gifts for boys and girls, Santa is adored by all and hated by none. He evokes good memories and nostalgic longings, childhood dreams and the sweet wish for something magical. Susan, from the 1947 film *Miracle on 34th Street*, declares, "I believe . . . I believe . . . it's silly but I believe."

Most people know that the beloved patron of Christmastime wish-granting has his origins in a vaguely historical personage. But fantasy and historical fact blur rapidly as soon as attempts are made to give the mythical/historical figure a name: Kriss Kringle, Sinterklaas, Santa Claus, Père Noël, Noel Baba, Father Christmas, Pelznichol, Nicolò, Nick, Nicola di Bari, Nicolaus thaumatourgos, and the myroblyte. The barrage of names points to a plurality of personas that makes it difficult to discover the identity of this quicksilver character or whether he did all, some, or none of the feats attributed to him. Although centuries of legends and pop-culture images can obscure the truth about things, historical evidence points to St. Nicholas of Myra as the man who would become Santa Claus. And uncovering the saint behind the myth will provide answers relevant to church history, the traditions of Christmas, and the heritage of Western civilization. The quest of this book is to find the historical man tucked behind the shadow of Santa Claus.

When a tiled mosaic icon of St. Nicholas was dredged up in the early sixteenth century from the Aegean Sea by fishermen near the Greek monastery of Stavronikita located on Mount Athos, metallic-shelled mussels were found clamped to it, covering the saint's forehead and halo. When the mussels were peeled back, some of the mosaic tiles popped off, and legend has it that the icon bled from the forehead during the procedure.[1] Reconstructing the life of Nicholas is like trying to clean that icon; it involves more than just locating the right historical documents and spiffing them up a bit. The barnacles of legend, myth, and exaggeration that have cemented themselves to the historical facts must be pried away. And yet, it should be kept in mind that the folkloric barnacles cannot be detached without permanently scarring—or even losing—the person. They are too tightly joined.

The history of Nicholas presents a tantalizing riddle. There is no early documentation of the man—no writings, disciples, or major acts. Then, curiously, story fragments and rumors begin to surface like driftwood in the water. A church is built in his honor at Constantinople, and suddenly he becomes an international symbol of holiday cheer and goodwill, an absolutely essential part of the Christmas tradition. It will take extra care and caution to reconstruct the most plausible account of his life.

The Bones Within

Luigi Martino could not have known what he would see on that day in May 1953 when he peered into the open crypt, which reportedly contained the bones of the *real* Santa Claus, St. Nicholas of Myra. Since 1087, when they had been removed by force from Myra, a town on the southern coast of Turkey known today as Demre, the bones of Nicholas had rested undisturbed here in Bari, a seaside city on the southeastern coast of Italy. They were interred inside a sarcophagus constructed of huge blocks of reinforced concrete for safekeeping. Then, some three hundred years after the bones had been brought to Bari, a Serbian tsar named Uros II Milutin donated a large quantity of silver that was molded to cover and decorate the rather plain and somber tomb. In a four-year renovation process beginning in 1953, Milutin's silver covering was removed in order to restore the original, gray, Romanesque design of the tomb. The Vatican made a special request to examine the bones of the saint during the restoration. Enter Luigi Martino, anatomy professor from the University of Bari.

Just an hour before midnight on May 5, 1953, with bands of visitors and pilgrims keeping candlelit vigil outside the Basilica di San Nicola, Martino, the Archbishop of Bari, and members of a specially appointed pontifical commission descended the granite steps leading into the underground, lamp-lit crypt. The contents of the tomb were more than a matter of historical reckoning—they were a matter of civic pride and religious devotion. In just four days, Bari would host its largest and most important annual celebration, La Festa di Bari, to commemorate the relocation of the bones to Bari. There would be parades and parties and pilgrims from Russia, Greece, France, and England.

Martino must have wondered what would happen if he did not have good news to report. When the heavy slab capping the tomb was lifted, he found to his relief human bone remains. A skull had been carefully placed at one end by Pope Urban II himself, instigator of the First Crusade, when he consecrated the tomb just two years after it arrived in Bari. The rest of the bones were scattered about the rectangular enclosure in no particular order and submerged in "a clear liquid, like water from a rock."[2] Pilgrims referred to this liquid as the manna or myrrh of Nicholas; once a year Dominican priests bent low to a small opening in the sarcophagus to collect the liquid in a vial. Martino took thousands of detailed measurements and x-ray photographs. Some sketches were made of the measurements of the skull and frame. But an authentic reconstruction of Nicholas would only come 50 years later, as advancements led to technology far more sophisticated than what was available to Martino.

By 2004 the imaging technology was ready. Caroline Wilkinson, a facial anthropologist with the University of Manchester, England, used the measurements taken by Martino in the 1950s and some luminous sound probes of the tomb to generate a three-dimensional digital reconstruction of St.

4

Nicholas' face and head for a one-hour BBC documentary. His skin was given an olive complexion, reflecting his Mediterranean ancestry; his hair and beard were colored white, signifying the fact that the bones in the tomb belonged to an elderly man, well over the age of sixty. Approximately five feet ten inches in height, his most distinguishing features were his heavy-set jaw and a broken nose. Wilkinson comments, "It must have been a very hefty blow because it's the nasal bones between the eyes that are broken."[3] In the media coverage of the story, this detail quickly became the most tantalizing tidbit.[4] How did it happen? Wilkinson shrugs her shoulders and conjectures, "I heard he once punched a bishop,"[5] referring to a legendary altercation between St. Nicholas and Arius, an infamous heretic, at the Council of Nicaea in 325. Others speculated about a hitherto unknown rough and rowdy past or an incident that might have occurred when he was arrested during the great persecution of Christianity in 303. No conclusions can be reached with absolute historical certainty. What is more, Martino had earlier reported that nearly all the bones were chipped or broken, reflecting the fact that they were hastily gathered by sailors and roughly transported from the southern coast of Turkey to the port of Bari in 1087. The break in the nasal ridge might be similarly explained.

But the bones present other clues about the man. From his study, Martino observes that Nicholas probably suffered from chronic arthritis and perhaps pronounced cephalic pain, evidenced by an unnatural thickening of the inside of the skull bone. Of course, it must be remembered that he died at an old age, so it is unknown whether the arthritis and head pressure were natural ailments of an elderly man or untimely pains that he carried in his body for years.

The Image of an Icon

The most pervasive cultural image of Santa Claus today has nothing to do with the digital reconstruction of the bones in the Bari tomb but originated with a landmark ad campaign by Coca-Cola. In an effort to boost winter sales, attract younger consumers, and improve its image after attacks from the Women's Christian Temperance Union, the Coca-Cola Company in the early twentieth century hired artist Haddon Sundblom to paint the big man into its advertisements. From 1931 to 1964, Sundblom produced warm and richly colored Christmas scenes featuring a larger-than-life Santa posing cheerfully in various locations, always with a bottle of Coke. Thirty years of nostalgic, Norman Rockwellesque paintings plastered on billboards and in magazines fixed the modern image of the saint.[6] The wide beard of white, the knobby nose, the wind-chapped cheeks, the bright eyes and grandfatherly smile, and of course, the red fur suit with white trim and black belt—this is Sundblom's Santa. Every movie or television or commercial depiction since is based in some degree on Sundblom's vision.

There is little connection between Sundblom's artwork and the oldest visual image available of St. Nicholas of Myra, which can be dated to between the mid-600s and the mid-700s.[7] That image is included on a panel painting divided into four rectangular boxes (fig. 1). In the top two boxes stand St. Paul and St. Peter; in the bottom two are St. Nicholas and St. John Chrysostom. It is noteworthy that Nicholas shares space with such highly honored men and testifies to the status accorded him when the panel was created. Painted by monastic artists in either Egypt or Palestine, the icon presents a full-length view of Nicholas. His beard is long and white, complementing his full head of white hair. Unlike those of Paul and John Chrysostom, Nicholas' beard is not neatly trimmed but slightly unkempt and bushy; unlike St. Peter's curly beard, Nicholas' is straight. Circling Nicholas' head is a bright and prominent halo. His eyes are wide and fixed on the viewer, and he wears Byzantine-style priestly robes of crimson and gold. Lobate crosses can be seen on his omophorion, the traditional vestment draped around his shoulders and neck that symbolizes the lost sheep carried by the good shepherd in Jesus' parable (Luke 15:3-7).

His right hand is raised in blessing, and a sacred book is positioned in his left.

FIGURE 1
Icon from the Monastery of St. Catherine, Mount Sinai, Egypt.
Image courtesy of Leo S. Olschki Publishers.

This icon resides in the historic Monastery of St. Catherine at Mount Sinai, present-day Egypt.[8] Its very existence is of special importance because Byzantine icons and religious art of antiquity suffered two cruel fates: first, the iconoclast movement of the eighth and ninth century eliminated most of the artwork, statues, and decorative pieces in churches, homes, and monasteries; and then, Western crusaders savagely laid waste to Constantinople and destroyed many of the remaining pieces in the Fourth Crusade of 1204.[9] Fortunately, the Monastery of St. Catherine, situated in the wastelands of Egypt, stood out of reach of both fates. And, by a special donation of protection, it was spared from mistreatment and plunder by Arabs, whose armies seized the area in the seventh century. In this uniquely preserved image of St. Nicholas, we catch a very early glimpse of the man. His strong eyes speak of fearless resolve and confident authority. His long white beard shows wisdom, maturity, and gentleness. His hand of blessing represents his pastoral concern, and the Gospel book signifies his Christian orthodoxy. His priestly garb reminds us that he was a man of ministry, devoted to the worship of God and the care of God's flock.

The contemporary picture of Santa Claus, however, is largely the byproduct of commercialization and advertisement. It is tied to the history of Coca-Cola, Hollywood's movie industry, Walmart's sales, shopping mall photo-ops, and the Internet. Of course, this Santa Claus image also tells an important story of American holiday culture, drawing on John Pintard's Dutch dream of the New York Historical Society, Washington Irving's *Knickerbocker's History of New York*, the enchanted scenery of "A Visit from St. Nicholas" ("T'was the Night Before Christmas"), the wily drawings and wood carvings of Thomas Nast, and the comical imagination of James K. Paulding. That image pulls from old and new alike, from old-world customs such as filling shoes and stockings with gifts to modern family traditions of watching animated Christmas specials on TV. Although all of these images are worth having, they do not get us any closer to the historical reality of Nicholas and shed no light on the fourth-century bishop who lived on the southern coast of what is now Turkey.

Interestingly, this subject has piqued the curiosity of more and more people in recent years. An uptick in the number of recent books and resources about the "real" St. Nicholas indicates a growing fascination with the topic. Titles include *The Real Santa Claus: Legends of Saint Nicholas* and *The Real St. Nicholas: Tales of Generosity and Hope from Around the World*.[10] A recent VeggieTales animated DVD for children includes silly songs and antics not about Santa Claus but about his predecessor, Saint Nicholas (*Saint Nicholas: A Story of Joyful Giving*, 2009).

Unfortunately, most popular offerings on the subject of Nicholas are frustratingly uninformative. Many books have the appearance of historical work but offer little substance. They tell wonderful stories, but in the process repeat errors that are at least a thousand years old. Two examples of such problematic accounts are Joe Wheeler's 2010 *Saint Nicholas* (Nashville: Nelson) and William J. Bennett's 2009 *The True Saint Nicholas: Why He Matters to Christmas* (New York: Howard Books). Wheeler is a gifted scholar and Nicholas devotee; Bennett is the former U.S. Secretary of Education and celebrated author of *The Book of Virtues*. Both enrich the holiday season with heartwarming tales and fascinating nuggets of trivia. But neither presents the best historical scholarship regarding the person of Nicholas. Instead, they weave together anecdotes—some factual and some fictitious—from a potpourri of sources lifted out of any and every era.

Most significantly, Wheeler and Bennett confuse the story of St. Nicholas of Myra with the story of another historical Nicholas. The mix-up dates back to the tenth century when Symeon Metaphrastes (c. 912–c. 982/7) made an ill-fated decision while compiling stores about the saints. He noticed two men in the historical record with the name of St. Nicholas: St. Nicholas of Myra, who died around 335, and St. Nicholas of Sion, who died in 564. Although they had lived near each other geographically, they were separated by two hundred years in time. Even so, Symeon must have reckoned that one grand story would be more edifying than two miniature ones. Or, more charitably, maybe he was unsure how to keep the two lives separate. Perhaps he did not recognize that they *were* different lives after all. The confusion of the two individuals must have been hard to avoid: modern archaeologists have found markers dedicating sites to *osios* Nicholas and *hagios* Nicholas. Both Greek words (*osios* and *hagios*) can be translated as "saint," but, in ancient times a subtle distinction was made between *osios*, which was used to describe ascetic and monastic saints like Nicholas of Sion, and *hagios*, used to describe martyrs, confessors, and churchmen like Nicholas of Myra.[11] A monastic saint was *osios*, and a priestly saint was *hagios*. Surely not everyone who told and retold the tales of *osios* Nicholas and *hagios* Nicholas knew or observed those fine-toothed distinctions. Nor have scholars been able to do so until very recently. In the early 1980s, Ihor Ševčenko and Nancy Patterson Ševčenko performed the valuable task of reproducing and translating into English the one complete Greek copy of the *Life of St. Nicholas of Sion*, indisputably demonstrating that it is a completely different story from a different time.[12] Not only have they made available a fascinating *Life* from late antiquity, they have shown that Nicholas of Sion is a distinct person from Nicholas of Myra. Symeon Metaphrastes either did not know or did not heed the important distinction between the two homonymous individuals. In consequence, he merged the two accounts and transmitted them as if they were one.[13] The product, of course, was not a true Nicholas but a new Nicholas, a third Nicholas that was little more than an amalgamation of biographies. Unfortunately, Symeon's error stuck, and subsequent biographers like Wheeler and Bennett have simply repeated it. The result is that the true history of Nicholas of Myra remains muddled.

New Evidence

The initial task in revealing the saint behind Santa Claus is to demonstrate that such a person actually existed. If there is no confidence in his existence, then it is pointless to discuss his deeds. The historicity St. Nicholas of Myra has been questioned by various persons in various degrees over the years. In recent times, it is not just children come-of-age who have doubted the Santa Claus myths, but two of the most important Nicholas scholars of the twentieth century: Gustav Anrich, the early-century German who compiled all the early Greek texts related to the saint, and Charles W. Jones, an esteemed Berkeley professor of antiquity. Anrich believes that, given the evidence, a definitive verdict on the historicity of St. Nicholas is not possible.[14] Jones expresses skepticism about every major "fact" of Nicholas' life, including his name, his deeds, and his death date.[15] Added to these indictments is the silence of Peter Brown, the preeminent authority on early Christian saints, who avoids a single mention of Nicholas of Myra in any of his major texts involving saints.[16]

Nicholas did not leave sheaves of letters, volumes of theology, collections of poetry, or codices of sermons for posterity's sake. His virtues were not touted by any famous theologian or churchman, as were those of St. Antony by Athanasius.[17] He played no major role in imperial politics, the rise of Constantine, or the shape of the institutional church in the fourth century. His name appears in some, but not all, of the lists of those that attended the Council of Nicaea in the year 325. Even if he were present, it is not clear that he contributed anything of importance to the proceedings. Most troubling, no contemporary witness testified to Nicholas' existence or deeds in the historical record. Not one of Nicholas' fellow bishops mentions him by name in any of their letters or writings, and no contemporary chronicler referenced him in the histories. The sprawling nineteen-volume *New Catholic Encyclopedia*, a product of mid-twentieth-century scholarship, claims, "No historically trustworthy evidence of his ancestry or the events of his life exists, except for the fact of his episcopate."[18] The encyclopedia groups the events of Nicholas' life, from his birth and attendance at the Council of Nicaea to his death, under the heading of "legend." Because of the lack of any substantive evidence, the 1969 edition of the Roman Catholic calendar of saints demoted St. Nicholas Feast Day, December 6, which had been a red-letter day for more than a thousand years, to the status of optional. The German scholar Walter Nigg, in his 1946 study of *Great Saints,* makes no mention of Nicholas.[19] *The Oxford Dictionary of Saints* likewise dismisses the historical existence of the man, saying simply that "Nicholas' life, although he was one of the most universally venerated saints in both East and West, is virtually unknown."[20] More recently, Tel Aviv scholar Aviad Kleinberg makes only three passing references to St. Nicholas in his *Flesh Made Word: Saints' Stories and the Western Imagination,*[21] and Thomas Craughwell's 2011 encyclopedia of relics gives little credence to the testimonies of the saint: "The stories that have come down to us about Nicholas are almost certainly legends."[22]

Into this gap of knowledge stepped Father Gerardo Cioffari. In defiance of the odds, Father Cioffari has staked his academic reputation on the historical person of Nicholas, and this book could not have existed without Cioffari's life's work. He has done for the historicity of Nicholas what Luigi Martino did for the body. In the same manner that Martino unvaulted and documented the physical bones, Father Cioffari has sifted and arranged and made sense of the boxes of documents and manuscripts collected in the archives of the Basilica di San Nicola. For the past thirty years, this humble Dominican friar has invested his life in the historical person of Nicholas. Throughout most of the twentieth century, an age of historical skepticism and suspicion, the idea of the very existence of a man named Nicholas was often under attack. Even if his existence were granted, scholars dismissed the facts and events of his life as untrustworthy. Undaunted, Father Cioffari returned to the sources and scoured the evidence, assembling previously unknown documents and witnesses to St. Nicholas' existence. He dates Nicholas' life to approximately 260–335 and has presented evidence for many of the deeds associated with the saint. He has also shown with a high degree of probability that Nicholas did in fact attend the Council of Nicaea in 325 as bishop of Myra, something that previous generations of scholars seriously doubted and at times completely denied.[23]

Father Cioffari serves as head curator of the archival library of the Basilica di San Nicola in Bari. Born in 1943, he was ordained a priest in 1970 and is a member of the Dominican order charged by the pope with maintenance of the famous basilica, an assignment they have faithfully kept since 1951. The modest archival library stands adjacent to the basilica, across a piazza and behind a small, unassuming door. Although Father Cioffari is a man of quiet demeanor, when he is talking about Nicholas, he speaks with fervor and passion. Pulling tattered books off tightly packed shelves in the archive library, he generously shares his intellectual discoveries with pilgrims, dignitaries, fellow scholars, and interested schoolchildren.

Early Literary Sources

Until about thirty years ago, the earliest mention of Nicholas that could be dated with precision in the historical record came from the imperial historian Procopius in the year 555.[24] Procopius reported the building of "a shrine to St. Priscus and St. Nicholas" in Constantinople, present-day Istanbul, Turkey.[25] Cioffari has worked to establish sources prior to this mention and has found two strong candidates. The first is the *Encomium* of Proclus, which dates to around the year 440, in which Proclus (c. 390–446) offers a laudatory speech on the many virtues of St. Nicholas. The patriarch of Constantinople, Proclus is known to historians for his many orations on the Virgin Mary and the incarnation of Christ and is counted as one of the major theological participants in the famous controversy between Cyril of Alexandria and Nestorius over the divine and human natures of Jesus Christ.[26] Of interest, his *Encomium* clearly draws its illustrations about Nicholas from an earlier source, a Greek recounting of the life of St. Nicholas.[27] This tantalizing but now-lost text is the second work that can be dated prior to Procopius' reference from 555. Written in the late fourth or early fifth century, the Greek account can be reconstructed from Proclus' *Encomium* as well as other later sources.

In addition to these sources, a number of important sixth-century works refer to Nicholas: first, the list of Nicaea contained in the *Tripartite History* by Theodore the Lector; second, the *Life of Saint Nicholas of Sion*, which mentions St. Nicholas of Myra multiple times; third, the *Refutation* of Eustrathius of Constantinople; and fourth, the *praxis de stratelatis* (story of the military officers), a famous story from the life of St. Nicholas that circulated in at least three different Greek versions in the sixth century.[28]

To these references, each independently testifying to the existence of a man known as Nicholas of Myra, another piece of evidence should be added, one that is indirect but still points to the presence of an important and widely known person named Nicholas in the early fourth century. Gustav Anrich has observed that prior to the fourth century the name *Nikòlaos* was virtually unknown in any country. After the fourth century, it appears in ledgers, city records, birth notices, personal letters, and official histories as well as on tombstones and other public markers. He also observes that the name first surfaced in the territory of Lycia (the region of southern Turkey where Nicholas was born and lived), and then in Asia Minor, Constantinople, Greece, and elsewhere.[29] Although Anrich's evidence stops short of creating a causal link, the sudden appearance and popularity of the name coincide with the timeframe given for the supposed existence of the bishop.

Council of Nicaea

Cioffari has devoted a major part of his life's work to demonstrating Nicholas' attendance at the council, whose general importance for church history will be discussed in a later
chapter. General opinion is not in Cioffari's favor. *The Oxford
Dictionary of Saints* reports that "attempts to make him one
of the fathers at the Council of Nicaea . . . have failed through
lack of evidence."[30] Gustav Anrich concluded that Nicholas did
not attend,[31] basing his verdict on the fact that the very earliest
lists, some of which were put together within a few years of the
council, contain only about 200 names, Nicholas' not among
them. Anrich's assumption is that the older and shorter lists
must be regarded as more accurate. However, it could be that
the earlier and shorter lists simply recorded the names of the
most prominent participants, or those who were most active in
the debates, or perhaps they did not take into account bishops
who arrived at Nicaea after the sessions began.[32] Paphnutius,
an Egyptian bishop known to have spoken at the council, is
not mentioned in the shorter lists.[33] Furthermore, the earliest
sources disagree to some extent on the exact number of attendees. Eusebius, bishop of Caesarea on the coast of Palestine and
author of the first major work of church history, figures about
250 attended, Eustrathius says 270, Athanasius and Galasius
more than 300, Hilary of Poitier exactly 318 (with regards to
this number, it should be noted that it is not as scientific as it
appears—318 is the traditional number of Abraham's servants,
and thus a holy number). Emperor Constantine, who not only
hosted the event but gave gifts to each bishop, estimates 300
present. Whatever the exact number, the scholarly consensus
agrees that it was closer to 300 than 200.

Cioffari investigated sixteen extant lists of attendees
and found that Nicholas' name is missing from ten lists, not
appearing in the lists that record 221 names, 225 names,
or 162 names.[34] On the other hand, his name appears in six
lists, all of which record 300 or more attendees.[35] Of these,

Theodore the Lector's list from the year 515 is by far the most significant since he had access to the best and most complete information available. As a lector (*anagnostis*) or "reader" of the church at Constantinople, he was perfectly situated to gather, trade, and investigate information regarding historical and ecclesial questions. All knowledge passed through Constantinople. Commissioned to compose an ecclesiastical history, Theodore produced his *Tripartite History*—a compilation of the three most authoritative church histories to date, those of Sozomenus, Socrates, and Theodoret of Cyrrhus.[36] He had clearly studied the documents and was convinced that the council consisted of more than 300 attendees. Number 151 in his list: Nicholas of Myra.[37]

Unfortunately, there is one more complication in Cioffari's analysis of Theodore's list: the physical manuscript of Theodore's list is not the original from 515, but a copy dating to the thirteenth century. Scholars have multiple reservations about this manuscript, and its authorship cannot be authenticated with certainty. Even assuming that it did originate with Theodore, scholars cannot guarantee that it was not altered: Nicholas' name might possibly have been added by an overzealous copyist.[38]

However, even noting these reservations, it seems more than plausible that Nicholas was in fact present at the great church council of Nicaea. The cumulative weight of the evidence is in his favor.

Physical Evidence

Beyond the textual documentation of the existence of St. Nicholas, there is the physical evidence. In 1998, Dutch scholar Aart Blom published an analysis of the historicity of Michael the Archimandrite's *Life of St. Nicholas*, the first full biography of Nicholas, which was written around A.D. 710. Blom studied Michael's use of historically and topographically identifiable clues, and his conclusions were quite favorable.[39] The city of

Myra did indeed have a temple dedicated to Artemis, which, according to Michael, Nicholas destroyed, as well as granaries, which were also mentioned by Michael. His description of the location of the tomb of St. Nicholas at Myra also fits well with the archaeological evidence. Blom found there are two churches in Myra built in the fourth century. One is located in Andriake, the port of Myra, and dates to the early 300s; it is most likely the one Nicholas built for his congregation. The other, known as the Church of St. Nicholas, contained the tomb of the saint and was built outside city walls on top of an older necropolis. This church was constructed by or before the middle of the fourth century, which would have been shortly after Nicholas' death, for the purpose of housing his bones.[40]

The historicity of a person named Nicholas is well attested from the physical and documentary evidence. The question remains as to who he was and what he did. How was it that "he became renowned and famous, not only among the faithful, but even among many of the unfaithful," as Symeon Metaphrastes relates?[41] This is the question for the remainder of this book.

The life of St. Nicholas of Myra is much more than a chapter in the story of Santa Claus. Yes, there is a fascinating link with the elf from the North Pole. But that link has been explored countless times. There is another story yet to be told—a story which is just as interesting if lesser known—of the life and times of a Christian minister at the turn of the fourth century. This book offers a microcosmic window on the grandest and most sweeping moment in church history: the conversion of the Roman Empire to Christianity. At the time of Nicholas' birth, the Christian population numbered around two million worldwide. Christians represented an illegal and persecuted minority. By the time of his death, there were as many as thirty-four million Christians. Over half of the Roman Empire claimed adherence. All of the growing pangs of this conversion process manifested themselves in the life of Nicholas. His was a life of faith, to be sure, but it was also one of adventure and honor, justice and charity, goodwill and thick resolve. Nicholas experienced tragedy and triumph, the miraculous and the mundane. His life is worth remembering, and his story is worth retelling.

Out of a Dying World
Comes a Light

In 1863 the British Museum funded an architectural archaeologist, John Turtle Wood, to search for a site in the ancient
city of Ephesus where once stood a temple dedicated to the
goddess Artemis. Once considered the crown jewel of the
world's seven wonders, not a single trace of it remained to
be seen when Wood and his team stepped into the hot sun on
the first day of the dig. They lacked even a basic sense of where
to begin digging. Six years later, having suffered a stabbing, a
broken collarbone, insufficient capital, and unreliable workers, Wood followed cryptic directions inscribed on a post in
the municipal amphitheater almost three-quarters of a mile
beyond the city walls to a swamp that was inaccessible and
clouded with insects. Undaunted, Wood's crew began to dig.
Twenty feet later, they struck the temple they had been commissioned to find.[1] Eventually, they cleared a foundation foot-
print measuring 413 feet by 214 feet. From ancient sources and
coin images, the British archaeologist knew that 127 huge columns once stood on this impressive foundation. The columns
propped up a massive roof that hung 65 feet overhead. The
temple had been populated with artistically carved, painted,
and fully dressed statues of the goddess and her associates, and
its sanctuaries and altars were decorated with vivid tapestries

and bright frescoes depicting the legendary deeds of gods and mortals. Nothing of this former glory was left in the brown layers of mud, silt, and detritus. Even so, Wood must have understood that he had unearthed more than column pieces, coins, sculpture fragments, and a temple base—he had uncovered a lost world.

Twilight of the Gods

The idea that any person might have trouble locating the temple of Artemis would have struck a first-century Ephesian as absurd. Upon his entrance into the city, St. Paul of Tarsus, the missionary of Christ, could see for himself—as could anyone—the white-marbled edifice towering in the hazy distance, presiding over lesser buildings and weaker mortals. He did not enter the city by way of the bustling sea-harbor, but, coming from the regions of Galatia and Phrygia—present-day Turkey— "Paul took the road through the interior and arrived at Ephesus" (Acts 18:23, 19:1). He entered through the southeastern gate and proceeded up the street that merged with roads from Colossae, Sardis, and Smyrna. As he went deeper into the city, Paul lost sight of the temple for a time. Merchant canopies and the smoke from meat-vendors obscured his view. He reached the heart of the city and found the *agora*, the "market," where everything could be bought and sold: Persian silks and Arabian carpets, Alexandrian glassware and locally produced clay pots, freshly baked artesian bread and beer loaves, olive oil, Syrian dates and fig cakes, wine, fresh and salted fish hooked on strings for display, live quail, leather belts, wooden staffs and handles, metal-fittings for horses and field equipment, and slaves. This was the bazaar of the greatest and most prosperous city in all of Asia Minor. For this reason, Ephesus was authorized to mint its own coins to feed the furnace of exchange and commerce.

Greek, Syriac, Latin, Egyptian, and Hebrew voices vied for attention. Pushing through the intestinal coils of the market, Paul suddenly found himself outside the walls of the city, in front of the white, geometric steps of the Temple of Artemis. He must have tilted his head back and allowed himself to gaze up, not forgetting to watch for pickpockets and purse-snatchers who preyed on disoriented sightseers. Yet even the savvy tourist could not help but be "captivated by pantomimes and occupied with the pyrrhic dance" that twirled in the temple's plaza, as one eyewitness noted. "The whole place teemed with piping, with hermaphrodites, and with castanets."[2] Philosophers, politicians, and religious orators took their places on the steps and attracted crowds to their speeches. Civic announcements were pasted at eye-level onto the thick columns. Pigeons swooped in and out, scavenging food while unabashed streetboys tugged at the sleeves of tourists, offering guided tours of the temple's splendor for a penny.

The temple was unique for many reasons, including its architectural orientation. Most Greek temples faced east, so that the first fingers of sunrise might caress the deified effigies within. But Artemis was mistress of the moon and so preferred shade to sun; her temple alone faced west. In front of the temple, merchants hawked trinkets and miniature statuettes of the goddess depicted with her arms outstretched and hands open wide in invitation. The invitation was not sexual in nature; her feet were together, her legs and back straight, her chin and eyebrows raised. This was a proud maternal figure, not a provocative, sexual one. Only her ebony face, hands, and toes were exposed. Over her legs, from ankles to hips, she wore a tight-fitting *ependytes* or tunic dress decorated with the animals of the field, from the lowly bee, deer, and oxen to the winged griffin and fierce lion. In addition, Artemis wore an ornate headdress made from a woven basket full to the brim with grain, and her torso was covered in a garment of breasts.[3] Swollen and round, they clumped together and symbolized her task: the provision of sustenance.[4] Artemis fed the world; she was the *magna mater* (the Great Mother; fig. 2). From her own bosom, she suckled the hungry. The breasts hung heavy like bovine udders, warm with life-sustaining milk and nutrients.

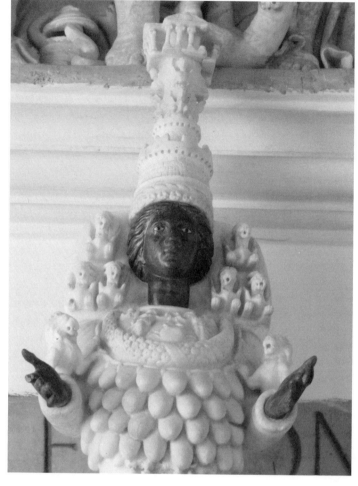

FIGURE 2
A statue of Artemis of Ephesus

"She will provide deliverance from your affliction," one inscription read.[5]

Artemis, known in Latin texts as Diana, kept a watchful eye and a gentle hand on every link in the food chain, from the farmer who bent low to plant the seed in the black earth to the sailors who transported grain from port to port, from the brick-oven tenders who baked and sold bread to the familial table where it was broken, dipped in oil, and consumed. Just before tasting it, the *paterfamilias*, the head of the house, would raise the blessed bounty in thanks to the goddess for her provision. And so the religious people of Ephesus asked Artemis to bless their crops and cattle with fertility and health, to protect the transportation of their goods with safe passage, and to enrich their daily meals with joy. In the tasks of protection and provision, the Great Mother followed the waxing and waning of the moon, whose mysterious magnetism pulled at the sea's tides, let down midnight vapors, and drew forth morning dew. People saw the glistening moon flickering into fullness each month only to be snuffed out again, and they understood that it was somehow connected to a woman's monthly (*menstruus*) menstrual cycle of womb, seed, gestation, birth, and death. Artemis—perpetually maternal and virginal, a field forever fertile yet unplowed—led the cyclical parade of life.[6]

St. Paul undoubtedly knew the longstanding veneration of Artemis. Having been to Ephesus once before, he took up a two-year residence in the city on this third journey. He taught openly in the lecture hall of Tyrannus, winning adherents but inflaming the traditionalists. Handkerchiefs and aprons that touched the holy man were taken to the sick that they might be cured (Acts 19:11-12), and other signs and miracles were performed. Evil spirits who would not submit to old cures and traditional exorcisms recognized the new names of Paul and Christ (Acts 19:14-18). Some practitioners of sorcery converted to Paul's teaching and publicly burned their scrolls of secret magical knowledge, which were valued at fifty thousand drachmas (Acts 19:19). All of these things infuriated the devotees of Artemis, who correctly perceived the gospel of Christ as a threat. Tensions mounted, and an ugly mood settled on the Ephesians. Sensing that his time in the city was coming to an end, Paul began packing his travel bags for Macedonia. Meanwhile, a silversmith named Demetrius, who made silver shrines of Artemis, fumed and fulminated against Paul and members of the Christian way. Not only was Paul dishonoring the city's goddess, he was siphoning off Demetrius' business. Why would anyone pay good money for an idol when Paul had convinced them that it did not work? His impassioned speech rallied other temple artisans to his cause, and shouts of protest went up: "Great is Artemis of the Ephesians!" (Acts 19:28). In an uproar, rag-pickers and spice dealers, bored youth, and excitable onlookers rushed to the open-air theater. A detachment went to seize Paul. Unable to lay hands on him, they grabbed Gaius and Aristarchus, Paul's Macedonian traveling companions, and dragged them through the crowd gathering at the theater. For two straight hours the frenzied cry—"Great is Artemis of the Ephesians!"—reverberated throughout the twenty-five thousand seats in the semicircular arena. In the end, however, nothing came of it. A brave city clerk talked the mob down. Gaius and Aristarchus were released unharmed.

Although Demetrius and the good citizens of Ephesus could not have known it that day, the winds of change were already stirring. In the year 262, Gothic invaders would descend from the Black Sea in swarms, with their coarse hair tied back in Suebian knots as they swung double-edged swords in circles over their heads. The settled, urban populations could only run in terror from this plague. The Gothic-born historian Jordanes relates in passing that the "leaders of the Goths took ship and sailed across the strait of the Hellespont to Asia. There they laid waste many populous cities and set fire to the renowned temple of Diana [Artemis] at Ephesus."[7] He says nothing further about the terrific sight of the fire that raged or the heavy chains used to pull down the temple's thick columns. This was not the first time the temple had suffered destruction. It had burned to the ground in a fire set by a madman in 356 B.C., but on that occasion, the city used the opportunity to construct an even more magnificent palace of stone for their goddess, an "eternal" monument to her glory and provision. By the time the Goths invaded, the "new" temple was well over four hundred years old and the worship of Artemis, adopted by the Romans under the name of Diana and diluted by the Egyptians under the name of Isis, had also grown old. The Ephesians, who had paid tribute to Artemis since the eighth century before Christ, were weary. The palace would not be rebuilt. Artemis would have to take up residence in the countryside, in sacred groves and trees, in local shrines and temples—a ghost of her former self.

About the same time as the Gothic sack of Ephesus, a boy was born to a happy couple in Patara, a city which lay about two hundred miles to the south of Ephesus. His name was *Nikòlaos*, Greek for "victory of the people." The victory his parents celebrated in the birth had nothing to do with the Great Mother, Artemis. They professed faith in the resurrected Lord, Jesus Christ, and saw in the events of the day signs of a new dawn gathering strength—the son of God ushering in an age of grace and peace and truth. "Wake up . . . and Christ will shine on you" (Eph 5:14).

A Child Is Born

High in the forested mountains of what is now southern Turkey, morning chill drew steam off thin pools of Lycian water. The steam rose and faded like the spirits of Sarpedon and Meleager—local heroes whose stories have long been lost but whose names can still be made out from rough etchings on half-buried monuments. Silvery streams of mountain water began to trickle toward the sea, choosing as they went between one of three rivers: the Xanthos, the Myros, and the Arykandos. Near the Mediterranean mouth of the Myros stood the ancient township of Myra, and near the Xanthos stood Patara (fig. 3). Both are important to our story—Patara the city of Nicholas' birth, and Myra the city where he served as bishop.

Patara, Nicholas' place of birth, prided itself on a long and rich religious heritage. Located just thirty miles west of Myra on the southern coast of the country that would become Turkey, in the third century it was the home to portent and

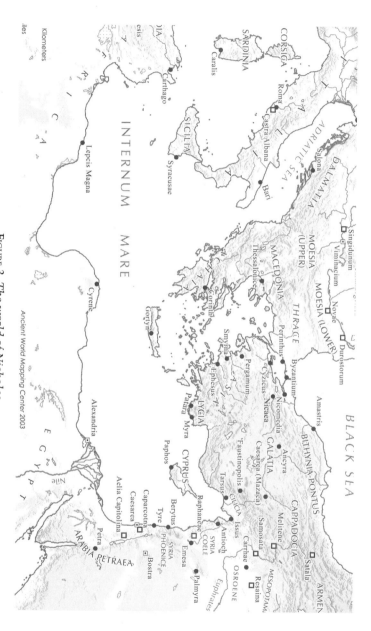

FIGURE 3. *The world of Nicholas*

Ancient World Mapping Center 2003

26

prophecy. The curly-haired and clean-shaven god Apollo, who was said to walk the island of Delos during summers, always made his winter lodgings in Patara, where troubled souls could go to his temple and receive an oracle from him. Niches in hallways, miniature shrines on street corners, the smell of incense, and the pageantry of periodic festivals all reminded the Pataran people of their divine obligations to the gods, which included Cybele and Asclepius in addition to Apollo and his charcoal-skinned sister Artemis. In addition to its sacred groves and divine augers, Patara was also a place of political action. Alexander the Great conquered the city in the fourth century before Christ. Brutus and Cassius conquered it in the first. St. Paul stopped at Patara at the end of his third missionary journey (Acts 21:1). The city, complete with its own amphitheater and ample archways, was one of the six main trade centers in the region known as Lycia. A huge lighthouse, the remains of which can be seen to this day, beckoned trade vessels and passing sailors to its harbors. Patara naturally became a major focal point for Roman administration. Despite being rocked by an earthquake in A.D. 141, Patara experienced unbroken growth and prosperity until it fell almost a thousand years later to Seljuk invaders.

Onto this ancient stage of Greek colonists and Roman legionaries, farmers and fishermen, sailors and tanners, a boy was born sometime after A.D. 260. Details of the birth and infancy were recorded by his earliest biographer, Michael the Archimandrite (life dates uncertain), who dictated his history around A.D. 700 or 710. Michael began the account with these prefatory words:

> O shining daybreak of piety and of famously wonderful works: Nicholas, the holy high priest of Christ, is presented to all of us gathered to give glory to God. I see that, as we annually celebrate him, he guides us, like a glowing and clear beam of light from the sun of justice. And so he radiates through the clouds, as one of gold, while showering sparks of his virtues.[8]

Michael's high and flourishing style is characteristic of the period. Writers of that day believed the written word should be elevated, refined, thoughtful, and poetic and considered straightforward prose gauche and uncouth; the inclusion of facts, dates, places, and names was disdained. Even so, Michael tucked important historical clues into his artistry. He observed that his reader, whom he identifies as Leo, was about "to celebrate his memory with hymns and songs," and that this celebration was occurring "as you prepare yourselves for the coming of God's Word according to the flesh from the holy Virgin."[9] From this description, it is clear that the season of Advent was at hand. St. Nicholas Day (December 6) was one of the first feasts of the season. Because churches everywhere made special use of the occasion to celebrate Nicholas' memory with hymns and songs, it was right and proper that Michael produce a complete account of his life and works. Michael commended the celebration of Nicholas to Leo, calling the saint "a help in danger and the defender of those living in various tribulations."[10] Nicholas was a ready aid to anyone, for he stood before God with the urgent petitions of those in need. "We who anchor our hope solidly in the Lord ask him to be guardian of our whole life."[11]

Michael, the author of these words, served as an archimandrite—an abbot who supervised a large monastery or perhaps multiple monasteries. His name is a testament to the pervasive appeal and allure of the angels, especially the archangel Michael, to Christians of his day.[12] Reverence for the angelic host was found on amulets and boundary markers throughout Asia Minor and was so popular that it spread into the religion of Islam. Michael, author of the *Life of St. Nicholas* and head shepherd over a *mandra* or "sheepfold," resided in a deserted province of Asia Minor, where the austere way of a monk's life attracted flocks of the devoted. Assisted by his *deuterarios*, or prior, he shouldered large administrative and disciplinary burdens on behalf of his monks. In spite of his busy routine, he took time to compose the *Life of St. Nicholas* as a favor to a certain Leo, about whom we know nothing beyond his request for an account of the life of St. Nicholas. In response, Michael promised, "by God's grace, and with all humility, to Leo, the most God-loving of people, a good friend, we will do what you ask—in your just way—when you urge us to produce a clear account of this great Archbishop."[13] Leo's request indicates that there were curious monks who ardently wanted to know more about this particular saint.[14] It also indicates that Nicholas' name was well known before Michael wrote his *Life*.

Michael appreciated the need for his monks and other Christians to become familiar with wholesome and venerable models of Christian living. Knowing that the biography would be read aloud in the refectory while monks ate one of their two vegetarian meals of the day, Michael wanted them to hear and meditate on an ideal Christian life. The churches and monasteries knew the deaths of the martyrs—Stephen, Philip, Peter, Antipas, Ignatius, Perpetua, Cyprian, and the forty martyrs of Sabaste—but they possessed few stories of Christian heroes who lived lives of faithfulness to ripe old ages. Models for dying they had; models for living they needed.[15] They wanted the Christian lifestyle demonstrated before their own eyes, especially so they could visualize the difference between Christian and non-Christian ways, and the *vitae* or *Lives* of the martyrs and the saints helped to concretize the victory of Christianity over paganism and demonstrate the Christian ideal. In the preface to *Life of Martin of Tours*, for instance, Sulpicius Severus justified his own work by saying, "it would be useful if I were to write a detailed record of the life of this most saintly man [Martin] as an example to others in the future."[16] Within the orbit of Christian sensibilities, Severus realized pre-Christian and non-Christian heroes could no longer serve as examples and models. Not only did Severus believe that imitating these men was foolish, but that Christians must "combat them most energetically."[17] "What benefit did posterity gain," he asked, "from reading about Hector's battles or about Socrates' philosophy?"[18] Faithful Christians needed new models to be elevated before their eyes so that they might

29

be roused to heavenly service and divine heroism.[19] Severus aimed to do more than present the worthy life of his subject; he wanted it to surpass all previous pagan attempts. A similar passion energized Michael the Archimandrite to "compose something simple yet profound, so that others, who do not know these things about him, might admire him, and so that the deeds of the saint might be presented clearly by ministers in sermons."[20]

Fragments of Nicholas' life had been in circulation for well over two hundred years before Michael composed his own. There was an anonymous biography, now lost, referred to simply as the *bios* ("life" in Greek). There were also multiple versions of a noteworthy episode from Nicholas' life known as the *praxis de stratelatis* ("the story of the military commanders"). Yet, because no definitive account of his life as yet existed, Michael ventured to compile the stories and produce what survives as our first full *Life* of St. Nicholas. To this end, Michael stood in the scriptorium of the monastery and dictated in Greek to a retinue of scribes hunched over wax-covered tablets. These *amanuenses* etched his words into the beeswax using metal or wooden styluses. They then rewrote their shorthand notes in a longhand transcription. Finally, a calligrapher stretched out and nailed into place a sheet of parchment. Taking a reed dipped in ink, he penned a master copy from which other copies could be made.[21] Possibly completed between the years 700 and 710,[22] the work bore the title, *Life, Works, and Miracles of our Holy Father Nicholas, Archbishop of Myra in Lycia*. Michael's *Life* recounts the story of Nicholas of Myra in twelve short episodes—the sacred number of Jesus' disciples and Israel's tribes—framed by a preface and a conclusion. Altogether, the work consists of fifty-two paragraphs.[23]

The story begins before Nicholas was born, when, according to Michael, the saint's unique vocation and character took shape *in utero*.

A strange thing happened to his mother at the time of his conception: from that moment she became sterile and was glad and happy to stay so for the rest of her life with no other children. In this way it turned out that Nicholas, his parents' one and only son, might be an image of the great John who baptized the Savior. Only the miracle occurred in reverse. John freed his mother from sterility when he was sent to the world as a candlestick for the light that is without beginning. Nicholas' conception instead led to infertility in the uterus of his mother. But she became fertile in the Holy Spirit, and was filled with divine power. She and her husband studied to please God and obey his commandments.[24]

At the time, the best medical descriptions compared pregnancy to cooking a loaf of bread in a fire-heated oven. The child Nicholas was refined, purified, and "cooked" at such a high degree of heat inside the womb that his mother was never again able to bear children. The cooking pot of her womb had overheated and cracked with this one—who was to be the image of John the Baptizer, the announcer of good news and salvation for the world. She was compensated with the gift of the Holy Spirit, so that instead of carrying babies on her hips she radiated the power of God's presence.

Like other children born in Christian homes, Nicholas received baptism as an infant. Water was ladled onto his head not once but three times, in the name of the Father, of the Son, and of the Holy Spirit. Words of blessing and covenant were spoken over him. Although historians are uncertain as to exactly when and how the practice of infant baptism started, it was most certainly common by the time of Nicholas. Origen (185–254) casually mentions infant baptism as the customary procedure of his day, the early 200s,[25] suggesting that the practice was widespread before Origen. However, it was not a consistent or universally followed rule—although Rufinus of Aquileia and Jerome were both reared in Christian homes, for instance, they were not baptized as babies but instead submitted to the rite as adults. Constantine received baptism very late in life despite the fact that throughout his adulthood he wholeheartedly professed faith. It is also worth noting that some Jews, like those in the desert community of Qumran, underwent ritual baptism regularly for the cleansing of sin. The Christian communities of the first few centuries had yet to work out the rules, regulations, and doctrines about the practice. With these facts in mind, historians wonder if New Testament Christians baptized not only adult converts but their entire families, including the babies (see for example Acts 10:44-48 and 16:31-34). If not, how long after the close of the New Testament did they begin to do so? These questions are most often addressed from a theological perspective, but they should also be considered from a cultural one. No one in the ancient world would have thought of children as "autonomous" individuals free to make up their own minds about God and religion. Religion revolved around the hearth and home. Each household kept and venerated its own household gods, known as *Lares*, deities who protected the family and who could also be the family's ancestral spirits. Figurine statues of the *Lares* could be found throughout the residence: in the atrium, the central living room, on the banquet tables, and on shelves of bedroom walls. The *paterfamilias*, or the head of the house, was ultimately responsible for his family's conduct and worship. In that sense, he was the chief priest of his household gods. Indeed, the father had the right to rule like a minor despot over the people who lived under his roof, divorcing or even putting to death his wife without cause, sending his children to school to learn or into the field to work, as it suited his needs and whims. As the *paterfamilias* went, so went the family. If the father decided for Christ, then it was expected as a matter of course that his entire household should follow him and be baptized accordingly. It would be hard to imagine any other scenario, and this must be the context to keep in mind for any investigation into the practice of baptism and religion in the early church.

But, even on this point, Nicholas broke the mold. He would do more than follow his family in faith; he would lead. Like all children, he learned to suckle at the breast of his mother; according to Michael the Archimandrite, "the child took breast-milk multiple times a day during the week as children normally do; but on Wednesdays and Fridays he took milk only once a day, and at a given time."[26] Innocently and unknowingly, the infant observed the traditional days of Christian fasting: Wednesday and Friday. "The blessed child adhered to the sacred observances regarding food, revealing even then a pure and holy heart."[27] We can well imagine the men in Michael's monastery, disciplined by prayer and regimented by regular fasting, nodding their heads in approval and delight at this. Michael interprets it as a sign, saying that God performed the wonder "in order to reveal something of the future life of the great Nicholas."[28] The medieval bishop of Chartres, Peter, drawing the attention of his parishioners in his magnificent Cathedral to one of four stained-glass medallions dedicated to St. Nicholas, rhapsodized in a sermon on how the infant Nicholas "reined in the vice of gluttony." Peter spoke with passion: "How weak, Nicholas lying at the teat! How strong, abstaining from the teat! If the boy is known by his studies, what of the infant and his milk!"[29] A later tradition added something even more spectacular: at his baptism, the meek and mild infant stunned all those present by standing up in his basin of water and pronouncing a blessing.[30]

At least three important pieces of information emerge from these miraculous infancy stories: one, Nicholas was born in the Lycian city of Patara; two, he was born to Christian parents; and three, he showed a certain precociousness and spiritual awareness at an early age. There is another, albeit indirect, reason to value these fantastical reports: they elucidate Michael's motive for recording them in the first place. By describing the miraculous phenomena that surrounded Nicholas' birth, Michael fulfilled hagiographic expectations. Hagiography, Greek for "holy writing," refers to the composition of reverential accounts of saints' lives.[31] In the world of Michael, such accounts were not written for mere entertainment, and they certainly were not intended for the sake of scholarly employment or academic documentation. Hagiography was done to promote moral edification, spiritual enlightenment, and religious zeal.[32] Athanasius (296/8–373), to give one example, documented the life of Antony for the high purpose of providing a "perfect path to virtue."[33] Biography blended with morality, fact converged with sermon, small truths gave way to the greater truth. Late antique and medieval Christians were more concerned with the spiritual, eternal value of a life than with its temporal, physical operations. They did not set about to distort; they simply wanted to draw out and enhance the lesson.

Legends and Lives

The lives of the saints were written down, collected, and bound together into what the Greek Byzantines called *synaxaries* and what the Latin Westerners called *legendries*—an example being Jacobus de Voragine's thirteenth-century *Golden Legend*. To an ordinary person today, "legend" connotes a fanciful tale that is not true. But the Latin word *legenda*, from which we get our English word "legend," simply means "what is to be read." It originally had nothing to do with the truth or falsehood of the narrative but referred to the devotional reading for the day.[34] During the *lectio* or reading portion of the Christian worship service, the *legenda* indicated what was supposed to be read.[35] The legendries, synaxaries, and the martyrologies were read aloud in worship services for the admonition and encouragement and instruction of the people.

Michael included the strange happenings associated with Nicholas' birth in order to teach a spiritual lesson. He believed learning about the saints would build character, inspire virtue, and draw the seeker closer to God.[36] The notion of sainthood derives its legitimacy from Scripture. The word "saint" appears in the Bible more than ninety times. Paul writes to the church at Corinth, "you were washed, you were sanctified, you were justified in the name of the Lord Jesus Christ and in the Spirit of our God" (1 Cor 6:11). To this end, Ephesians 2:19 declares, "you are fellow citizens with the saints and members of the household of God." Those Ephesians who were sanctified or made clean in Christ and pure before the heavenly throne rightfully received the title of *hagioi*, Greek for "saints," holy ones of God. Psalms 31:23 encourages worshipers to "Love the LORD, all you his saints!" Matthew 27:52 documents tombs opening upon the death of Christ "and many bodies of the saints who had fallen asleep were raised." The Pauline epistles are addressed "to the saints" at Corinth, Ephesus, Philippi, and Rome (Rom 1:7, for example). New Testament books as diverse as Acts, Hebrews, and Jude refer to Christians as saints (Acts 9:32; Heb 13:24; Jude 1:3). Revelation identifies saints as those who have suffered for the name of the Lord (Rev 13:7-10, 14:12, 16:6, 17:6). It could be concluded from the evidence that all God's children are, in the words of Scripture, holy, chosen, and consecrated by God's Spirit. It has always been the case, though, that some exercise their holiness better than others. For this they should be admired and held up as examples. These exemplars—both dead and alive—function as vehicles of God's grace. They communicate God's word, deliver God's verdict, and enact God's will. For this they are to be honored.

In the late fourth century, Augustine of Hippo (354–430) regularly preached at what were called "feasts of roses," which were annual festivals of martyrs held by torchlight on warm spring evenings. The anniversary of a martyr's earthly death-day was also a celebration of his or her heavenly birthday: passing from the travail of this world to the joy of God's presence (Phil 1:21),[37] and it was celebrated with cooked meat, new wine, lentils, and breads.[38] Augustine allowed that it was right to honor the saints and the martyrs, but he reminded those attending that they should worship God alone.[39] Too often the festivals, though worthy events in themselves, devolved into raucous revelries and thin excuses for drunkenness, chambering, and wantonness. Women stayed all night or slept next to the tombs, and Basil of Caesarea (330–379) complained that some of them became inebriated and danced provocatively.[40] The men were no better; they tended to get drunk, play dice, and leave the martyr's memorial only to end up in brothels.[41] These cases were extreme, to be sure, but they hinted at deeper problems with the memorial customs.

The drift toward a veneration of deceased saints was natural since Christian worship itself commemorated Christ's death: the wine and bread elements of communion represented his spilt blood and broken flesh, the smell of incense recalled burial preparations, and the arrangement of altar linens brought to mind the spreading of a burial shroud.[42] Because Christ's death was memorialized, it seemed fitting to do likewise on behalf of other holy men and women. And, just as the remembrance of Christ's crucifixion was both an event of mourning and an anticipation of resurrection, so the festivals of the saints were more than graveside memorials—they were celebrations of life, for the saint lived on in heaven. Unfortunately, the veneration of the martyrs and saints tended on occasion to serve as substitutes for the glory of God. People pocketed handfuls of dirt, rock, and anything else they could pry loose from the tomb areas as souvenirs and charms. Others left prayers and petitions written on scraps of parchment and woodchips. From the beginning, thorny tensions existed between honoring the saints and idolizing them.

Two examples can be offered here, one showing the extent of veneration and the other of condemnation. The first example comes from Anselm of Canterbury, England (1033–1109), the master of rational argumentation and inventor of the ontological proof for the existence of God. Anselm visited the tomb of St. Nicholas in 1098 and, struck by a genuine sense of angst about his own sinfulness, prayed the following lines:

But my sins are without bounds or limits,
my prayer will not be heard,
all this is not enough without an intercessor.
I will pray to one of the great friends of God
and perhaps God will hear him on my behalf.
I will call upon Nicholas, that great confessor,
whose name is honoured throughout the world
　　Nicholas!
If only he will hear me!
　　Great Nicholas![43]

Anselm's heartfelt words reveal the depth of his veneration. For him, the saint acted as an intercessor, a mediator between the God who sits above the rainbow and the sinful soul who wallows in misery; he was friend of heaven and of humans. The second example comes from the mid-1500s, the height of the Protestant Reformation, a time when stained-glass windows were smashed, statues toppled, legend books burned, and saint days outlawed. A poem written in Latin by Thomas Naogeorg (1508–1563) expresses the Reformation's condemnation of saint-worship. Naogeorg feared that saints took the place of God:

The mothers all their children on the Eve do cause to fast—
And when they every one at night in senseless sleep are cast,
Both apples, nuts, and pears they bring (and other things
　　beside,
As caps and shoes and petticoats), which secretly they hide—
And, in the morning found, they say "This, Saint Nicholas
　　brought!"
Thus tender minds to worship saints and wicked things are
　　taught.[44]

St. Nicholas bought the affections of tender minds with gifts and goodies. Why, Naogeorg wondered, would children worship God if St. Nicholas delivered the presents? The attack on St. Nicholas extended even to the baking and distributing of

Christmas cookies, which counted as a criminal offense in the puritanical realm of Massachusetts until the late seventeenth century.[45] Because the invocation of the saints was so easily abused, it was thought best to avoid the practice altogether.

The Second Council of Nicaea, held in 787, insisted that God alone was to be worshiped and adored (*latria* in Greek). Saints deserved to be respected and honored (*dulia* in Greek).[46] There was a proper distinction between worship and veneration. The difficulty, however, was that the veneration of saints was not the neatly packaged product of theology or a mere idea for consideration; it represented pop spirituality in its rawest form. Popular religiosity did not always observe the fine-toothed distinctions between *latria* and *dulia*, adoration and veneration, worship and honor. Theological abuses were inevitable. The personalities of the saints connected with the masses—their needs, their hopes and fears; the legends of the saints found their home in spoken sermons, in popular storytelling, and with family customs. In times and places of low literacy rates—when people were not absorbed in heavy theology and most often could not read the Bible for themselves—the oral traditions of the saints offered tangible support, encouragement, and practical ways to relate to God. These traditions fell somewhere between sermon illustration and entertainment, biography and mythology, fact and fiction, stock story and creative license, strange-but-true anecdote and the miraculous legend, melodrama and comedy, the rigorously ascetic monk's life and the everyman's journey, deep Christian spirituality and local superstition, morality tale and gory martyrdom.

Symeon Metaphrastes (c. 912–c. 982/7) stitched together ten volumes of saints' lives, Nicholas' among them, in his magnum opus known as the *Menologion*. This work earned him the nickname "Metaphrastes," which means the "translator," "compiler," "paraphraser," or "re-writer."[47] He was also called the *logothete tou dromou* and the *magistros*, both terms indicating offices he held at the courts of Constantinople. In

38

the *Menologion*, Symeon placed genuinely historical characters side by side with fictitious ones. Andrew, Ambrose of Milan, Daniel the Stylite, and Gregory of Neocaesarea (an apostle, a preacher, a hermit, and a missionary bishop) were widely attested and renowned historical characters. Others characters were obviously not historical. Symeon Metaphrastes celebrated a saint named Lucian, who was purportedly tied to a stone and thrown into the sea by the emperor Maximian, only to have his body brought forth from its watery grave and deposited on the shore fifteen days later by a dolphin.[48] The reason? St. Lucian's feast day coincided with the feast of the Greek deity Dionysus on the fifteenth day of the month of Dionysus, and Dionysus is represented pictorially by dolphins.[49] Another example is St. Barbara, one of the "fourteen holy helpers" and the patroness of those who work with explosives.[50] Barbara was put through rigorous tortures on account of her Christian faith, but, according to Symeon, found that her injuries were healed every morning. And when her tormenters put torches to her body, their flames were extinguished. The virgin martyr was finally beheaded by a member of her own family, her father, who was righteously struck down by lightning on his way home afterwards.

In order to interpret and fully understand the life of Nicholas, it is important to appreciate the vehicle by which it has been preserved—the hagiographic *vita* or *Life*. Symeon spoke of the purpose of his work as a hagiographer in the preamble to his biography of Nicholas. He compared his work to that of a painter who "knows how to imitate true things beautifully, and how to show the significance of things." He went on to say: "Now the lives of those who have lived for God, when portrayed in speech, attract and call many to virtue and kindle all to copy their zeal. Such is the life of our divine father Nicholas. He, more than any other, delights our ears, causes our souls to rejoice, and stirs up our devotion for honorable things."[51] Symeon's aim was to delight the ears, cause the soul to rejoice, and inspire good works. His concern with Nicholas, as with the hundreds of other saints he chronicled, was edification, not necessarily historical documentation. The same could be said of Michael the Archimandrite, who expressed his desire that the life of Nicholas be talked about in sermons and duly admired by all.[52] Symeon, and to a lesser degree Michael, exercised poetic license to edit, paraphrase, and invent stories wherever he deemed appropriate. His commitment was to the spirit more than the facts, and, like so many hagiographic writers, this was his first aim.

Into the Teeth of the World

For much of the world's history, childhood has not been an oasis of innocence, joy, nurture, and shelter. Childhood in antiquity was not enjoyed but survived. The average number of births per household was about five, but only two or three of those newborns would make it through childhood. The infant mortality rate was one in two or three births. This stark reality fostered two harshly pragmatic attitudes. Because infant mortality rates were so high, society as a whole did not encourage early emotional attachments with offspring—better not to get too invested. But while downplaying emotional affection, society and even government encouraged childbearing, knowing that not all babies would survive. Indeed, beginning with the first Roman emperor, Augustus, tax penalties were levied against infertile couples while monetary rewards were given to families with more than three children. Girls as young as age fourteen could marry and commence their reproductive duties to society. Homemaking was not optional; it was required. Census records from Roman antiquity confirm that active mothers were expected to reproduce once every two to three years to keep up with population demands. Over this reproductive pressure loomed the ever-present specter of death. The raw fact was that men and women could not reasonably expect to live much past the age of twenty-five; Ulpian, a famous third-century Roman lawyer and scholar, put the average life expectancy even lower, at twenty-one. Only four out of every hundred men lived past fifty. The fourth-century preacher John Chrysostom (347–407) observed sadly that the people were "grazed thin by death."[53]

As if disease, malnutrition, unhygienic conditions, and poor medical treatment were not dangerous enough, children were regularly threatened by infanticide. It is almost impossible to know with certainty how frequently infanticide was practiced, mainly because it was a matter for the *paterfamilias*, the father, to decide. Because it was not a state matter, it was not reported. The head of the house, not the government, decided the fate of the child. Roman law did not regulate or in any way prohibit fathers from exposing their children to death. Acceptable reasons for abandoning children included the following: the child was "maimed or monstrous from birth," not the preferred gender, or physically unimpressive, or the family was simply unable to feed one more mouth.[54]

The ancient world offered countless ways to die—war, famine, plague, bad luck. Between A.D. 169 and 180, a pestilence (possibly smallpox) swept through the Roman Empire, killing approximately five million, or 10 percent of the population. In the years surrounding Nicholas' birth, a separate but equally devastating epidemic raged closer to his home in the provinces of Asia Minor (A.D. 251–270).[55] On the whole, childhood was not a time to cherish and adore but a time to endure and overcome. People survived and flourished not so much because of their childhood experiences, but in spite of them. The parental impulse in every age is to love, care for, and nurture offspring. Yet families simply could not allow themselves to grow overly attached to their progeny until they had evidence that life would take hold. The legend of Romulus and Remus, the fabled founders of Rome, provides the quintessential example. The two brothers were abandoned at birth to the wild and survived by drinking milk from the teats of a she-wolf. Even into late medieval times, the fourteenth and fifteenth centuries, society looked coldly and dispassionately upon childhood. In popular literature of that day, the chief role of children, according to Barbara Tuchman, "was to die, usually drowned, smothered, or abandoned in a forest on the orders of some king fearing prophecy or mad husband testing a wife's endurance."[56] In illustrations and tapestries, *adults* were depicted going about all sorts of endeavors—sleeping, eating, washing, praying, hunting, planting, plowing, harvesting, building, dancing, fighting, traveling, writing, sailing, getting married, having sex, dying. Rarely were *children* pictured. Equally rare was a parent interacting with his or her child. Certainly the Christ-child was a prominent theme in religious art. Painters manufactured Madonna with child for churches, businesses, and homes. In both Byzantine and Latin representations, however, the infant Jesus never looks like a baby, but almost always like a miniature man. He is often shown raising two fingers in a blessing. The placid face of Mother Mary communicates contentment, serenity, and sanctity, but rarely maternal affection. Mother and child do not make eye contact but contemplatively look out at the viewer.

Mitigating these cultural severities, Nicholas had the good fortune of being born to parents who were, by all accounts, financially prosperous, socially secure, and religiously committed. Michael the Archimandrite does not provide their names, nor does any other source from antiquity. Although later tradition supplied them with names, Epiphanius and Nonna,[57] this must be judged a case of mistaken identity. Epiphanius and Nonna were the parents of Nicholas of Sion who lived some two hundred years later, from 480 to 564.[58] It was this other Nicholas, born in Pharroa in the region of Traglassi, who was said to have stood in his baptismal water basin for two hours blessing his parents and the people congregated for the church service. After showing remarkable signs of spiritual maturity at a young age, this Nicholas was consecrated a "reader" in the church and then, at the age of nineteen, was ordained a priest. He retreated into the nearby wilderness and built a cloistered monastery called Sion and eventually was appointed as bishop of Pinara. Sometime in the ninth or tenth century, the biographies of the two men named Nicholas were merged, and many of the anecdotes and elements from the life of Nicholas of Sion were simply swallowed up and incorporated into the stories of the life of Nicholas of Myra. The confusion is understandable for a number of reasons: the two men shared the same name, had similar life experiences, lived geographically near each other—the monastery of Sion was carved out of the mountains halfway between Myra and Fenike—and their death dates fell within days of each other, Nicholas of Myra on December 6 and Nicholas of Sion on December 10. Even so, the two men were separated in time by nearly two hundred years.

Although we do not know the names of the parents of Nicholas of Myra, what seems clear from the biographer Michael and other reliable sources is that he was reared in a good home. His diet consisted of fish from the sea—pike, grouper, mullet, and tuna, as well as a variety of items cultivated in the interior such as grapes, figs, dates, chickpeas, lentils, olives, and olive oil. Because his hometown of Patara was on the coastal trade route, corn, wheat, barley, and cheese could be readily acquired, although certain crops became hard to find during Nicholas' lifetime on account of the fact that the population dropped off in the mid-third century and some farmlands went untilled. Rural and remote areas experienced food shortages, some of them severe. From his devoutly Christian parents, Nicholas learned not to be anxious about uncertainties; life was more than food and work. They taught him the saga of Abraham who, thinking he was hosting three ordinary wayfarers, entertained angels. We might wonder if Nicholas met any descendants of Abraham while growing up in Patara, as a Jewish synagogue was located on the outskirts of town. Even if he did not, Nicholas knew their Scriptures. He heard the story of Esther who risked everything, including her life, to petition the king to stop the wicked plot of Haman. He sang the Psalms in worship. From the senior members of the church, he heard the saving message of Jesus—his birth, ministry, death, and resurrection—as passed down generation to generation from St. Paul himself, who had personally delivered the good news on his visit to the city. It was this message that captured Nicholas' heart and directed his life's calling.

Nicholas joined with his parents and other Christians as they met on the first day of each week before sunrise and on some days at sundown to celebrate the Eucharist—breaking bread as a sign of Christ's body broken on the cross and sharing wine as a sign of Christ's blood. Eucharist, Greek for "thanksgiving," was the word most commonly used at this time to refer to the communion event. The rite constituted the oldest known form of uniquely Christian worship. St. Paul, writing in the mid-50s, instructs the unsteady and underdeveloped church at Corinth on the proper way to perform this basic liturgy. He reminds them that, "I received from the Lord what I also handed on to you," namely how the Lord, on the night he would be betrayed, celebrated a Passover meal with his intimate band of disciples. He broke bread and passed around a cup of wine, investing each element with spiritual meaning. He commanded his disciples: "Do this in remembrance of me" (1 Cor 11:23-25). Paul's letter shows that within twenty years of Jesus' death and resurrection the Christian community had already established the standard pattern for Eucharistic liturgy, which the church of Nicholas' boyhood would have certainly followed.[59] The memorial meal was sacred, its elements "the medicine of immortality,"[60] and so its recipients should be clean of heart. St. Paul warned the church about taking communion unworthily (1 Cor 11:27). Unbelievers and unbaptized initiates or catechumens, as they were called, could not participate.

When Nicholas was a boy, Christians met by and large in homes, not in independently constructed religious buildings or churches. Christianity was still a "frontier" religion. When Gregory of Neocaesarea (c. 213–c. 270) was ordained bishop to the backwater diocese of Neocaesarea, there were said to be only seventeen Christians in all; when he finished, there were only seventeen pagans.[61] Gregory had settled the land for Christ, baptized thousands out of their rustic superstitions and rituals, and built his own church cathedral.[62] This pioneering trend changed during Nicholas' lifetime; Gregory "the Wonderworker," as he was called, died before Nicholas was quite ten years old. The missionary frontier of Asia Minor was shrinking. As the territories accepted Christianity in greater numbers, freestanding church structures began to appear. In Duro-Europas, Syria, a church has been found that began as a private residence but was converted into a church sometime around 250.[63] By the year 300, chapels, basilicas, and shrines could be found in important cities such as Nicomedia, just four hundred miles to the north of Nicholas' hometown and in plain view of the emperor's personal residence. In Nicholas' childhood, however, Christians continued to meet in the cramped quarters of private homes. The people constituted the church, not the building. The *ekklesia* (Greek for "church") referred to the community, not the brick and mortar. In addition to meeting in houses, Christians occasionally participated in communion services in the catacombs or at the cemeteries—gathering around the tomb of a famous martyr or well-loved saint. The cemeteries of Patara were located outside the city's walls in peaceful solitude. Believers gathered together there to be reminded that the story of God's Son did not end with his death on the cross or his burial in the tomb but that he rose again on the third day. They remembered that their ultimate resting place was not the grave, but with God (Rom 6:5). Believers found reassurance of their bodily resurrection in the rising of the sun after the darkness of night, the budding of a new plant from a hard seed buried in the earth, and the mysterious resurrection of the Arabian bird, the phoenix, said to cocoon itself, die, and come back to life as a worm, growing new wings and a new body.[64] After death came new life, the day of judgment, and the hope of eternity.

In connection with the graveyard, Nicholas would have been told of the great Christian witnesses who had recently died for the faith. Just a few years before his birth, in fact, four names from Patara and Myra were added to the roll-call of martyrs. In Myra, a man named Crescentem was put to death for refusing to sacrifice to the gods, while at the same time, two pillars of the church, Dioscorides and Themistocles, were hunted down in the mountains to the north of the city.[65] In Patara, a courageous Christian known as Leo incurred the wrath of the authorities when he marched into the temple of Fortuna in the city square and smashed her candles and votive objects. For this shocking offense, Leo was beheaded.[66] Throughout Nicholas' boyhood, the whole region of Lycia convulsed in religious tumult. The church endured years of discrimination, intolerance, and outright persecution. Christians took courage in the words of St. Peter, "Dear friends, do not be surprised at the painful trial you are suffering, as though something strange were happening to you. But rejoice that you participate in the sufferings of Christ" (1 Pet 4:12-13).

Michael the Archimandrite reports that the boy grew into the strong name he had been given—*Nikòlaos*, victory for the people. Keeping in mind the young monks under his charge, Michael assures his readers that "he hated useless pastimes and the bad advice of bad characters and treated them as something harmful to the virtue that reconciles us to Christ."[67] The hand of God could be seen on Nicholas' life, and from the beginning he looked and acted like a saint.[68] He had a strong moral compass and avoided "public life," where he might be obliged to take oaths, swear by the genus of the emperor, or participate in pagan ceremonies; he abstained from "economic activities" where he might be tempted by cutthroat competition and greed; he closed his ears to the profane and vulgar talk of "uncultivated people," hid his eyes from the "lust of women," and kept his heart from "theatrical performances."[69] "Instead," Michael says, "he nurtured continence."[70] He kept alive "the lamp of virginity"—a phrase that implies more than sexual purity. Moral integrity, compassion, politeness, humility, and self-control also counted as marks of holy virginity.

Purity was holistic, involving mind, body, and soul and requiring the doing of certain things and the avoidance of others. Nicholas lit such a lamp with "the oil of active generosity."[71] His story was not the story of someone who finds God late in life. But like the biblical hero Samuel, Hannah's son who served Eli in the house of the Lord from his boyhood, Nicholas devoted his life to prayer and Christian service at an early age, forsaking worldly pleasures and embracing compassion and generosity. "He never strayed far from the church and, like a nest to a dove the church was to him a refreshment and a comfort." According to Michael, "His mind was illuminated by the teachings, and day by day he grew towards a pure and genuine compassion."[72]

From the information provided by Michael's *Life* we can surmise that Nicholas was not only spiritually minded but also had the privilege of a basic education: "The wonderful young man was educated and trained conscientiously according to the custom of his parents."[73] Although schooling was not universally accessible, it was readily available throughout much of the Empire. Grammar schools flourished as far west as Portugal. Without a terrible strain on finances, parents could hire a tutor or send their boys to school. Sometimes the town's "big-man" or patron would personally finance the creation of a grammar school; at other times the town council would provide funding for scholarships. In the backwaters of African Numidia, for instance, a donor supplied finances to help make education possible for Augustine. Schooling consisted of two basic levels of achievement. A "school of letters" under the care of a "primary" teacher (known as a *ludi magister* or *grammatistes*) offered instruction in the basic skills of reading, writing, and arithmetic. The school was small, as a teacher could not facilitate more than about thirty students, who met in a public colonnade on warm days and a rented room when the weather grew foul. If the school had a classroom, it was not equipped with a blackboard and desks; instead students sat on individual stools or long benches and mastered the art of balancing wooden tablets or papyrus rolls on their knees. They copied words and sentences using a pointed stylus to scratch letters into the thin film of wax that coated their writing tablets. When finished, they rubbed the wax smooth and started over. The noise of commerce, wagons, and daily activity constantly defied the teacher's best attempts. Distractions lurked everywhere, leading frustrated teachers to box the ears of boys with wandering minds.

Like other boys, Nicholas began his education at the age of seven and was led to his teacher by a pedagogue, a household slave assigned with the task of taking the boy to school. The pedagogue carried reading and writing supplies and protected the child from danger; he also monitored the child's progress, kept him from diversions, and disciplined him when needed. Nicholas attended for five years, until he was twelve. School lasted six hours a day, eight days a week—every ninth day was market-day.[74] Education was not year-round; students tended to evaporate during the hot summer month, forcing schoolmasters to close operations for three months, from July to the beginning of October. Nicholas, being a member of the more fortunate middle class, continued his education beyond this first stage. From age twelve to eighteen he was placed under the care of a "secondary" teacher (grammatikos), who could command as much as four times the fee of the primary teacher. He would have read classics like Homer's Illiad and Odyssey as well as the tragedies of Aeschylus and Euripides. Although Nicholas' homeland was under Roman administration, the prevailing cultural and educational force was Greek. The Hellenistic bias was such that, while Latin-speaking instructors in the West exposed their pupils to Greek literature and language, Nicholas' Greek schoolmasters in the East did not bother their students with Latin. In addition to conquering the basic building blocks of the Greek language, Nicholas memorized large sections of Greek literature and composed speeches and responses to prompts. A few students who finished the first two levels of schooling went on to a post-secondary study of rhetoric or natural philosophy, either by hiring a *rhetor*, a teacher of rhetoric, or by traveling to a metropolitan city like Alexandria, Carthage, Athens, Ephesus, or Pergamum. It seems unlikely that Nicholas continued past the first two stages of education.[75]

Nicholas' strength of character came not only from his well-received education and his fervent Christian faith but also from the support of his parents. He enjoyed their nurture and protection for a tragically short amount of time, however. They died while he was still young, probably near the age of eighteen. We are not told how they departed from this life, but it is quite likely they were victims of the terrible plague that swept across the countryside of Lycia in the mid-third century (A.D. 251–270). The plague cut down young and old alike. It ravaged families and entire villages, leaving countless voids of population in its wake. We can only imagine how deeply this loss affected young Nicholas. It was a heartbreaking way to end childhood.

—St. Nicholas' Association with Children—

The mercy of St. Nicholas was associated in the early legends with children, especially children who could not fend for themselves. And in one heroic tale told about him, Nicholas did for another boy what no one had been able to do for him—reunite him with his parents.

Adeodatus Is Saved

Sometime in the late 800s, John the Deacon of the Church of St. Januarius in Naples, Italy (d. 910?), translated the *Life* of St. Nicholas from Greek into Latin. Scholars believe that the popularity of St. Nicholas in the western half of Europe can be traced directly to John the Deacon's work. Although Nicholas had long been a popular saint in the

Greek-speaking, eastern half of Europe and Asia Minor, those in the west had no way of learning about him until John supplied his Latin translation. Then, about one hundred years after John's translation, his work was supplemented by Reginold, bishop of Eichstätt (d. 991), who added various miracles and events.[76] In Reginold's version of John the Deacon's translation, we find the rescue of Adeodatus.[77] A certain man, Cethron, and his wife, Euphorsyna, made a pilgrimage to Nicholas to ask for his blessing that they might conceive a child. When they arrived in Myra, they were disappointed to find that Nicholas had just died and was being buried. Nevertheless, the infertile couple took a relic and returned home to Exoranda, still hoping that their prayers might be answered. Their reverence for the holy man was so great that Cethron planned to build a chapel in honor of him on the outskirts of town. As the edifice began to take shape brick by brick, the belly of Euphorsyna began to bulge. Their prayers had been answered—Euphorsyna was pregnant. The chapel was completed, and Apollonius, the local bishop, dedicated it to Nicholas. The relic taken from Myra was affectionately placed inside. A son was born to the happy couple exactly one year to the day after Nicholas died. He was named Adeodatus, meaning "gift of God."[78]

So the little family enjoyed contentment and prosperity. Seven years later, however, as grand preparations were being made by Cethron and Euphorsyna to celebrate St. Nicholas' feast day and Adeodatus' birthday, a terrifying scene unfolded. Arabs from the east descended into Exoranda, wreaking havoc as they went. In the turmoil, the boy was yanked up and taken to be sold as a slave in Babylon. Adeodatus was auctioned and made a cupbearer in the palace of King Marmorinus of Babylon. One day, so the story goes, Adeodatus entered the presence of King Marmorinus with his face hanging low in deep sadness. King Marmorinus noticed and asked what was wrong. In the Old Testament book of Nehemiah, Nehemiah the exile also served as cupbearer to the king of Babylon, one named Artaxerxes. King Artaxerxes noticed Nehemiah looking especially dejected and sad one day and asked, "Why does your face look so sad when you are not ill? This can be nothing but sadness of heart" (Neh 2:2). Timidly, Nehemiah answered that his heart ached to return to the land of this fathers, to Jerusalem. He expected rebuke, but none came. To his surprise, the king gave him his blessing and let him depart for home. Such was not to be the outcome of Adeodatus' tale. We pick up the story in Reginold's Latin edition at the point where Adeodatus responds to King Marmorinus' inquiry.

The child indeed had reason to fear, and though trembling, he began to speak to him, saying, "My Lord King I remembered for a moment in my mind that today it has been one full year since I was taken captive by you, because my mother was on that day performing a solemn observance in the church of Saint Nicholas our lord."

After listening to these things, the king responded and said to him: "O wretched child, what benefit is it to you to think about that, since I have you with me? And who is it that can take you from my hand unless our god wills it? You should think about that. Bring me something to drink!"

The child picked up a goblet in order to prepare a drink, and put water in his hands in order to wash the cup. Suddenly Nicholas appeared before the man, and he grabbed the child by the hair on the top of his head, and carried him back and restored him to his mother. When the child was returned, everyone looked outside the gate of the church at him standing there with the goblet of water in his hand. Some went out to take hold of him and talk to him, saying, "Who are you?"

And he said, "I am Adeodatus, Cethron's son."

When his mother Euphrosyna heard this, she ran to him for her heart was moved and she embraced him with tears of joy. And putting her arms around the neck of her son, she began to rejoice and said, "Thanks be to you, Lord Jesus

FIGURE 4
Nicholas saves Adeodatus, painted on a bottle of myrrh

Christ, that our son is alive! You have not deprived me of your grace, but behold my son! I have seen him with my eyes before I have been called out of this world, so that with the Father and the Holy Spirit you live and reign, God for ever and ever. Amen."[79]

It should not come as a surprise to learn that this story became the basis of a very popular theatrical production in the Middle Ages. As early as the 1100s it was being performed on stage.[80]

The story of Adeodatus was not the only medieval legend to associate Nicholas with children. In another story, a man pledged to give a golden cup to the altar of St. Nicholas but changed his mind and decided to keep the precious thing and had a second cup made to donate to the altar. The act of dishonesty cost the man the life of his son, who fell overboard and drowned in the sea. The man tried to rectify his offense to the saint, though imperfectly. He placed the second cup as a gift on the altar, but it tipped over. The cup was set upright but it fell off again. The man was confused and ridden with anxiety when unexpectedly his son reappeared to him, alive and well. The tale concludes with the son taking the original cup and placing it as a gift on the altar, thus helping his father fulfill his vow in good faith. These and other stories helped strengthen the connection between Nicholas and children, and he became the especially beloved patron saint of children. By the twentieth century, children pervaded the pictures and stories of St. Nicholas such that the two were bound together; the modern-day St. Nick cannot be imagined apart from his relationship to little ones.

53

3

Three Gifts and One Election

The boy Nicholas, now about eighteen, grieved for his dead parents. He had received from them love and the blessing of baptism. He had seen in them the virtues of service, selflessness, and devotion. In death, they bestowed one more gift: all their worldly wealth. In their will they had left their son, their sole heir, a hefty inheritance. "When his parents departed from this earth to return to the Lord, they left him great wealth in gold and property."[1] It was his to do with as he pleased. Like the prodigal son, he could squander it on trifles. Like the slave given a talent by his master, he could bury it in the ground and do nothing. But Nicholas was destined to do something different.

The biographer Michael the Archimandrite records Nicholas' personal musings during this time of transition: "Thinking hard about God's goodness, he asked God that he might dispose of his life and his assets in accordance with His will."[2] He prayed the prayer of the Psalms: "Teach me to do your will, because you raised my soul" (Ps 143:10).[3] He remembered the Psalmist's caution about material wealth: "He keeps me away from all kinds of greed and worldly ambitions" (Ps 143:8) and "Do not be attached to riches, even if they abound" (Ps 62:11).[4] Nicholas was wary of the temptation his inheritance presented; it opened the gate to greed, worldly ambition, pride, gluttony, and self-destruction. He wondered what he should do to avoid such pitfalls. Michael tells us that he called to mind Proverbs 11:17, "The person who has compassion on the indigent and on the poor does good for his soul."[5] Perhaps Nicholas also recalled his parents saying it was better to give than receive. This well-worn proverb once sprang with startling freshness from the lips of Jesus, as quoted by Paul in a speech he gave to the church elders of Ephesus (Acts 20:35). And Jesus had more to say on the subject. His challenge had gone beyond the occasional act of kindness as he commanded his followers to give food to the hungry, drink to the thirsty, shelter to the homeless, clothes to the naked, care to the sick, and comfort to the imprisoned (Matt 25:34-40). His message was radical and demanding. To the rich young man, he said: "Go, sell your possessions and give to the poor, and you will have treasure in heaven. Then come, follow me" (Matt 19:21). Nicholas read in Scripture about how the first believers took care of one another and met each other's needs out of their resources: "From time to time those who owned lands or houses sold them, brought the money from the sales and put it at the apostles' feet, and it was distributed to anyone as he had need" (Acts 4:34-35). Indeed, one of the first official acts of the church was to elect seven individuals to see to the daily distribution of food to the poor (Acts 6:1-7). Christians were supposed to take care of each other.

More than that, Christians were supposed to take care of *anyone* in need, even those they did not know or like. And the early church did these things to the astonishment of their neighbors. When non-Christians initially encountered the new-fangled religion of Jesus, they immediately noticed how its members took care of one another. Unlike other religious cults and spiritual societies, the Christians did not collect dues or charge induction fees. Tertullian (160–220), explaining Christian behavior to outsiders, said that members of the Christian community treated each other like family—mothers, brothers, sisters, fathers—and contributed money voluntarily.[6] Not only did they take care of each other, these people of the Way provided for others as well—food and shelter for orphans and widows, clothing for prisoners who worked the mines, medicine for the sick and bedridden, and even graves and coffins for the recently deceased.[7]

And so it was that when young Nicholas uncovered the existence of three young maidens in Patara, all daughters of a once-wealthy man who had lost everything, he decided to act and in so doing "revealed his true character."[8]

Nicholas' Most Famous Act

In the callous world of late antiquity, Fortune's wheel could be unforgiving. People did not have liquid assets, savings accounts, retirement plans, or credit lines to draw upon when hardship struck. A bad crop, a lost ship of merchandise, a debilitating injury, or a failed deal could spell ruin for a small family. Michael the Archimandrite tells of one singularly unlucky man who had become so desperate that he resolved to sell his daughters one by one into prostitution. Although Michael withholds the man's name, he does provide two details about him: he "came from well-to-do and noble parents" and "lived near the house of the Blessed One," that is, Nicholas.[9] "Because of the malice and snares of Satan, who always envies those who have chosen to live according to God, and having fallen suddenly into great poverty and distress so that he was plunged from happiness into extreme poverty, the man reasoned that since he has three beautiful daughters he would prostitute them so that he and his family might live."[10] Michael gives something of a rationale for the father's deplorable actions by saying that no bachelor, however rich or poor, was willing to marry any of the girls because of their poverty. Even those men who might advance their social standing by marrying one of the daughters stayed far away. With no money, no prospects, no food, and no provisions, the family was left no other options. And so, "desiring to provide for his own survival and abandoning hope in God," the father decided to do the unthinkable, and sell the sexual services of his daughters.[11]

Contemporary readers might well wonder if the father had the right to sell his girls like merchandise. This extreme course of action was not as uncommon as it might at first seem. The historian Zosimus confirms that during this period mothers sold their sons and fathers their daughters to pay the provincial tax collectors.[12] The Roman emperor Constantine enacted legislation in Africa and in Italy to make available public funds so as to provide food, clothing, and even cash for families in crisis, lest they be tempted to abandon their children or sell them into slavery or prostitution.[13] A similar measure had been enacted by the Empire two hundred years earlier—an indication that the sale or abandonment of children was a real and recurring problem. For those caught in the clutches of poverty, such a move was a way to survive. In a sermon, Basil of Caesarea remembers a desperate sight he witnessed in the marketplace: a father selling his children because of debt.[14] Ambrose of Milan recounts something similar. "Who," he asks, "should be sold first?"[15] The father miserably sifts through his pathetic options and decides: "I will sell the firstborn. But, he was the first to call me father. He is the first among the children and the one who will bring me honor in my old age. So, I will put up the younger. But that one is so tender and in need of love. I am ashamed to sell one and I pity the other."[16] Ambrose makes the pain of the decision palpable. Who could possibly look his child in the eye and say, "My son, I am selling you so I can eat"?[17] The historical record shows that children, both boys and girls, occasionally went to the auction for just this reason.

The Christian community attempted to put some boundaries and limits on a father's whims. The Council of Elvira met near Granada, Spain, sometime around or before 310 and promulgated eighty-one canons or rulings on a wide variety of domestic and liturgical matters, including the prohibition of household idols and pictures of any kind—whether hung or painted—on the walls of the church. In regard to the father's rights over his daughters, three relevant canons collectively forbade Christian maidens from being given in matrimony to pagans, heretics, Jews, or priests of the idols.[18] The injunctions were not aimed at restricting the freedom of girls to marry; they were aimed at the rights of the fathers who made those decisions for their daughters. Canon 16 specified, "If parents do anything contrary to this prohibition, they should be out of communion for five years." The parent, not the child, was being addressed.[19]

The father in Michael's story could in fact sell his daughters one by one into slavery or prostitution, despite society's general disapproval and the church's condemnation. "But the loving God, who does not want the work of his hands to slip into the guilt of sin, sent his holy angel—I mean the divine Nicholas—in order to save him [the father] and his entire family from poverty as well as from perdition, and also to help the man regain his former good fortune."[20] If the physical remains at Pompeii on the western coast of Italy give any indication, the business of prostitution thrived in classical and late antique times. That city supported a number of brothels, one of which was divided into ten separate rooms. Provocatively painted scenes and lurid inscriptions on the walls of Pompeii's baths suggest that sexual services might have been obtained there as well. Nicholas must have wondered what he might do to rescue these girls from such a fate. Michael the Archimandrite says Nicholas turned once again to the Scriptures for consolation and guidance, refreshing himself with the words of the Proverbs, whose strong emphasis on charity, virtuous action, and care for the poor fortified his mind.[21] He resolved in his heart "as one standing before the judgment of God" to become their protector.[22] It was a bold and brave thing, but Nicholas was convinced it was the right thing to do. Compelled by the Scriptures and his Christian convictions, he placed a few gold coins in a small money-purse, tied the string, and in the dead of night tossed it through an open window into the man's house. When the miraculous gift was found the next morning, the family praised God and cried tears of joy. Here Michael re-creates the scene in his own words:

> Acting with caution, he gathered in a cloth a sufficient sum of gold coins which he secretly threw through the window of the man's house, and quickly returned to his home. When daylight came, the man got up from bed and found in the middle of the house a pile of money. He could not hold back his tears but was overjoyed, amazed and stunned. He gave thanks to God but also tried to understand the meaning of this good fortune. Deciding to accept the gift as if it had been given by God, the father of the girls took the serendipitously found gold and noticed that the sum corresponded to the amount of money needed for a dowry. Without delay he adorned the bridal chamber of his eldest daughter. And so his life once again became good, full of joy and peace of mind, thanks to the intervention of the holy Nicholas, who had created a way for his daughter to marry.
>
> Becoming aware of what the father had done, the man of God and generous alms-giver, Nicholas, seeing that his charity work had resulted in the festivities of a beautiful wedding and created an atmosphere of new joy, went again to the same window, tossed in a similar amount of money, and quickly returned to his home.
>
> When the father of the girls awoke and got up in the morning, he picked up the new and completely unexpected gift of money and fell on his face before God with cries of gratitude. He was almost unable to open his mouth at the arrival of this new gift. Deeply moved, he turned to God with words half-formed in his mind, praying in his heart with sincere supplications: "Tell me, O Lord, what good angel from among the people you designated for us. Tell me who has prepared this banquet full of delicious treats. Who is administering the riches of your immense kindness to humble people like us? Thanks to that person we have been

60

released, beyond all hope, from misery and the spiritual death of sin that had ensnared us. Behold, for your indescribable gift allowed me to legally marry my second daughter, freeing her and me from the ugly desperation and wickedness in which we had fallen. Glorify your holy name, and glory be to your great goodness without end—which is for us, your unworthy people."[23]

Michael's tale of unexpected generosity tugs at the heartstrings. One might say that it verges on melodrama and that the narrative becomes overly sentimental. And yet, in spite of this criticism, it makes for a delightfully memorable and compelling story. This may be in part due to the fact that Michael fixes our attention on the father's spiritual journey, and this is what he communicates with clarity.[24] The father's salvation was not only from the misery of financial catastrophe but from spiritual crisis: the spiritual death of sin. In his prayer, the man shows gratitude to God and to God's secret agent of grace. The gifts were divine answers to desperate prayers. By law and by custom, the family of the bride must give a dowry of property, business, or money to the husband's family as part of the marriage agreement. It was a tradition that dated back to the Code of Hammurabi (c. 1790 B.C.) and continued as a widespread practice into the nineteenth century of our own era; it is still in effect in some cultures to this day. After Nicholas' generosity, the father was able to provide a dowry, thus affording his daughter the opportunity to marry and saving his family's honor from public disgrace.

Twice the family had been saved from ultimate despair. The father must have wondered if the unknown benefactor could be counted on a third time. Michael intimates that he vacillated between hope and despair, watching the windows every night and praying to God for just one more miracle.

Having conducted the marriage of his second child like the first, the father, who had enjoyed the gifts that God had sent him through his servant Nicholas, spent the following nights in vigil. Staying sober and alert throughout the night, he hoped that the stranger would bring a dowry to his third daughter also. Because he had brought gifts to the other sisters without being recognized, [the father] would have to remain watchful so as not to miss him while sleeping.

While the man tried with great effort to remain awake through those long nights, Nicholas, the worshiper of the Trinity and a servant of the one Christ of the Holy Trinity, our true God, came in the night to the usual place. He wanted the third daughter to be able to marry in the same way as the others. Surreptitiously throwing an equal amount of money through the window, he turned away in silence. But soon as the gold landed inside, the father of the girls, who had been expecting the return of our saint, immediately ran out and caught him. Recognizing who he was, [the father] fell prostrate at the feet and broke into tears and sobs. He thanked him warmly and with many words praised him before God as the savior of him and his three daughters. He said: "If it were not for your goodness, which was stirred up by our Lord Jesus Christ, I would have long since consigned my life to ruin and shame."[25]

In his fifteenth-century English translation of the story, William Caxton reports the father's actions in an abbreviated but touching way: "he kneled doun & wold haue kyssed hys feet, but the holy man wold not, but requyred hym not to telle ne descouer thys thyng as longe as he lyued."[26] Nicholas, though caught off guard by the father's actions and embarrassed at being recognized, asked for nothing in return except a promise that his identity would remain secret as long as he remained alive. According to Michael, "Saint Nicholas raised the man from the ground and forced him to swear not to tell anyone how he came by those gifts until the end of his life. So let the man go away in peace."[27] In his tenth-century retelling of the story, Symeon Metaphrastes says, "he made [the father] take an oath never to tell anyone what had happened his whole life long, or to make public his benevolence," only to add the following line: "Now of all the deeds done by the magnificent Nicholas, this one is the most charitable and he best known."[28] It is ironic that in the same breath that Symeon dutifully notes Nicholas' wish *not* to make his action known, he happily declares that it is the "best known" of them all.

And like that, Nicholas entered the pages of history as one of the greatest gift-givers of all time. He answered the plea for mercy by transforming his handsome inheritance into marriage dowries. From the legacy of two deaths came the promise of three new beginnings, turning his parents' gift into a father's answered prayer. In this endearing and enduring story, we see all the raw materials for the magical Santa Claus tale: a mysterious night visitor who silently enters the home to bestow wonderful gifts to children. As the story was told and retold, new details were added. In one version, the money bags landed in the girls' shoes. In another, Nicholas found that the windows of the house were shut, so he was forced to drop the bags of gold down the chimney where they fell into one of the girls' stockings, which had been hung by the fireplace to dry.

63

—Nicholas and Apollonius—

Just as interesting as the connection of this story about Nicholas to the Santa myth is its connection to paganism. In order to read this story correctly, we must read it in its cultural context: the clash between Christianity and paganism. The episode not only elevates Christian virtue and generosity, personal faith, and love of neighbor, it also upends pagan expectations of the day. While the story does not present an open challenge to paganism, there is an implicit challenge that should not be missed. The tale of the three dowries, as it turns out, has a parallel in pagan literature, where we find a remarkably similar story told to a strikingly different end.

Written around A.D. 216 in Greek by the Athenian author Philostratus (170–245), at the request of Julia Domna, mother of the emperor, *The Life of Apollonius of Tyana* follows the saga of a certain Apollonius who serves as a philosophical substitute for Jesus.[29] Said to have been born in A.D. 2, Apollonius joined the Pythagoreans as a teenager and learned their habits of abstaining from meat, strong wine, marriage, immorality, and haircuts. He became a magnetic teacher of philosophy and a spiritual guru who performed miracles and could even fly from one location to another. Known as "the Sage," Apollonius became a luminous icon for the proud spirit of paganism in its twilight years. He emerged in the minds of many as a Greco-Roman counterpart to Christ: "Why do we need Jesus when we have Apollonius? Apollonius did the same kinds of things as Jesus, true or false?"[30] The name of Apollonius was bandied about in debates between Christians and pagans. The anti-Christian philosopher Porphyry appealed to him as an example of virtue in a treatise *Against the Christians*. The Christian apologist Macarius Magnes refuted Porphyry.[31] Hierocles held up Apollonius as a rival to Jesus in a tract called *The Lover of Truth*, against which the Christians issued their own tract, *Against Hierocles*.[32]

Forming part of a long rebuttal to the pagan alternative, Michael the Archimandrite's *Life of St. Nicholas* might be read as something of an answer, or echo of an answer, to Philostratus' *Life of Apollonius*.[33] Apollonius was born in Tyana, on the southern coast of Turkey near present-day Anatolia; Nicholas was born in Patara, also on the southern coast of Turkey. Nicholas was virtuous from his youth, as was Apollonius.[34] Both gave away their possessions. Both intervened at a trial to save someone condemned to death.[35] Most interesting, both provided dowries to a poor father so that his daughters might marry. According to Philostratus, a certain businessman was sacrificing to the Earth when he saw Apollonius coming and prayed to him for help. The man claimed to be the most unlucky person in the world and lamented, "I have four daughters and need four dowries, but while I have twenty thousand drachmas for now, when my daughters each get a share, they will seem to have got only a little, while I will be ruined and destitute."[36] Apollonius took pity on the wretch and directed him to use his twenty thousand drachmas to buy an olive orchard that had fallen into disrepair. When the man inspected the property he had risked his money on, he discovered a jar full of gold coins, making him rich, so that "his household was full of eager suitors."[37]

The similarities between the stories of Apollonius and Nicholas are obvious. What should be noticed, however, are the differences. The opposing religious orientations of the two stories immediately pop out. Nicholas saves the poor man from ruin by giving out of his own wealth; Apollonius concocts a secret plan. Nicholas sacrifices; Apollonius resorts to cleverness and a bit of prophecy. In the Nicholas narrative, no magic is performed, nor does the father need to do anything to earn the reward. Nicholas acts as a servant (*servus*) and worshiper (*adorator*) of the "Trinity and the only-begotten one of the Trinity, Christ, our true God."[38] The poor man in Apollonius' story, by contrast, makes offerings to mother Earth and prays to Pandora, the "giver of all." Another point of difference, albeit a minor one, is the Trinitarian motif that runs throughout the Nicholas story. There are three daughters, three bags of gold, three nighttime visitations. Apollonius' story has no interest in this theological theme—there are four daughters instead of three, and Apollonius makes one appearance, not three.

A New Kind of Saint

As has been said, Michael composed his biography of St. Nicholas primarily to edify, instruct, and improve the moral conduct of his monks who were lodged in the high hollows of central Turkey. So, what lessons emerge from the story of the three dowries? What ethical truths does it bestow upon the reader? At least four major moral lessons are embedded in the story. First, Nicholas demonstrated the value of intentional, targeted giving, that is, giving in order to meet specific needs as opposed to giving randomly for the sake of generosity or for ridding oneself of possessions. Second, Nicholas' choice of recipients imparts important implications. By giving his money to three world-forsaken girls so that they might marry, Nicholas affirmed the moral value of marriage in an age when its worth was being severely tested. Third, Nicholas offered a compelling model of ordinary goodness in which good deeds need not be miraculous, angelic, or incredible. The episode shows that Christian generosity can be mundane; anyone might do what Nicholas did. Fourth, Nicholas laid down the highest challenge to those who would strive for Christian virtue: anonymity. Nicholas' example calls those who would take pride in their good works to give in secret.

Know to Whom You Are Giving

Nicholas did not exactly follow the saintly mandate of "giving all you have to the poor." He did not indiscriminately disperse his property to an unidentified mass of poor people but targeted his charity so as to produce the maximum effect. Michael informs the reader that Nicholas spent some time pondering his actions, taking into account the needs of the girls, the dignity of the father, and the preservation of his own humility.[39] Curiously, he does not say exactly how Nicholas learned of the family's needs. Gustav Anrich, however, has found one tenth-century manuscript that does.[40] According to

Anrich, an anonymous author reworked the original story to make it about Nicholas of Sion instead of Nicholas of Myra. In this variation, there are only two daughters, and their plight is disclosed to Nicholas by an angel in a dream. Young Nicholas wakes up and decides to act. Not once, but twice, he steals fifty gold pieces from his parents—who, it should be noted, were still alive—and throws the money through the window of the girls' home and onto the dinner table. The text is interesting not only because of its alterations to the standard telling but also because of the specificity of its details: the attire and words of the angel, the exact amount of gold, the fact that the bags of money land on the dining table. Whatever we make of this other version, it is important to note that it retains the theme of purposeful and planned works of mercy.

Nicholas of Myra certainly could have "gotten credit" for his charity without spending so much time on investigation. An almost exact contemporary of his, Antony (c. 251–356), who made his home as a monk in the desert of Egypt, inherited a sizable estate from his parents when he was still a young man. Six months after their death, he stood in church one day and heard the command of Jesus to the rich young man to sell all his possessions and give the money to the poor. He felt the words directed at him. Immediately, he gave his family's land, three hundred acres in all, to the villagers and liquidated all other assets, giving the proceeds to the poor, "that they should be no more a clog upon himself and his sister."[41] We are not told what his sister thought of the arrangement. Nor are we told exactly who benefitted from his gifts: who received the proceeds and the land and what did they do with them? It does not seem to matter. Antony's example of giving everything to the poor—whoever they are—in order to free himself from earthly concerns is not unique. He encouraged others to do the same. Once a man decided to renounce the world and enter the desert to live as a hermit like Antony. But, instead of giving all his possessions away, he kept a little of his money in case of emergency. Antony told him, "If you want to be a monk, go to the village over there, buy some meat, hang it on your naked body and come back here."[42] The man did as he was told. To his dismay, birds and dogs began picking and tearing at the meat hanging from him and in the process their beaks and teeth caught and ripped his flesh too. Antony looked at him unsympathetically and said, "Those who renounce the world but want to keep their money are attacked in that way by demons and torn in pieces."[43]

Nicholas' actions were qualitatively different. He did not relinquish his wealth solely to edify his soul or test his mettle. His charity was not simply flung out the door and onto the poor. He was compelled not only by a love of God but by a profound concern for the needs of his neighbors. He gave to a family in despair—to three daughters at the end of their rope. In this he followed an old Christian proverb, "Let your alms sweat in your hands until you know to whom you are giving."[44]

In Defense of Marriage

Nicholas certainly knew to whom he gave. What he could not have known at the time was the theological statement he was making about marriage. By supplying the girls with dowries for marriage, he was giving his tacit support to the estate of marriage as something good and noble. While people today argue about the morality of same-sex marriage or the rising levels of divorce rates, the third- and fourth-century Christian wondered if anyone, male or female, should marry—ever. Disciples were to imitate Jesus, who was himself unmarried and who said that in heaven no one would marry or be given in marriage (Mark 12:24). In 1 Corinthians, the apostle Paul indicated his personal preference on the subject: "I wish that all men were as I am . . . [that is] unmarried, as I am" (1 Cor 7:7-8). Paul goes on to give a number of reasons for this preference— unmarried people are not tied down to home and hearth; they do not have the responsibilities of raising children and caring for a family. Because of this, they have more energy, time, and freedom to serve God and go where they are needed, especially since "the time is short" (1 Cor 7:29).

Later Christians who read the Gospels and Paul's words nodded their heads and came to the conclusion that the preferred life must be the single life. Jesus called his followers to separate from the world and its desires.[45] Ambrose, Augustine, Cyprian, Jerome, John Chrysostom, and Tertullian all wrote treatises, pamphlets, sermons, and letters on the blessedness of virginity. To be completely devoted to God, one must clear away all worldly commitments and bodily entanglements. Restraint of sexual desire displayed superior self-control and often became the supreme test of virtue. It demanded full command of spirit, mind, and body. St. Hilary (d. 368) counseled his daughter Apia not to marry but remain in a perpetual state of blessed virginity. Apia consented, but her father must have had his doubts about her resolve because he "prayed the Lord to call her to Himself, rather than let her live any longer."[46] A few days later, Apia died. A similar tale was told about St. Peter and his daughter. Benedict of Nursia (480–547) soothed his own flames of desire by throwing himself into dense bushes of thorns and nettles.[47] Jerome (c. 347–420) told an even more shocking tale: one young "soldier of Christ" was taken by his persecutors to a lush garden where he was tied down. A prostitute entered and began touching and kissing him; since he could turn neither to the left nor the right, he bit off his own tongue and spat it at her rather than besmirch his chastity.[48] These examples represent an extreme attitude, to be sure, but they resonated with a broader conventional wisdom about such things. The flesh must be disciplined so that it is not easily distracted by food, sex, money, pride, and the rest. Every temptation must be removed. As the true disciple divests himself or herself of worldly wealth, rich foods, and strong wines, so he or she must forego interaction with the opposite sex. In the camps of the monks, for instance, no females were allowed to enter, not even a female donkey. And ministers were expected to set the example for the rest—to be chaste and preferably celibate. Some priests and monks went so far as to castrate themselves so as to remove the temptation from their bodies literally—and become "eunuchs for the Kingdom of heaven's sake" (Matt 19:12).

When Nicholas arrived at Nicaea many years later for the historic and monumental council of 325, this, in fact, was one of the issues raised. Fortunately, the council showed as much good sense as spiritual wisdom: young men should not be encouraged to maim or castrate themselves out of devotion to God. Eunuchs were permitted to join religious orders only if their castration had been for medical reasons or if it had been done against their wills by an owner or a barbarian.[49] The following motion was also made: all married ministers, priests, and bishops should put away their wives. Nicholas surely must have winced at hearing such nonsense. Paphnutius, an Egyptian bishop who had suffered the loss of an eye and the use of a leg from grueling torture he had endured during persecutions, made a passionate defense of marriage before the bishops and other church leaders attending the council.[50] Marriage was an honorable estate, and separating married couples would put an undo strain on all parties involved. The motion against married ministers ultimately failed, but the impression had been made: marriage was not the ideal for the committed Christian. It was a concession to the weak.[51] Nicholas' actions argued otherwise. He could have spent his inheritance money on any cause—lepers, the blind, prisoners of war, the homeless—but instead he enabled three daughters to marry. Nicholas gave his money to the cause of marriage.

Ordinary Goodness

Most anecdotes in circulation among the early Christian communities involved miracles, exorcisms, and martyrdoms. Some were far-fetched, such as the legend of Peter bringing a smoked tuna back to life or Paul baptizing a repentant lion.[52] Others were factual but no less amazing—stories about sons who turned their backs on their family fortunes and walked away from everything to follow Christ and mothers who would rather have their entrails spilled out on the Colosseum floor than renounce Christ.[53] The exemplars of the faith were martyrs like Vibia Perpetua (d. 203), who was publicly scourged and made a plaything for the crowds at Carthage's amphitheater before being beheaded, and Sebastian (d. 300?), whose arrow-filled body was depicted again and again in early Italian altarpieces. Saints worthy of memory and veneration appeared also in the roles of sacred teachers and enlightened instructors, as is the case with Macrina (324–379), the older sister of Gregory of Nyssa. On her deathbed, "although the fever was burning up all her energy and leading her to death, she was refreshing her body as if by a kind of dew, she kept her mind free in the contemplation of higher things and unimpeded by the disease."[54] According to Gregory, Macrina proceeded to discourse on the soul, the meaning of life, and the resurrection. On other occasions, holy men and women inspired the faithful and awed the masses by their extreme asceticism. Symeon Stylites (390–459) was dismissed by his abbot from the monastery at Eusebona near Antioch for mortifying his flesh by wearing a rope of twisted palm leaves so tightly and for so long that it began to eat through his skin. Once beyond the reach of the abbot, he found other ways to practice his self-mortification, first atop a nine-foot pillar, then an eighteen-foot pillar, a thirty-three-foot pillar, and finally a sixty-foot pillar that was only six feet wide. The historian Theodoret of Cyrrhus (c. 393–457) recounted "incalculable numbers" of pilgrims who came to see him. "Not only those living nearby, but also those separated by a journey of many days" flocked to Symeon, "all trying to touch him and to gain some blessing from his clothing of skins."[55] Daniel (409–493), the immediate successor to Symeon's mantle and pillar, became an even greater tourist attraction—the Emperor Leo saw to it that his pillar was reinforced and expanded so that he could be exhibited to imperial guests.

71

Nicholas' story was different, though. Here was a young man—not even a bishop and certainly not an ascetic monk nor a trained theologian—performing a seemingly random act of kindness on behalf of three poor girls. There was no voice from heaven, no blinding light, nothing paranormal, nothing bloody or gruesome. The girls were not daughters of the emperor or some other celebrity; they were like anyone else caught in the trap of poverty and hunger, a trap that ensnared millions of faceless and nameless individuals in the ancient world. Their choices were enslavement, forced prostitution, homelessness, starvation. And Nicholas saved them. This was a story to which ordinary people could relate. "He who teaches others by his life and not his speech is truly wise."[56] Nicholas taught his faith by his actions. He was living up to his name, "the people's champion," and for him, the miracle was in the mundane. Jerome relayed a similar story in his *Life of St. Hilarion*. Hilarion (291–371), a contemporary of Nicholas, lived an ascetic lifestyle in Syria and on the isle of Cyprus. One day he received a visit from Aristaenete, the wife of Elpidius the Praetorian prefect. Her three boys lay in bed feverishly ill, and she begged the saint to go to them. In a tearful apology, Hilarion had to refuse, saying he could never leave his hermitage. Undaunted, Aristaenete said his visit could be kept secret if he would only come to Gaza at night. This Hilarion did, and the children were healed.[57] As in the story of the three poor maidens, there were in Jerome's story three youngsters in dire need and a parent in distress. In both instances, the saint made a nighttime visit to the distressed families. But—and here is the crucial difference—in one account the dilemma was resolved by a material gift, in the other by a miraculous touch. Nicholas' deed was memorable precisely because it did not depend on supernatural intervention but on common Christian charity.

Giver Unknown

In the second part of his massive and labyrinthine summation of Christian beliefs, the *Summa Theologiae*, Thomas Aquinas offers a lengthy discussion of virtues. Topics include justice, prudence, temperance, fortitude, hope, and charity. At one point, Aquinas wonders if ingratitude counts as a sin. His logic is swift: because gratitude and thankfulness count as virtues, neglect of these virtues must be reckoned as sinful and inexcusable. "It is evident that every ingratitude is a sin."[58] Having made his argument, Aquinas feels satisfied with his position until he remembers the words of Seneca, who said, "sometimes it is necessary to deceive the person who receives assistance, in order that he may receive without knowing from whom he has received."[59] It seems like wise counsel to avoid doing good deeds only to be noticed and praised for them. But performing deeds in this way could put the recipient unavoidably in the way of ingratitude. And that, Aquinas remembers, is exactly what happened in the story of the blessed Nicholas and the three dowries. The poor man had no idea who was slinging gifts through his window in the middle of the night. Nicholas had purposefully hidden his identity because he wished "to avoid vainglory" and "popularity."[60] The man did not know to whom he should be grateful and give thanks. Aquinas realizes he must rethink his position: "He that is unaware of a favor conferred on him is not ungrateful, if he fails to repay it, provided he be prepared to do so if he knew."[61]

73

Young Nicholas demonstrated himself to be a true disciple of Jesus. He showed concern for all people by providing for the needs of the town's unwed daughters. But he went one step further: he preserved his modesty and humility by remaining anonymous, choosing not to "sound his own trumpet."[62] Even so, the impulse of the story will not allow his deeds to go completely unnoticed and unhonored. Michael the Archimandrite cannot resist exclaiming his praise: "O strong saint of compassion toward the destitute! O beatific Nicholas, worthy of the noble counsel of Christ!"[63] By the end of the story, Nicholas is duly recognized and praised for his charity, even as he shuns the attention and obliges the father not to tell anyone.

Why anonymous? Why would Nicholas want his charity to remain unknown? Acts of generosity were not out of the ordinary in the ancient world; they occurred frequently. Leading men regularly lavished their wealth on public works, Olympic games, colonnades, temples, statues, and art. Households with money not only gave freely, they were expected to give. But never was it imagined they would give anonymously. The name of the benefactor would be boldly inscribed on the monument he had commissioned, often with the price tag posted prominently too. The host of the game, festival, or party would be elevated to the seat of honor. Honor and merit were bound tightly with generosity. They were one and the same. To the average listener, Jesus' words must have sounded radical and countercultural when he said, "when you give to the needy, do not announce it with trumpets, as the hypocrites do in the synagogues and on the streets, to be honored by men" (Matt 6:5). Such people deserved no honor or admiration because their actions were driven by arrogance, not charity. Instead, Jesus advised his disciples in the following manner: "When you give to the needy, do not let your left hand know what your right hand is doing, so that your giving may be in secret" (Matt 6:6). Not much in these statements strikes the modern reader as revolutionary. Many people today prefer to give anonymously and certainly without blowing trumpets. But in Nicholas' world, anonymous giving was simply not done. A story of three girls receiving bags of gold on three separate occasions from an unknown benefactor was something novel and worth retelling. It made an extraordinary impact on the Christian communities who first encountered it. The tale of the three daughters was more than an anecdote. It was something totally new—the likes of which had never been imagined. It became the story with which people identified Nicholas.

When the common worshiper of old gazed at great church frescoes, basilica mosaics, or stained-glass portraits of Jesus, Mary, John the Baptist, the apostles, and saints, he or she had to look for small visual clues, like keys or a sword or a scythe, to distinguish St. Luke from St. Matthew or St. Paul from St. Peter or St. Ezekiel from St. Elisha. There was even less to distinguish nonbiblical saints from each other. There was slight to no difference between one bishop wearing a miter hat and carrying a crozier staff from another bishop wearing a miter and carrying a crozier. In the midst of all these monotonous characters, St. Nicholas stood out. He could always be recognized as the one carrying three bags of gold, or, more often, three gold spheres or three gold discs.

The story of Nicholas' generosity to the three maidens caused him to jump off the dry page of history and into the minds of artists and the imaginations of young girls, and boys, and adults. Whenever Nicholas was depicted in art, he was always shown with his three golden gifts. Some theologians would allegorize the three gifts they saw in the pictures as faith, hope, and charity.[64] Others saw in the three gifts a reference to the Trinity or a sign of wealth and good fortune.

In Raphael's 1505 painting known as the *Ansidei Madonna*, a work of technical perfection and symmetry, mother Mary sits upright in an elevated and canopied seat, looking serene and stately (fig. 5). The fleshy newborn Jesus is propped on her lap. John the Baptist stands to one side, wearing a rough camel-hair garment with a red, toga-like palla draped over his sun-darkened skin. His eyes are turned upward; his thoughts are not of this world. It is hard to know to whom the viewer should relate. Certainly not John the Baptist—he is far too unearthly, nor the Virgin Mother. Seated high on her gilded throne, her attention is devoted to her beautiful and divine son. But then there is Nicholas, standing on the other side of Mary. He is decked out in full ecclesiastical regalia, but, almost comically, he does not look at all comfortable in them. The pointed miter pushes down on his forehead. His oversized cloak restricts his arm and leg movement. He cradles an open book in both hands while trying not to drop his decorative crozier staff. He has had to put his three gold spheres on the floor. The viewer wonders if he is searching for a prophetic word to fit the occasion

FIGURE 5

*The Madonna and Child with St. John the Baptist and St. Nicholas of
Bari, 1505 (oil on panel) by Raphael (Raffaello Sanzio of Urbino) (1483–
1520) (National Gallery, London / The Bridgeman Art Library)*

or a bedtime story to read to the infant. Either way, his face
reveals that he is having trouble finding what he is looking
for, and the book is tilted as if to catch a little more sun on the
page. In the holy presence of Jesus, Mary, and John the Baptist, Nicholas is approachable, likeable—dare we say—friendly.
Despite the high formality of the Renaissance style, Raphael
has painted everything we love about Nicholas. His frump-
ish, ill-fitting attire endears him to the viewer. His preoccupation with his book humanizes him—one day Santa Claus will

likewise occupy himself with long lists of children's names which he'll study through a pair of spectacles perched on the end of his nose.

If nothing else, the story of the three daughters in distress made Nicholas preeminently likeable. He was likeable not only because he was generous with his wealth, but more importantly, he was trustworthy; he did not let down the girls in their hour of need—the money showed up on time. To pawnbrokers, money lenders, bankers, and financiers of all kinds, St. Nicholas became the gold standard, the guarantor of payment: "I swear by St. Nicholas that I will repay this loan in thirty days." The Lombards, who were the great moneylenders of the early Middle Ages, adopted the three coins of Nicholas as their symbol.[65] The emerging classes of pawnbrokers, bankers, and moneylenders followed their lead. To this day, the universal symbol of pawn dealers is the three gold balls of Nicholas, and three gold spheres in a triangular formation can be seen on the marquees of pawn shops everywhere (fig. 6). Because thieves were also associated with money—namely by stealing it!—they also adopted him as their patron saint, referring to themselves as "the blades of St. Nicholas."

It is perhaps in connection with moneylending that the following story of a Jew and a dishonest moneylender came into existence. In the historical record, it appears in countless

FIGURE 6
Local pawn shop sign showing the three spheres of St. Nicholas

forms and versions, indicating its popularity throughout the Middle Ages. Here it is retold by the medieval compiler of legends, Jacobus de Voragine:

> A certain man had borrowed some money from a Jew, giving him his oath on the altar of Saint Nicholas that he would repay it as soon as possible. As he was slow in paying, the Jew demanded his money; but the man declared that he had returned it. He was summoned before the judge, who ordered him to swear that he had repaid the money. In the meantime, the man had placed the money that he owed in a hollow staff, and before giving his oath, he asked the Jew to hold the staff for him. Whereupon he swore that he had returned the money and more besides. Then he took back his staff, the Jew handing it over all unaware of the trick. But on the way home the defrauder fell asleep on the roadside and was run over by a chariot, which also broke open the staff in which the gold was hidden. Learning this, the Jew ran to the spot; but although the bystanders pressed him to take his money, he said that he would do so only if, by the merits of Saint Nicholas, the dead man was restored to life, adding that in this event he himself would receive baptism and be converted to the faith of Christ. Immediately the dead man came back to life, and the Jew was baptized.[66]

The presence of the Jew in this narrative is, on one level, a shameful reminder of an old stereotype and longstanding prejudice. The Jew serves as little more than a stock character—the moneylender. And yet, it is interesting to note that he is not demonized as the "bad guy" in the story. In fact, the Jew is the victim, the one taken advantage of, the one deceived and abused, and ultimately the one whom St. Nicholas avenges. In this story, St. Nicholas is not only the defender of Christians, but also of Jews. In some versions, the villain is actually identified as a Christian—revealing that Nicholas stands up for the innocent even against fellow believers. The episode also reveals the fears of ordinary medieval people who worried about finances, about being cheated, and about losing money. This saint enacts the justice of God on behalf of those who suffered such losses and indignities. He acts swiftly to guarantee fairness and restore property. He shows himself to be a saint for all people, even those outside the fold of the pious and the chaste and the enlightened.

Unexpected Election

As a young man, Nicholas searched for direction, for God's will, and for consolation in the wake of his parents' death. He found purpose in his spiritual labor and worked for "the fruit of justice."[67] He cultivated a habit of good works and service to God. According to Michael the Archimandrite, "Justice and greater justice came forth from Nicholas: from the root of faith and the fear of God his life's work in the world flourished, and many more, it should be said, of his works came to fruition, from the anointing of his oil."[68] More than public charity or personal purity, Nicholas devoted himself to justice, to righting wrongs and correcting inequities. These were the concerns that characterized his life. He was more than a public defender, of course; he was a minister of God. "He praised God in the right manner, and kept the light burning brightly on the high candles, where many people greeted him so that he might speak a good word over them."[69] By all appearances, he was at this time preparing for ministry, perhaps serving as a subdeacon, deacon, or as a reader of the Scriptures—a consecration often given to individuals too young for the more formal ordination to the priesthood. Depending on his age, of course, it is possible he was already a priest. Either way, Michael said his actions ministered God's grace to the people, and he devoted himself to the daily office of worship and ministry. He spoke words of blessing over the people; he kept the candles of devotion lit and the fragrant incense burning. He was finding his calling in life.

—*The Other Nicholas*—

Symeon Metaphrastes, who was the next major biographer of Nicholas after Michael, says that after Nicholas' parents died he was taken in by his uncle, who tended a monastery in the wilderness beyond Patara. Nicholas joined the monks, learned the Scriptures, the liturgies, and the discipline of the monastic way. According to Symeon's account, after a period in the wild, Nicholas boarded an Egyptian boat and made a pilgrimage by himself to ancient Israel, the Holy Land. There he dipped into the Jordan River where Jesus had been baptized, stood on the hill outside of Jerusalem where he was crucified, and knelt at the empty tomb where his body had been laid. But these extraordinary details are not found in the *Life* written by Michael the Archimandrite, who makes no mention of a monastery or a trip to Palestine. Most likely, Symeon Metaphrastes took these biographical tidbits from the anonymously authored *Life of St. Nicholas of Sion*, and so, again we have a case of mistaken identity. As we saw earlier, Symeon and later biographers conflated the fourth-century bishop of Myra with the homonymous sixth-century monk of Sion. The two separate lives were combined to make one grand life.[70]

In actuality, there are no records of Nicholas of Myra joining a monastery or making a pilgrimage to the Holy Land. Nicholas of Sion did these things. At an early age, Nicholas of Sion showed a remarkable spiritual sensitivity, stopping on his way to school to heal a woman named Nonnine when he was just seven. His parents, Epiphanios and Nonna, noticed his gifts, and soon his uncle, who was also named Nicholas, encouraged them to send the boy to Myra. There, the archbishop of the region might be persuaded to ordain him as a reader. The *Life of St. Nicholas of Sion* reports how it happened.

While the child Nicholas was growing up, guided by the Spirit, the church [of Sion in the vicinity of Pharroa] was being completed by the grace of God. Nicholas' most holy uncle, the Archimandrite Nicholas, joined to him the priest Konon, the overseer for the construction of the Church of Holy Sion, and took him to the blessed and most holy Archbishop Nicholas [in the metropolis of Myra],[71] so that the latter would ordain him reader. When the most holy Archbishop saw the features of the child, which were full of grace, he recognized in spirit that the child was to become the "chosen vessel" of the Lord, and he took and blessed him and ordained him to the rank of the readers without receiving of him anything at all for the act of ordination.[72]

Looking at this short excerpt, it is easy to see how readers and listeners blurred and confused the different individuals named Nicholas: young Nicholas was sent by his uncle Nicholas to be ordained in Myra by the Archbishop Nicholas while paying homage at the tomb of Nicholas. Symeon Metaphrastes untangled the jumble of identities by simply rolling all the different personas into one: St. Nicholas the Wonderworker, as he came to be called.[73] The Greek word *thaumatourgos* carried over into Latin as *thaumaturgus* and is rendered in English as "Wonderworker" or sometimes transliterated as "thaumaturge" or "thaumaturgist." The title was reserved as a special designation for certain miracle-performing saints like Nicholas. Given this new identity, Nicholas the Wonderworker transcended place (Myra and Sion) and time (he was not bound by death). He was said to work miracles and wonders (*thauma* in Greek) anywhere his suppliants had need.

On his pilgrimage journey to the holy city of Jerusalem, Nicholas of Sion stopped in the town of Myra for a second time to pay his respects to his namesake at the tomb of St. Nicholas. While staying in Myra, he met a certain skipper from Askalon named Menas who offered him

81

transportation, saying, "I have heard that Your Holiness is about to sail on a pilgrimage to the Holy City of Jerusalem to reap benefit from the power of the Venerable Cross. And if it pleases Your Holiness, come aboard my little boat and bless us [by your presence]."[74] Nicholas of Sion boarded ship with Menas and sailed first to Egypt and then on to Jerusalem, where he made a votive offering, looked inside the open tomb of Jesus, and visited the River Jordan.[75] He was also able to fulfill a vow he had made: to adore the true cross in the Church of the Resurrection.[76] The celebrated discovery of the true cross had drawn pilgrims from all over the known world since the mid-300s; they came to touch, kiss, and sometimes bite off pieces of the wood.[77]

The destiny of St. Nicholas of Myra lay not in Jerusalem to the east or in desert monasteries to the north, but much closer to home. Around the year 295, news reached Patara, where Nicholas was living, that the bishop of the neighboring town of Myra had passed away. Nicholas decided to visit the church and pay his respects. Inside the small facility, bishops from the surrounding area gathered to elect a successor for their recently deceased colleague. It was not an easy task. No willing candidates presented themselves. The church as a whole was weighed down by a great strain—imperial persecution. Christianity was at the time considered an illegal religion. Religions were required to register with the government in order to gain legal standing as private cults. Christianity refused to do so. As a show of loyalty, civilians were required to honor the emperor as a deity. Christians honored only Christ. Upstanding citizens were expected to pay their respects to the gods in public acts of reverence at city festivals, gladiatorial games, and bath houses. Christians refused to attend. Pliny, a Roman governor, thought Christians should be put to death if for no other reason than their stubbornness. The Empire found it hard to trust this new religious movement. Their founder, Jesus, whom Christians worshipped as a god, was put to death by the duly constituted authorities of the Empire for treason, and it appeared his followers promoted the same treason. They were rigid in their worship, calling all other gods demons and all other religions false.[78] Christians refused the normal customs of society, setting themselves apart by their strange lifestyle and practices.[79]

Christians were not the only group singled out for persecution by the Roman Empire, as emperors held in suspicion any guild, society, or association they could not directly control. Domitian expelled all philosophers from Italy and banned actors from the stage because they too often satirized his prestige. Trajan did not permit fire brigades to form lest they turn into political organizations. Any guild might potentially become a nest of treachery and rebellion. Emperors lived apprehensive and distrustful lives, knowing their hold on power could be jeopardized in a moment. Caracalla, emperor in the year 215, had the boys of Alexandria parade in front of him only to have them butchered on the spot for nothing more than a supposed insult against his dignity. Jews suffered sporadic but intense persecutions as well. After the siege and destruction of Jerusalem in A.D. 69, some 97,000 captives were taken to work as slaves in Rome. Many of these slaves had a hand in building Vespasian's fifty-thousand seat Colosseum, and the outline of their pilfered menorah can still be seen in the triumphal arch of Titus. Demoralizing social conditions and discriminations led to a violent uprising in Alexandria in 116, resulting in the death of thousands. Less than fifty years later, a prohibition against circumcision proved the tipping point for another bloody Jewish revolt, this one led by Simon bar Kochba.[80] In response, the Roman governor Tineius Rufus "moved out against the Jews, treating their madness without mercy." According to the church historian Eusebius of Caesarea (263–339), "He destroyed in heaps thousands of men, women and children, and under the law of war, enslaved their land."[81] The butchery knew no bounds. To add insult to injury, Jews were forbidden to enter the sacred city of David, Jerusalem, which was recolonized and renamed Aelia Capitolina.[82] Jewish communities lived in constant fear and regular conflict with the Roman authorities.

The Christian church was one among many groups that suffered imperial harassment and oppression. It should be noted as well that Christians who lived in the first three centuries did not experience persecution everywhere or all the time. Like hot spots along the edges of tectonic plates, persecution would flare up here and cool down there, depending on the public mood, the persons in power, and the activities of the church. Much of the time, Christians were left alone to build churches and convert their neighbors. Occasionally, major shifts in the plates opened fissures, created earthquakes, and unleashed fire. In the latter half of the third century, the ground trembled with mounting tension. Civil wars and barbarian invasions had wrecked the countryside. Frequent famines and outbreaks of plague had disemboweled the cities. The armies were fragmented and disgruntled. Inflation skyrocketed. Corruption among government officials was rampant. No less than fifty different men proclaimed themselves the true Roman emperor at some point during the tumultuous 200s, each one backed by his own military detachment, and each one assassinating and being assassinated in turn.

Diocletian (244–311), a common soldier who rose through the ranks, grabbed at the reins of government in 284; after a series of maneuvers he was declared the senior Augustus, or emperor. After fifty years of militarized anarchy during which time two dozen claimants to the imperial purple fell, he fully appreciated the fragility of the Empire and the precariousness of his situation and understood that the frustrated masses were hungry for a scapegoat. He asked for a sign to know who was to blame for the calamities. Soothsayers came into his presence and sacrificed animal after animal, examining their livers for mystical markings, but to no avail. Nothing could be determined. Something was interfering with the sacrifices and making the markings impossible to interpret. Tages, the chief priest, looked up and pointed his bloodied ritual knife at some of the onlookers. He claimed the sacred omens had been profaned by their presence because they were Christians and had been making the sign of the cross. Diocletian was enraged. He ordered that any Christian in his service or in the service of the army who refused to sacrifice to the gods should be discharged immediately.[83]

Diocletian's co-ruler, Galerius, urged him to go further. On February 23, 303, at Galerius' prompting, Diocletian issued an edict that ordered all copies of Scriptures to be surrendered and burned, churches to be pulled down brick by brick, and Christians to cease and desist from gathering for worship. The day the edict was read, a unit of troops marched to the Christian church that stood in view of the emperor's own palace at Nicomedia and demolished it. One brave soul tore off the edict and ripped it to shreds. He was arrested, flayed, and burned alive.[84] At Nicomedia alone, 268 Christians joined him in death. In areas as disparate as Phrygia, Palestine, and Egypt, Diocletian's edict was carried out with morbid enthusiasm. In Alexandria, 660 believers were executed. Leaders of the church were rounded up, tortured, sent to work in the mines, beheaded, or burned alive, while their properties were confiscated and their homes ransacked. Eusebius of Caesarea reports that "a vast multitude were imprisoned in every place; and the prisons everywhere, which had long before been prepared for murderers and robbers of graves, were filled with bishops, presbyters and deacons, readers and exorcists."[85] Even in more tolerant territories, Christians could not feel safe. They were at the mercy of their fellow citizens in more than one sense; the edict of 303 stripped Christians of every legal right to defend themselves against accusers in a court of law, regardless of the charges.[86]

These conditions were on the minds of the bishops who gathered furtively in 295, hoping and praying that God would lead them as they chose the next bishop of Myra. They committed to pray through the evening for an answer. In the course of that night, one of the senior bishops received a vision: "Go to the house of God with the others this night and lie in wait in the atrium. Take the first person to enter and ordain him bishop. His name will be Nicholas."[87] True, God had revealed his will in mysterious ways before—Gideon asked God for a very specific sign when he laid out a fleece one night to see if God would soak it wet while leaving the surrounding ground dry; the apostles chose Matthias to replace Judas Iscariot as the twelfth disciple by casting lots; tradition said Fabian was elected bishop of Rome when a white dove fluttered down and lighted upon his head while he was standing as a mere citizen in a crowd of people who had come to hear the name of their new bishop. Even so, the other bishops present in Myra must have felt at least a twinge of skepticism at the plan to choose the new bishop. The likelihood of someone named "Nicholas" walking through the doors of the church was slim. The old pastor who had announced his dream was looking for a miracle. Just then, in came a quiet young man dressed in the simple tunic. Michael describes the scene:

> In the early hours of the morning the great Nicholas was sent by God and was the first to cross the threshold of the church. Taking hold of him, the bishop asked, "Son, what's your name?"
>
> His simple voice and mild response was heard by all: "Sir, I am the sinner Nicholas, a servant of your Excellency." Upon hearing this, they were stunned by the humility of such a just man. The bishop said, "Son, come with me, I must explain something to you."
>
> He brought him to the other bishops with whom he had lifted those prayers to God. Praising Almighty God, he brought him to the center of the church. Addressing the crowd of faithful believers gathered and indicating the man chosen by God, he said: "This, sisters and brothers, is the

one whom the Lord foreknew and predestined to hold the office of bishop in the presence of all of us and of your holy church."[88]

If the amazement of the bishops and the church was great, one can only guess Nicholas' reaction to the senior bishops crowding around him with congratulations and blessings and instructions. He was surprised, embarrassed, and speechless.

As best as can be reconstructed, Nicholas was about thirty or thirty-five at this time. Jesus did not begin his earthly ministry until he had attained the age of thirty, so it became a tradition that young men could not be ordained as bishops until they reached thirty. By the late 200s, the tradition had taken on the force of church law. To give one example: Athanasius, a near contemporary of Nicholas, was often accused by his Melitian detractors—and he had many—of being installed as bishop of Alexandria on the coast of Egypt in haste and while he was underage.[89] If this were indeed the case, then there was no question that his ordination could be declared invalid. Athanasius never argued with the canonical law on age of ordination even as he consistently denied the accusation. The example shows that the rule of thirty might be powerful enough to get one disqualified, even if he were prominent. If we follow Cioffari's dating of Nicholas' birth as sometime after 260, then the year of his installation as bishop must have been close to A.D. 290, 295, or perhaps even closer to the year 300.

Thirty years of age made Nicholas an adult in society's eyes, but, measured in terms of pastoral experience, he was a baby. The office of the bishop was typically reserved for senior clergymen with white hair, wrinkles, and years of leadership. The bishop, or "overseer," was the head shepherd of the flock.

—Boy Bishop—

Over the years, each telling and retelling of Nicholas' election made him younger and younger. Boys attending cathedral schools in the heyday of Charlemagne's educational renaissance latched on to the tantalizing figure of Nicholas, the "Boy Bishop." The tradition of the Boy Bishop dates back at least to A.D. 912, when King Conrad I paid a visit to the monastery at St. Gall to watch children make procession during Vespers at Christmastime. The initial idea seems to have been to allow the children to conduct a service, perform the rites, read the lessons, preach the homily, and even name a bishop for a day. In this way, they would, theoretically, learn to take ownership of their faith, gain insight into the liturgy, and develop a greater sense of respect for the church's worship. Conrad I seemed genuinely impressed with the behavior of the young boys leading the service. According to an onlooker who witnessed the event, Conrad ordered apples to be strewn down the middle of the church's aisle to tempt the boys as they processed, but "not even the tiniest lad broke ranks or stretched his hand out to get one."[90]

As the practice developed over the years in medieval France and England, it became customary for a choirboy to be elected bishop on Nicholas Day, December 6, or the eve thereof. His duties and rights would continue until Holy Innocents Day, December 28, when he would officiate Mass. In the meantime, the Boy Bishop would put on a miter and pallium, the official costume of the bishop, and appoint his friends as priests and cardinals. He would assign the adults to the tasks of the choirboys and decree self-serving canon law and new feasts. If he were industrious, he would make rounds and take up collections—sometimes peacefully and sometimes by way of boisterous and indecent threats. It seemed that the good intentions of the adults quickly backfired. The Boy Bishop had power to legislate whatever he liked and overturn whatever he disliked. Feasts would be thrown, and someone would be dubbed the Lord of Misrule—a title and role dating back to the winter celebrations of classic times; masks would be worn and the revelries became raucous. Most noticeable in the historical records are the number of prohibitions against Boy Bishops, Nicholas Day carousing, Feasts of Fools, Feasts of Innocents, and holiday begging, known as "mumping" or "thomasing."[91] The restrictions and condemnations serve as testaments to the trouble that such practices must have caused. The good behavior witnessed by Conrad I at St. Gall proved to be more of an exception than a norm. In a remarkably short amount of time, the custom devolved into silliness and worse.

The unrestrained frenzies that often accompanied the weeks of the Boy Bishop are no more shocking or unprecedented than the orgies of decorating and spending and partying in the twenty-first century. Societies have always needed release from the pent-up energies brought on by the doldrums of winter. Ancient Rome celebrated the Sigillaria, Juvenalia, Brumalia, and Saturnalia in the cold month of December, and the Kalends on January 1. Heavy drinking and game playing marked these topsy-turvy festivities. Gifts were distributed to children, labor came to a halt, prisoners were unlocked, slaves released, bread was handed out, wax tapers were lit, and people dressed in costumes—slaves as masters and men as women. A yearning for a golden age when all are one and everything is shared and enjoyed together elicited the best—and the rowdiest—in people. Karl Meisen reminds us that the Boy Bishop custom was not a new invention but actually an attempt to reform an older custom, the Feast of Fools, that had become unwieldy and improper over the years.[92] Whatever the noble goals of these winter celebrations, they tended inevitably toward frivolity, hilarity, and debauchery.

There must have been much rejoicing and good cheer the day Nicholas was elevated to the bishopric in Myra. Michael continues the story: "So the one who bore the name 'Nicholas' was raised to the episcopal throne."[93] Reluctantly, Nicholas accepted God's will and allowed himself to be anointed with oil and ordained a minister of the gospel. The bishops laid hands on him and conferred the authority and responsibility of shepherding the flock at Myra, a flock which St. Paul himself had started. For Nicholas it was an incomparable and unanticipated honor. He was surely humbled by the weight of the new charge and by the prayers of those who ordained him: "that you may stand firm in all the will of God, mature and fully assured" (Col 4:12). In the days before Alexander the Great conquered the world, in another part of eastern Turkey there arose the need in the province of Phrygia for a new ruler. The divine oracles revealed that the next person to enter the city driving an ox cart would be their next king. Gordias, a simple man from the country, nearly fell out of his wagon when he was declared king of the Phrygians as he rode into town on an errand.[94] Nicholas must have felt the same kind of shock and bewilderment. Perhaps he remembered Thecla, an Iconian woman who, according to tradition, was ordained by Paul to Christian ministry at Myra. Whether or not she was a genuine historical character is beside the point; Nicholas would have certainly heard her story, which had been in circulation for well over a hundred years by his time. As he faced his new position, he must have recollected Thecla's memorable and heartfelt prayer to "Christ Jesus, the Son of God, my helper in prison, my helper before governors, my helper in the fire, my helper among the wild beast—you yourself are God. To you be the glory forever. Amen."[95]

The role of bishop was not an easy one. A saint of a different age, Dominic (1170–1221) had told the town of Conserano he would rather die than be made bishop. Some candidates had to be tricked into the position. Because St. Martin (316–397) would not leave his wilderness cell, a certain citizen of Tours, in Gaul (France), named Rusticius went to him on the pretense that his wife was ill. He managed to draw Martin out of his cell and into the city, where an expectant crowd was waiting to hail him as their new bishop.[96] In order to avoid an unexpected and undesired election, Augustine admitted that he purposefully avoided entering churches that lacked bishops. He thought himself safe as he stepped out of the hot African sun and into the shade of the cathedral church in the port city of Hippo, which he knew had a fine and perfectly healthy bishop, Valerius. He was wrong. Valerius saw in young Augustine his chance to name a successor and ordained Augustine to the priesthood on the spot.[97]

The office of bishop has developed in many directions over the course of time. By Nicholas' day, its duties and dignities had evolved from the simple requirements sketched out in 1 Timothy 3:1-7 and Titus 1:7-9. The bishop or "overseer" (*episkopos* in Greek) operated something like head minister for a town or an area. Ignatius of Antioch, an early second-century martyr, treated the office with dignity, saying that the honor accorded to the bishop should be equal to that of Christ, because he stood before the Lord on behalf of his people.[98]

He fulfilled the role of high priest as does Christ, "who is holy, blameless, pure, set apart from sinners, exalted above the heavens" (Heb 7:26). In one manual from fifth-century Gaul, we find instructions on the behavior of bishops: they should live in a humble dwelling not far from the church; they should devote their time to reading, prayer, and preaching; their furniture should be practical and of minimal cost.[99] Michael the

Archimandrite relates that Nicholas "became a great shepherd of those sheep of Christ, always leading first by example."[100] A bishop in Nicholas' day was responsible for distributing money and food to the needy, caring for the members of the church, preaching, baptizing, and instructing new converts. He did not wear embroidered silk robes, gold chains, white gloves, or his seal of ecclesial authority—the signet ring—as bishops of a later age would; instead, he donned the simple black garb of the peasants.[101] The bishop was a man of the people and for the people. He served God above all else and executed the ministries of Christ and the church with diligence and prayerfulness. Nicholas did these things, and, according to Michael, "his name became well known to all, and inspired by God he became the guide for those requiring an interpreter worthy of the Spirit, and even among those in the sacred ministry."[102]

The Terror of Persecution

No sooner had pastor Nicholas settled into the routine of his new assignment than he was arrested on religious charges. The official policy of the imperial persecution was to target the leaders of the church. The inexperienced Nicholas was snatched up and carried to prison—he was not read his rights, he was not permitted a lawyer, and he was not brought before a judge so that he might be informed of the charges. Instead, he was led to the torturers where he was peppered with questions and accusations. He was threatened and beaten. Nicholas steadied himself with thoughts of Christ's sufferings. Infuriated by his unwillingness to renounce his faith or hand over Scriptures to be burned, his examiners ordered torments of various kinds to be applied. Meanwhile, his colleague at Patara, bishop Methodius, was put to death. Nicholas must have counted himself blessed that he was "only" tortured. According to early fourteenth-century Byzantine historian Nicephorus Kallistos Xanthaopoulos, many of those attending the Council of Nicaea who had "persisted in professing their faith" through the dark days of the persecutions "still showed the wounds and scars in their flesh, and especially among the Bishops, such as Nicholas, Bishop of Myra, Paphnutius and others."[103] These especially "shone with apostolic gifts."[104] We do not know what kinds of wounds and scars Nicholas showed his brothers in Christ at Nicaea, but a common torture dealt to recalcitrant Christian prisoners of that time was to blind their right eyes and cut the sinews of their left ankles. For his courage, endurance, and faith in God through it all, Nicholas wore the badge of "confessor." Those who died for the faith were revered as martyrs; those who suffered torture but lived to tell were honored as confessors.

For the majority of Nicholas' tenure as bishop of Myra, Christians were a hated minority—a target for angry mobs and imperial displeasure. Eusebius of Caesarea testifies that "we saw with our own eyes the houses of prayer thrown down to the very foundations, and the Divine and Sacred Scriptures committed to the flames in the midst of the market-places, and the shepherds of the churches basely hidden here and there, and some of them captured ignominiously."[105] Even so, Eusebius assures, by the Holy Spirit's provision the gospel survived and the church thrived. Nicholas preached, sang hymns, and conducted the ministry God had ordained for him, come what may. Michael states that "when the oppressions of the persecution [*tribulationibus*] happened, a cloud of sorrow fell on many, and they came into his presence to get help."[106] The people came to Nicholas for protection and direction, for guidance and reassurance. Some wanted to know if they should flee or take up arms against their oppressors. Nicholas counseled peace and perseverance. "Behold therefore!" Michael exclaims, "Behold that God directed him and promoted him to the dignity of the pastoral office in order to bring peace!"[107] By God's mercy, they would overcome these dark days.

Before long, cracks appeared in the imperial policy of intolerance. Diocletian's great persecution of 303 did not have the results he had hoped for. His subjects were no more unified

93

because of it, nor were the Christians any weaker. Diocletian soon retired from public life. His successor, Galerius, at first redoubled the persecution efforts, strengthening and re-enforcing anti-Christian laws. But his furor eventually softened. Then, something happened in the far west that no one could have predicted. Constantine (c. 271–337), ruler of the western half of the Empire, including Italy, Gaul, Spain, North Africa, and Britain, declared toleration for the Christians. He would no longer permit discrimination against them in his lands. Going one step further, he announced himself a disciple of Christ.

Every Christian who heard the news, including Nicholas, must have felt encouraged and cautiously optimistic, even if somewhat puzzled by the fact that a Roman ruler would associate himself with them. There was, however, a cost. The backlash of Constantine's open hand to the Christians was that Licinius (263–325), whom Galerius had appointed as a successor and who ruled the eastern half of the Roman Empire—Greece, Asia Minor, Palestine, and Egypt—began to have grave suspicions. Constantine had inherited from his father a legitimate claim to the title of senior Augustus, that is, emperor, and had already put together and brilliantly executed a number of military campaigns. He was extremely popular with the troops and the people alike, and Licinius now worried that he was plotting to overthrow him and become sole emperor of West and East. Since Constantine was a Christian, Licinius reasoned that the Christians who lived in his lands were probably acting as secret agents on behalf of Constantine. Licinius had good reason to be concerned. Prayers were being lifted up on behalf of Constantine, not Licinius, and a letter was intercepted from Constantine to the churches of the Eastern Empire in which he promised to soon liberate Christians from Licinius the tyrant. In Licinius' mind, Christians could not be trusted. They were the enemy.[108] In retribution, he ejected all Christians from his court and from the civil service. Citing public health concerns, he prohibited believers from meeting together in large groups for worship and forbade men and

women worshiping together in the same place. He also can-
celed the tax privileges enjoyed by the clergy and required
them to enroll in the public liturgies of the town councils.[109]
In another edict, he forbade bishops from leaving their cities
of residence. So it was that Nicholas, like many other bishops,
was again placed under house arrest and confined to Myra. Fortunately, the new persecution did not last long. In the summer
of 324, Constantine's army pounded through Thrace, blowing
back enemy forces from Adrianople to Byzantium. Licinius
surrendered at Nicomedia, present-day Izmit, Turkey, located
on an inlet of the Sea of Marmara.

Constantine, now supreme and uncontested ruler of the
vast Roman Empire, did not delay in ending the persecutions
and making good his promises to the Christians of the east.
Nicholas lived to see not only the end of persecution but also
the rebuilding and revitalization of the church. Those who had
been imprisoned or sent to slave camps or into the mines were
set free; exiles were brought back to their homes. Confiscated
property was ordered returned to its rightful owners. Those
who had lost their rank in the army because of their religious
beliefs were given the choice of either re-enlisting or receiving
honorable discharge. Those stripped of their nobility and their
privileges were to be restored. Bishops were empowered to set
things right and so were given legal authority to judge in civil
matters and adjudicate cases. Constantine ordered Christians
to begin building new churches immediately at public expense.
Provincial governors and administrators were directed to give
them whatever they needed to repair, rebuild, or build new—no
expense spared.[110] As news of these provisions spread, a buzz of
excitement sparked the wearied community of Christians at
Myra. With tears of joy they praised God their protector. "The
Lord is the stronghold of my life—of whom shall I be afraid?"
(Ps 27:1). Nicholas, now nearing the age of sixty-five, wore his
clerical robes in public with dignity and grace. His beard and
hair had turned white with more than thirty years of pastoral experience. Because he had stayed with them through the

good times, the slow times, and the dark times, his congregation trusted him. The city of Myra also showed him respect for standing his ground through the trials of persecution.

Winter came to an early end in 325. At the first signs of spring, Myra's civil administrators approached Nicholas to ask what materials and manpower he would need to build his new church. Although these were the same administrators who had earlier harassed him, Nicholas wasted no time nursing petty resentments; there was much to do. He set to work approving building plans and overseeing the laying of a foundation near the harbor of Andriake.

4

The Work of Victory

Within months of liberating the eastern provinces from Licinius and outlawing the persecution of Christians, Constantine, who now bore the title of *maximus Augustus* and ruled everything from the sun-baked borders of Persia to the ocean's edge of Portugal, sent out a sealed notice to every known bishop. Nicholas broke open his letter, prepared for anything. To his surprise, it was a request that all bishops assemble at the emperor's personal residence in Nicaea in order to convene a council. The letter read as follows:

> I announce to you, my beloved brothers, that all of you promptly assemble at the said city, that is at Nicaea. Let every one of you therefore, as I said before, keep the greater good in mind and be diligent, without delay in anything, to come speedily, that each may be physically present as a spectator of those things which will be done.[1]

Nicholas might have looked at the piles of brick and stone of his new church and sighed. Everything would have to wait. In May of 325, he obeyed the emperor's summons, packed his bags, and headed north toward the small town of Nicaea, present-day Iznik, Turkey, more than 400 miles away. He might have proceeded with trepidation, thinking of the uncertainty that must accompany any audience with the emperor. He certainly would have wondered if the new emperor would allow the bishops to conduct their business freely or try to seize control of church affairs. The Christian religion, as anyone could observe, was porous and diffuse. It had no centralized structure, universally recognized chain of command, or agreed-upon standard of belief, making its operations vulnerable to manipulation. There were many good reasons for Nicholas' anxiety, but his thoughts were most likely interrupted by the abrupt chill of a spring rainstorm. The storm proved to be more than a passing shower; it was the onset of heavy rains which prevented a number of bishops from attending. Only one bishop from Italy was present at the council; the bishop of Rome refrained from coming but sent two deacons in his stead. Even so, the number and variety of bishops who were able to attend inspired awe and delight. According to Eusebius of Caesarea, it was a miracle that Nicaea's single house of prayer could contain nationalities as diverse and incompatible as the Syrians and Cilicians, the Phœnicians and Arabians, the Palestinians and Egyptians, the Thebans and Libyans.[2] The council even attracted one prelate from Spain in the far west and one from Persia in the far east.

After many days of soggy travel, Nicholas arrived in the small town of Nicaea, where the emperor had taken up residence while his capital, the New Rome, was being raised on top of a much older city, Byzantium. The site of the new capital was perfectly located to unite the eastern and western halves of his realm and stood within striking distance of the river Danube. It also had the advantage of being situated on a peninsula of land that connected the Sea of Marmara to the Bosphorus, and thus the Mediterranean to the Black Sea. This new seat of power, which took six years to complete, would eventually take the name Constantinople from its patron, Constantine.

Despite modest accommodations at Nicaea, Nicholas must have been overwhelmed by the experience. It was, after all, the first ecumenical or "worldwide" council of the church ever convened. With representatives from Egypt and Gaul, Greece and Palestine, Syria and North Africa, this was truly the church *katholikos*, "catholic," a Greek term well in use by this time. At Nicaea, the Church universal was drawn together in one place. Eusebius of Caesarea has left us a description of the June 1 majestic opening ceremonies. According to his account, the bishops arranged themselves before long benches. They sat down and waited. At a sign they all rose as the Emperor Constantine himself, decked out in purple robes and wearing a crown of gold studded with jewels, entered the room. In deference to the bishops, he waited for their gesture before taking his seat on a gilded stool. He then received speeches of praise and commendation from the most prominent bishops. But he also gave his own speech exhorting the bishops to unity and brotherly love and charging them to overcome their differences for God's sake.[3]

FIGURE 7
Large head of Constantine in Rome, formerly part of a larger statue

At Nicaea

The bishops were presented with a full agenda. One issue was the date of Easter, which different regions celebrated on various days. As most understood the matter, Easter could be reckoned from the date of the Jewish Passover, for the Gospels said that Christ died and was raised at the time of Passover. Herein lay the problem. The Jewish lunisolar calendar set Passover on the fourteenth day of Nisan, but ministers unfamiliar with its calendric calculations found the date difficult to determine. Even when figured correctly, from equinox to equinox, the Jewish calendar might yield two Easters in one solar year or none at all. Constantine wanted conformity in the practices of the church as much as he wanted the Christian holy day to be disassociated from its Jewish predecessor.[4] In the end, the council did not devise a mathematical formula but commended the methods of calculation used in Rome and Africa, Italy and Egypt, but not in Syria or Mesopotamia. The solution was more appearance than substance, however, since Rome and Alexandria, for instance, differed in their dating systems. Something more precise would have to wait for another council. For the time, it was enough for the bishops to affirm the principle that Easter should be observed on the same day by all faithful believers.

Beyond this, the delegates at the council laid down a variety of rulings: the ordination of a bishop must be confirmed in the presence of at least three fellow bishops and by other regional bishops in writing; the appointment was lifelong— once consecrated to a province a bishop could not move or accept another see. The practice of ordaining to the priesthood converts immediately after their baptism was disallowed, as was the ordination of those guilty of major crimes or serious moral infractions. Deacons were forbidden from serving the Eucharistic bread and wine to the priests or to themselves. Kneeling at prayer on Sundays and during the seven weeks between Easter and Pentecost was prohibited. Conditions under which a person might reenter the church if he or she had abandoned it during the persecutions were arranged. The council also sorted through the various rogue groups and dissidents within the Christian fold such as the Novatians, the Paulianists, and the Melitians. Then there was the problem of the Arians.

Arius (256–336), a charismatic presbyter (priest) originally from Libya, served the church of Baucalis in Alexandria at the same time that Nicholas served at Myra. The philosophically minded Arius had been trained at Alexandria's book-filled Museum, the intellectual nerve-center of the world. Using the sharp tools of logic, he accused the bishop of the city, Alexander, of a seemingly minor intellectual heresy. Arius said that bishop Alexander could not in good conscience maintain that God the Father, Son, and Holy Spirit were equally divine, equally changeless, and equally unbegotten while professing at the same time that the Father begat the Son and sent the Spirit or that God himself had become flesh for our salvation. It could not be that the Father, Son, and Spirit shared equally in the eternal unchanging perfection of God. The Father alone was everlasting and unbegotten. The Son was not unbegotten but begotten, that is, born of the Father. This meant that the Son had a beginning. To quote from a letter Arius sent to his friend and compatriot, Eusebius of Nicomedia, "God had an existence prior to that of his Son . . . before He was begotten, or created, or purposed, or established, He was not. For He was not unbegotten."[5] Only God the Father existed in pure perfection—all-powerful, all-knowing, and untouched by the whims of change. The Son, the "first born among creation" (Col 1:15), was an offshoot, a product, a creation of the Father. The two did not share the same existence; they were different substances.[6]

Alexander, the elderly bishop of Alexandria, rebutted the upstart Arius by accusing him of an even greater heresy—saying that God was not eternal and that the Son was not fully divine. According to Alexander, if there was a time when the Son was not, then, "God was not always the Father, but there

101

was a time when God was not the Father."[7] Alexander's main insight was that, if Arius were correct, then the Father had not always been Father but only *became* Father by begetting or creating the Son.[8] Before the Son, God was not the Father, only afterward. And so, the very thing that Arius was trying so desperately to protect, God's unchangeability, would be compromised and lost. A dual dilemma ensued: first, the Trinity—God the Father, Son, and Spirit—could not always have existed but must have begun at a certain point in time when the Father made the Son, and second, the Son could not be as divine as the Father, but could only be a creation (even if a very special creation) of the Father.

Since the beginning of the controversy, local councils had convened sporadically in Alexandria and Palestine to denounce or defend Arius' theology, but the disagreements only became more heated and the two sides polarized. One council met early in the year 325 at Antioch, modern-day Antakya on the border of Turkey and Syria, and condemned Arianism but failed to resolve the controversy. Its results revealed to Constantine that the problem was festering and growing into something much larger than a local dispute. Acting with decisiveness, he changed the venue of another upcoming council originally scheduled for Ancyra to a new location—his imperial residence in Nicaea. He expanded the invitation from just the eastern bishops to the entire church body. Constantine understood that Arianism needed to be confronted on a larger scale.[9] He himself would preside over this assembly.

Everyone who attended the great council worshiped Jesus the Christ as the Son of God. On one point all agreed: Jesus was and is divine. But *how* divine? Was Jesus the Son equal to God the Father? All confessed that the Father was "the God," *ho theos*, while the Son was "God," *theos*, but there was a lingering uncertainty as to whether the two were identical.[10]

The Council of Nicaea was to be a watershed event in the history of the faith. The outcome would forever shape the basics of Christian belief and worship. It had to address and resolve a real ambiguity in Scripture. In Arius' defense, a number of Scriptures seem to suggest a subordination and even distinction between the Father and the Son: Mark 13:32, John 14:28, John 17:3, Acts 2:36, Romans 8:29, Philippians 2:5-11, and Colossians 1:15. "No one knows about that day or hour, not even the angels in heaven, nor the Son, but only the Father"; "Therefore let all Israel be assured of this: God has made this Jesus, whom you crucified, both Lord and Christ"; "For those God foreknew he also predestined to be conformed to the likeness of his Son, that he might be the firstborn among many brothers." These verses indicate a differentiation between Father and Son and seem to imply that the Son ranks lower than the Father on the grounds that the Father is his maker. On the other hand, Alexander's camp could muster an equal number of Scriptures: Matthew 25:31-46, Mark 2:5-10, John 3:13, John 8:58, John 14:9, John 20:28, Romans 10:13, Hebrews 1:3, Colossians 2:9, 1 Timothy 4:1, and 1 John 1:2. "Anyone who has seen me has seen the Father. How can you say, 'Show us the Father'? Don't you believe that I am in the Father, and that the Father is in me?" "The Son is the radiance of God's glory and the exact representation of his being, sustaining all things by his powerful word"; "The life appeared; we have seen it and testify to it, and we proclaim to you the eternal life, which was with the Father and has appeared to us." These verses speak of an identity and equality between the Father and the Son. The Son is not a creation of the Father or a lesser being than the Father but is equal in glory and power and being. The Son and the Father were and are one.

Theologically sound and biblically supported arguments could be made for either position. The Arians accumulated Scriptures for their position just as easily as Alexander and the orthodox theologians did for theirs. The dilemma demanded a clear answer, a Yes or a No. What was needed was a definitive rule, an outside term, or a single phrase to sum up and interpret the Scriptures. Alexander's camp sought a term that would express with precision the absolute unity of the Father and Son and the genuine equality of the Son with the Father. Eusebius says that Constantine himself proposed the Greek word ὁμοούσιος/*homoousios*, "same substance," "consubstantial," or "of one being," as it is variously translated.[11] The Son and the Father share the same substance; they are of one being, equally divine. The Son is God from God, light from light, true God from true God. It is not the case that the Son, though divine, was a lesser divinity than the Father, nor is it the case that the Father created the Son from a different substance or nature than himself. After much debate on the point, the council assembled a creed, a statement of faith taken from the traditional baptismal confession of new believers and amended to specify the parameters of orthodoxy.

> We believe in one God, the Father Almighty, Maker of all things visible and invisible. And in one Lord Jesus Christ, the Son of God, begotten of the Father, the only-begotten; that is, of the essence of the Father, God of God, Light of Light, very God of very God, begotten, not made, being of one substance [ὁμοούσιον/*homoousion*] with the Father; by whom all things were made both in heaven and on earth; who for us men, and for our salvation, came down and was incarnate and was made man; he suffered, and the third day he rose again, ascended into heaven; from thence he shall come to judge the quick and the dead. And in the Holy Ghost.[12]

It might be interesting to note that this profession of faith, known simply as the Nicene Creed, is a slightly different version than the one recited in churches today. In the year 381 it was revised and expanded at the Council of Constantinople so that the Nicene Creed confessed by Christians today is, in actuality, the Niceno-Constantinopolitan Creed of 381.

The Council of Nicaea concluded its creedal statement with some pointed stipulations aimed at Arian objectors. That there be no confusion or misunderstanding or alternate interpretation, the council anathematized or condemned those who might say things like, "There was a time when he was not" or

"The Son is of another substance than the Father."[13] The "anathemas" called out the key phrases of the Arian position and forbade them. No wiggle room remained for Arius or his followers.

Where was Nicholas in these debates? With whom did he side, Alexander or Arius? Undoubtedly, more than a few of the bishops must have felt exasperated by the idea of the debates altogether and wondered why the whole council needed to be plagued with the trifling philosophical disputes of the Alexandrians.[14] Initially few bishops opined strongly for one side or the other. Michael the Archimandrite, however, makes plain that Nicholas' position was neither neutral nor Arian. He gives special emphasis to the orthodoxy of his beliefs and teachings. He "taught and worshipped God the Father, His Word and only begotten Son, our Lord Jesus, according to the doctrine handed down by the Apostles, as well as his Spirit equal in power, in addition to the consubstantial Trinity."[15] Nicholas aligned himself from the beginning with the tradition handed down by the apostles. In specific terms, the good bishop confessed that the persons of the Trinity "should not be confused because of their identical nature, as if there were three attributes to be traced to a single person like the fool Sabellius taught, nor, on account of the three divine hypostases, should they be divided into three separate and different kind natures, as the abominable Arius taught."[16] In opposition to the doctrines of Sabellius and Arius, Nicholas, according to Michael, taught that the Father, Son, and Spirit are not just three names for the same thing nor are they three separate things. They are three, and they are one. "This God is revealed in three persons and is identified by the same glory. . . . So Nicholas believed and preached."[17]

Later tradition affirmed Michael's verdict about Nicholas' orthodoxy and attested to his zeal for the truth. In one legend, he stood up before the eminent council and held out a brick for all to see. He declared that it was an analogy of the eternal being of God: just as God is Father, Son, and Spirit, though one, so the brick was one uniform substance, though it came from the combination of earth, water, and fire. At that very moment, the brick burst into flames while water dripped from it onto the tiled floor. All that was left in Nicholas' hand was dust. He had proven his point.[18]

Another tradition reported that when the good bishop from Myra heard Arius spouting blasphemy before the council and declaring that the Son was not equal to the Father and that Jesus was less than fully divine, he leapt to his feet and slapped Arius on the face.[19] Although Nicholas might have been justified in his righteous indignation, his example of poor collegiality and lack of self-control could not be tolerated. No one should ever commit an act of violence in the presence of the emperor. Constantine deferred Nicholas' punishment to the bishops. They had him bound and incarcerated for a time; he was stripped of his bishop's robes, and Roman guards burnt off his beard. In essence, he was defrocked. While Nicholas was confined to his sad and dark cell, the Virgin Mary and her son Jesus appeared in resplendent light and placed on his shoulders a stole of pastoral ministry and in his hands copy of the Gospel—a symbol of sound teaching. The heavenly visions also appeared to Constantine, who immediately ordered Nicholas released. Nicholas' robes were returned to him, but at the time of the celebration of the Mass he still could not bring himself to put them on. His heart had been defeated. Then, at the moment he was to pronounce the opening words of the celebration, Mother Mary and the angels descended from on high with stole and miter in hand. When those in attendance came to greet him after the service, they found his face glowing and his charred beard restored to its former thick, black luster.[20]

These dramatic scenes from Nicaea—of the flaming brick and the slap—are rendered in bold, vivid lines on ceiling paintings inside the Basilica di San Nicola in Bari, Italy.[21] The legends of the brick and the slap place Nicholas squarely within the orthodox camp and depict him as full of conviction and bravado. He was on the winning side of history. But, there is something that does not ring true about these legends. They display none of the compassion and tenderness and concern for which Nicholas was so well known. The theologians who circulated the stories wanted to prove that their hero, Nicholas, was one of the key defenders of the faith at Nicaea; they needed Nicholas to enthrall his colleagues and steamroll his enemies. Michael, our first and foremost guide through the story of Nicholas, presents us with a different picture. Instead of thundering down wrath on the heads of theological deviants, Nicholas shepherded them back into the fold with gentleness.

> Holy Nicholas was so revered and angelic in appearance that he gave off fragrant scents of holiness to the effect that, with only his appearance he made everyone better. Moreover, since he was zealous in the salvation of others, he pushed everyone he encountered to be better. When a heretic, who had contracted the evil of wickedness and been held by it for many years, came into contact with him, he was soon freed. Following his conversion he became a fearless preacher of the true faith.[22]

Who was this "heretic" vaguely identified in the text? Michael's text gives no further information, saying only that he had "contracted the evil of wickedness and been held by it for many years." Andrew of Crete (660–740) fills in the rest of the story,[23] revealing that the heretic in question was Theognis, bishop of Nicaea and a major player in the events at the council. Andrew calls him a Marcionite bishop after Marcion, the heretic who divided the God of the Old Testament from the God of the New Testament, declaring in essence two deities. Marcionites followed his divisive dualism. More damning than this, other ancient historians like Eusebius of Caesarea, Socrates, and Theodoret identify Theognis as an Arian sympathizer.[24]

Andrew, from whom we receive our report about Theognis and Nicholas, was born in Damascus and devoted himself as a monk to the desert monastery of St. Sabbas near Jerusalem. His gifts for hymn writing and poetry were quickly noticed, however, and he was transferred to Constantinople as a secretary to the patriarch. Eventually he acquired the bishopric of Crete. Both at Constantinople and at Crete, he would have heard stories from sailors, read key texts in the libraries, and visited shrines and churches dedicated to Nicholas. He had plenty of opportunity to gather information about Nicholas, and after researching the matter, he came to the conclusion that Nicholas was just as concerned about the unity of the church as he was about the triumph of truth. Those who had sided with the Arians needed to be reconciled with the truth and reunited with their brothers in Christ. Using an appropriate nautical metaphor, Andrew compared Nicholas to Noah calling on all people of good will, even the Arian brethren, to enter the common ship of salvation.[25]

According to Andrew, Theognis irritated everyone with his stubbornness. Theognis had subscribed to the Creed at Nicaea, but at the close of the council, when Constantine ordered that word be sent to Alexandria to excommunicate and remove into exile Arius and his supporters, he and Eusebius of Nicomedia protested that the punishment was unfair and extreme. The various priests from Alexandria had not been given a chance to speak for themselves and had been prematurely judged. However, the emperor and the council had no patience with such objections, and so Theognis and Eusebius received temporary excommunication.[26] They were not stripped of their titles, but they were removed from fellowship and ordered to think about their sins. Meanwhile, Constantine vented his frustrations in a heated letter to the Christians of Nicomedia explaining why their bishop had been chastised and exiled. The other bishops in attendance must have also felt exasperated with Theognis' protest. It was clear to them who had won; Theognis and Eusebius needed to get on board. Arian belief was heresy, and heresy could not be tolerated. Nicholas, however, did not give up, lose control, slap his face, or stand him in front of a flaming pyre and ask him to reconsider.[27] Instead, according to Andrew of Crete, Nicholas wrote a string of letters to

Theognis patiently persuading him of what was right. Nicholas quoted Psalm 133:1 to him: "See how good and pleasant it is for brothers to live together in unity."[28] He urged Theognis to put aside his pride and be reconciled with his fellow bishops although it would take a lot of humility and courage to submit for the sake of unity.

In the end, Theognis was convinced. He agreed for the cause of peace to conform to the will of the council and the emperor. Theognis and his cohort, Eusebius of Nicomedia, submitted a letter of reconciliation and submission to the bishops, reuniting themselves to the Church at a second convening of the Council of Nicaea in the year 327. They affirmed in no uncertain terms the Creed of Nicaea and in particular the *homoousion*, professing belief that the Son is consubstantial and of one substance with the Father.[29] They reiterated that they had only objected to the anathemas and the prejudgment of Arius and the others. In their joint statement, preserved by the historian Socrates in his *Ecclesiastical History*, Theognis and Eusebius of Nicomedia explained that at the Council of Nicaea in 325, "we subscribed the declaration of faith; we did not subscribe the anathematizing; not as objecting to the creed, but as disbelieving the party accused to be such as was represented, having been satisfied on this point, both from his own letters to us, and from personal conversations."[30] After stating their initial objections to the anathematizing, they went on to give their full assent to the orthodox creed and the Nicene faith and, beyond that, to the wisdom of the council in all its decisions. "If therefore you should now think fit to restore us to your presence," Theognis and Eusebius conclude, "you will have us on all points conformable, and acquiescent in your decrees."[31] The council accepted their statement, and the two bishops, now in good standing, were restored to their bishoprics.

Nicholas returned to his rocky, seaside home of Myra having accomplished a good work. Not only did he enjoy the satisfaction of participation in the council, but he also had a renewed sense of mission and purpose. That his new church was still under construction near the docks of Andriake did not stop people from the city, the wharf, and the countryside from streaming in and asking questions about the religion that Emperor Constantine now touted. Nicholas did his best to meet everyone and answer their inquiries. Citizens and city administrators sought him out not only with questions about Christianity, but also in hopes of gaining his support and backing. Christian leaders like Nicholas suddenly found themselves prominent in civil affairs.

The Daily Task of Ministry

Bishop Nicholas lived an extraordinary life—he endured persecution, witnessed the crowning of the first Christian emperor, and attended the first major ecumenical council in church history. These things make up the major events of his life. His routine activities were, of course, much more mundane. As bishop he performed regular worship services or *liturgies*, "the works of the people," also referred to as *sacraments* or "holy mysteries." The principal liturgy was the Eucharist, or communion, conducted on Sunday—some Christian pastors recommended that believers simply say "the first day of the week" and not "Sunday" since this word had its roots in the old pagan celebration of the *dies solis*, day of the Unconquered Sun. Wednesdays and Fridays—in contrast to the Jewish days of prayer, Tuesdays and Thursdays— were also set aside for fasting and devotion.[32] Many churches practiced a "daily office," primarily observed by monks and nuns, in which prayers were offered, Psalms sung, and Scriptures read.

The Christian worship service typically featured processions—of the Gospel-book, of candles, of incense, of the gifts of the altar, of the sacramental elements of Eucharist, of the clergy. In a series of grand entrances and exits, the bishop, priests, deacons, and other clerical ministers walked slowly down the aisle of a church, carrying the various objects for all to inspect and revere. The architectural design of newly constructed churches permitted and perhaps fostered this trend. Funded by Constantine's treasury, church buildings across the Empire were being patterned after public assembly halls, the basilicas. These rectangular spaces created long halls or naves ideal for ceremonial processions.

The liturgy began with the Word, the Scriptures. Although the codex or book-form had come into circulation by the second century, the Holy Writ was often kept in the traditional way, on scrolls. A single scroll for the entire Bible was not practicable. Instead, the sacred text was divided up into multiple scrolls: one each for the Gospels, the Epistles, the Psalter, the Pentateuch, and the Prophets. In worship, the divine Word became a sacred object whose presence was announced to the congregation by the sweet aroma of incense that preceded its entrance. When Nicholas performed a liturgy, the scroll or book was processed into the sanctuary ahead of him, held high for all to see. Nicholas would greet his beloved Scriptures with a kiss. Multiple readings, from the Psalms, the Gospels, the apostolic letters, and the Hebrew Scriptures, would be read aloud and meditated on during a single service. Many congregations ordained readers who kept the books safe in their homes and performed the duties of reading from them. Some scrolls were marvelously illustrated, such as the *Exultet Rolls* from Apulia, so that as the reader unrolled a scroll over the lectern, the congregation could look at colorful pictures of the story being read.

The liturgy of the Word led to the high point of the service, the Eucharist, in which baptized church members shared the mystical bread and wine. This portion of the service began with another procession, at which point nonbelievers were asked to excuse themselves. The words and motions of the Eucharist did not vary; they were fixed, and the minister conducted them with solemnity and awe. The elements had taken on powerful and deep meaning; the people were ingesting the body and blood of their Lord.[33]

Nicholas' first task as bishop was to conduct the sacraments, lead faithfully in worship, and give instruction from the Scriptures. Second to that was the broader task of practical ministry, conceived as it was in the nomenclature of "patronage." Early Christian holy men—who were already being venerated as saints by the third century—served the volatile world of late antiquity in the capacity of patrons, that is, as go-betweens who could mediate town and country, powerful and poor, imperial representative and local resident. In a traditional Roman province, agricultural colony, or village, the patron was the big man—προστάτης, *patronus*—the boss. He could settle local disputes, negotiate with the Roman garrisons and tax collectors, and offer protection when conflicts arose with neighboring villages.[34] He was indispensible to the daily operations of commerce, law, and community, especially in the more rural towns. The scattered breadth of the Empire demanded the help of strong, local, big men. For example, in the third century, the city of Rome was able to count a million inhabitants, and other important cities could claim one-hundred thousand, but most of the towns throughout the Mediterranean hovered at five thousand or fewer. Peter Brown, one of the world's foremost experts on late antiquity, calls them "mere 'agrotowns' by modern standards."[35] As the foremost city in the Lycian province, Myra could boast of a population of fifty thousand, but much smaller hamlets dotted the maps by scores. The control Rome exercised over villages, towns, and rural communities was unavoidably loose and indirect. Even in an important province like Egypt, with its key city of Alexandria, there was one imperial official for every ten thousand citizens.[36] Roman governors and bureaucrats, like Roman soldiers on the borderlands, were spread thin. Quite naturally then, the need arose in smaller localities for unofficial managers to fill in the governmental voids and provide some kind of communal stability.

The *ordo curialis*, the duly constituted town council made up of individuals from the area's wealthiest families, not only provided local governance but also patronage and munificence. Powerful landowners, well-to-do aristocrats, up-and-coming merchants, and ambitious farmers viewed it as a high honor to sit as a *decurion*, or councilor, on the town council. The *decurions* were the patrons of the people, and as such, were highly respected. Though a privilege, the position came with the heavy public responsibility of financing games, distributing food to the needy, and initiating public works.[37] Law required them to perform the duties of legislators, adjudicators, and executors; custom called for them to play the roles of benefactors and "fathers." Despite the burden of the office, it was nevertheless a coveted position for many years, not easily won even by those who held the requisite amount of land to qualify. However, at some point in the late third century, the prestige of the *decurion* lost its appeal, in part because the primary duty of the position had become tax collection on behalf of the out-of-breath Empire. No longer honored and cherished, the *decurion* was now dreaded and avoided.[38] He was the taxman. The more unpopular the position of *decurion* became, the more individuals excused themselves from it and withdrew from the city councils. According to Brown, "The crisis of the late Roman Empire is precisely the crisis by which the traditional hinge-man withdrew from the village scene."[39] By the fourth century, Libanius, a famous Roman orator, complained of "hunting after patrons" in the villages of Syria.[40] Like sand slipping through fingers, community leaders and town councilors slipped away.

Who would fill the void left in the local economies and communities by the exodus of the traditional benefactors? Who would arrange loans? Who would protect the interests and property of the towns? Who could be trusted to resolve disputes with fair and unbiased judgments? According to Peter Brown, "It is precisely at this point that the holy man came to the fore as a figure in village society and in the relation between the village and the outside world. For what men expected of the holy man coincides with what they sought in the rural patron."[41] The connection became so close that in many localities the words "saint" and "patron" were

113

interchangeable, or were often the same word. Even today, the vocabulary of "patron saint" is still used. The ministers of the church—whether holy men, pastors, priests, or bishops—stepped into the gap and served as civic mediators, negotiators, and arbitrators.[42] The minister, by freeing himself from family obligations, economic greed, gluttony, sexual desire, and worldly needs in order to serve God, became a natural go-between. He was a neutral party, an objective and dispassionate observer, an ideal judge, mediator, and protector. John of Ephesus (c. 507–586) reports that a certain holy man named Habib traveled the districts of Syria, assisting in civil matters wherever he was needed. He cured one woman of infertility and helped another collect unpaid fees. Whether dealing with landlords or moneylenders, he effectively resolved disputes, and when "a widow or poor woman or poor man begged him to go with him on any business whatever, he did not, as a man of high reputation, refuse to go, but, in order to satisfy him, would go with him at once."[43] A holy man like Habib could be trusted to be continent—in full control of his body and mind. He did not debase himself by spitting or scratching or slobbering or slurring.[44] He was a man of power who could inflict curses on recalcitrant souls who did not abide by his judicial arbitrations, be they laundry girls or Persian judges.[45] He could expel demons from individuals and towns and could reconcile troubled families. He could restore peace to ostracized individuals and heal fragmented communities. He was the protector of the region.[46]

Nicholas grew into this role of holy patron. His primary pastoral ministry was the ministry of patronage. Townspeople nodded their heads and noted him as a man of discipline and chastity, action and respect. Nicholas' biographer Michael commends his "resolute and immediate aid in the various times of trouble."[47] With his newfound authority and imperial recognition, Nicholas turned on his greatest ideological threat and Christ's greatest rival in the region: Artemis of Ephesus. Though the traditional worship of the ancient goddess permeated the landscape and was part of the fabric of the culture, the battle-tested *communio sanctorum,* the "communion of saints," did not value religious toleration as we might today: they believed paganism was the enemy, its gods were demons in disguise, its religious rites and rituals were superstitious nonsense, its beliefs were transparent falsehoods.[48] The history of the rise of Christianity recounts an epic conflict. The conversion of the Roman world from polytheistic paganism to Christian faith became nothing less than a tournament of narratives, a contest of wills, a fight for the hearts and minds of the people. It represented a clash of cultures—the old ways of divinities and spirits and festivals versus the new way of Jesus Christ. The two could not coexist.

Michael the Archimandrite represents in his biography the process by which pre-Christian beliefs and practices were expunged and replaced by Christian ones. He writes of the triumph of Nicholas over the last of the gods. And behind these stories we can discern the outlines of what might be called the "grey time between the gods, when pagan practice had been prohibited and when Christianity itself, though officially triumphant, was by no means, as yet, the religion of the 'cognitive majority' among the populations of Europe and the Middle East."[49] Nicholas was more than a smiling grandfather of the people; he was a facilitator of change from paganism to Christianity.

Contest with Artemis

The *Thargelion,* the birthday celebration of Artemis, had been a holy day in Nicholas' region from time immemorial. Held alternately on the sixth day of either May or June, it featured ritual reenactments of the birth of Apollo and Artemis with song, images, and the cacophony of noise and foot-stamping created by youngsters playing the parts of the Amazonians. More popular still was the *Artemisia,* celebrated between March and April in the month known as Artemision. So economically successful and entertaining was the holiday that by the second century A.D. "it was decided," as one inscription from Ephesus decreed, "that the whole month of Artemision be sacred in all its days, that there be held during these days every year in this month the festivals, both the festival of the Artemisia and the cessation of public business throughout the whole month."[50] The *Artemisia* functioned as a time of courtship. Eligible young men and women engaged in ritual dances and processions in the long shadows of the evening, touching hands and making eye contact while eating, drinking, laughing, and singing. The more adventuresome would clad themselves in revealing animal skins and sling quivers of arrows over their shoulders in imitation of the huntress. Wooden wagons carting green wreaths and painted terra-cotta images processed through torch-lit streets out of the city to the shrine of Artemis. At the front of the procession, young maidens carried baskets of incense, sacrificial knives, and other utensils—the baskets of Artemis. Behind them walked the sacrificial animals and those chosen to perform the sacrifices. Trailing these were the flute players and musicians and the other participants.[51] Once at the temple, worshipers took the sacred images of the goddess through a hallowed grove of cypress trees and to the river. They would purify the statues in the waters, anoint them with oil, clothe them royally, and return them to their places. The ceremonies culminated with a glorious banquet inside the torch-lit temple.

Such rituals formed the backbone of society. Even as intellectual ideas and spiritual values shook and shifted, the familiar traditions and holidays clung tight. Although huge swells of new converts entered the Christian sanctuaries where they were genuinely won over by the gospel and baptized, they struggled to separate themselves from the seasonal festivals and religious holidays of their childhood. It was one thing to convert souls, another to change habits. The victory of Christianity over its rivals did not come instantaneously but was the result of a long and intense process.

Intellectually, Christians had made and remade their case in order to gain legitimacy. The *apologia*, or apology, had been a standard genre of Christian literature since the second century writings of Justin Martyr. The steady stream of Christian defenses and refutations culminated in a profusion of productions during the late fourth and early fifth centuries, including Theodoret of Cyrrhus' *Treatise on the Greek Disposition*, Lactantius' *Divine Institutes*, Gregory of Nazianzus' *Orations against Emperor Julian*, Augustine's *City of God*, Prudentius' *Against Symmachus*. Christians out-narrated and out-argued their pagan opponents with vigor.

Politically, the struggle had to be fought at the local level, town by town, district by district. After about A. D. 330, Constantine allowed the destruction of pagan temples as long as the artwork and precious items taken from them were brought to the imperial treasury.[52] He ordered that bronze doors and tiles be stripped along with the gold overlay on idol statues. Local oracles were gradually closed, and public sacrifices disallowed. The Palestinian town of Aelia Capitolina was given back its former name, Jerusalem, and public funds were lavished to beautify it with new churches like the Church of the Holy Sepulcher, which replaced a temple of Aphrodite that had existed since the time of Hadrian. The Christian victory was consolidated formally in A.D. 391 when Theodosius I named Christianity the official religion of the Empire.[53] In 529 Justinian the Great required every citizen of the Roman Empire to be baptized.

Practically, however, the intellectual and political victories were not enough. The cultural habits of buying temple meat, consecrating the seasons, and lighting votive candles endured the passage of time and the criticism of Christians. In Rome, for instance, more than ten years after imperial law had officially excoriated paganism, the ornate Codex-Calendar of 354 featured pagan holidays and martyrs' feasts, the symbolism of traditional polytheism and Christian monotheism side by side.[54] The world, though perhaps tamed by angels and saints, was brimming with sprites and spirits, demons and mysteries. Pious individuals did not hesitate to "call on Neptune in the sea, on Lamiae in the rivers, on Nymphs in spring, on Dianas in woods," complained Martin of Braga (c. 520–580) in a sermon.[55] Superstitious habits proved hard to break; according to Martin, stubborn men and women continued "to observe the 'days' of Vulcan [August 23] and the first days of each month, to adorn tables and hang up laurels, to watch the foot, to pour out fruit and wine over a log in the hearth, and to put bread in a spring."[56] Women were quick to invoke Minerva in their weaving and sure to hold weddings on Fridays, the day of Venus, for luck. People were willing enough to embrace Christianity as long as the winds of fortune were behind it, but they did not see the need to relinquish all other loyalties. The challenge to take off the old self and put on Christ completely (Col 2:6-23) required coaxing, convincing, and at times cajoling.

And yet, a new day was dawning in the Mediterranean world, a day in which Christian ministers stood shoulder to shoulder with civic authorities and advised the emperor himself. In the newly Christianized Empire, the old religions and customs began to evaporate like puddles of water before an afternoon sun. By the end of the fourth century, the uneven varieties of polytheistic worship, local superstition, and Greco-Roman mythologies that had dotted the Mediterranean like wildflowers in an open field were all labeled together as "paganism," from the word *paganus*, "second-class participant," or "peasant."[57] Those who persisted in the old ways and the old gods were pagans, backwards country-folk, *rustici* ("rustics") or *agrestes*, another word for "peasants." Christianity was the way of truth and enlightenment—the way of the future.[58] The old ways were gradually consigned to the flames like unwanted weeds.

The Temple of Artemis and the Demons Therein

Nicholas' most direct confrontation with the gods of old occurred in his battle with the goddess Artemis. Andrew of Crete, in his *Encomium of St. Nicholas,* sings the following praise: "Most surely you cleaned and cleared all the spiritual fields in the region of Lycia, pulling up the thorns of disbelief." Like a vinedresser in an unkempt vineyard, Nicholas pulled up the weeds of wrong belief and trimmed back the tendrils of error. To him fell the task of pruning described by Jesus in John 15:2. Andrew continues, "By your teachings, you toppled idol altars and leveled the houses of horrid demon worship. In their place, you raised Christ's sanctuary."[59] Andrew attributes the gospel's success to Nicholas' communication powers. With his sublime teachings, he flushed out pagan falsehoods and felled the altars of idols. It was not the statues of Artemis that needed washing in the river, he told them, but the people themselves. They were the ones in need of Christ's cleansing power and the repentance of baptism. It was not by the fecundity and protection of Artemis that the harvests and granaries were secured, it was by the mercy of the great God and Creator of all. Michael the Archimandrite says,

> Nicholas, a pastor imbued with divine wisdom, preached the faith sound without blemish to the sheep who depended on him. He was so moved by zeal from the heavenly divine Spirit that dwelt within him that his blood began to boil and he ached to exterminate the demons once and for all. Reflecting on the aberrations of the deceptive and idolatrous altars which still existed in the metropolis of Myra and thinking about those who still enjoyed their demonic evils and fed on the most foolish false prophecies, he rose up mightily against these kinds of wickedness.[60]

Nicholas did not confine his preaching to the church walls but took his message to the villages and roadside markets. "Strongly agitated with zeal for God," he went out and "began to scour every corner of the diocese with his faith in Christ."[61] Michael's reader is reassured that Nicholas did not use violence against anyone in his holy crusade. He did not take up "visible weapons," but relied on the invisible weapons of prayer and righteousness and "armed himself with hope and firm confidence."[62] Not everyone followed Nicholas' example. Mark the Deacon reports that in Gaza the demolition of pagan sites devolved into frenzies of looting, pillaging, and rioting. There were even casualties.[63] Pagans retaliated with their own forms of violence. In one incident recorded in the *Life of St. Theodotus*, seven devout women were taken captive by a mob at an annual pagan ceremony just outside the city of Ancyra. The women were stripped, chained, and paraded to a lake, where statues of Artemis and Athena were to be ceremonially washed and cleaned. The ringleaders of the mob presented the women with a choice: become pagan priestesses or be drowned. The women made their choice and were forced into the lake. Pitiably, their friends, Theodotus and Theocharides, returned to the scene late that night, waded into the water, found the limp bodies, and pulled them out. A memorial shrine was erected to mark the spot.[64] Such was the tension between Christians and pagans at this time.

In Myra, the action—though it stopped short of violence against persons—escalated rapidly. Nicholas not only spoke out against the false gods and goddesses, but also destroyed their temples and sacred groves with his own hands. "He turned upside down the temples of the idols and cast out demons, exposing their deceptive and wicked impotence."[65] Michael adds that, "the holy one openly fought the evil spirits in order to put an end to their false ways once and for all."[66] Nicholas was "determined to root out and destroy the worship of demons in the entire region."[67] Around the year 333, as the holy man approached the age of seventy, he took it upon himself to demolish the local temple of Artemis.[68] "He had a divinely inspired idea to carry out a major undertaking, namely to destroy the temple of Artemis which stood large and imposing."[69] According to Michael, it was the tallest temple in the area, had the greatest number of decorations and, of course, the greatest number of demons. At about the same time, a zealous group of believers in Ancyra, a major city to the north in the region of Galatia, dismembered a sister shrine. And in Myra, the will of the people firmly supported Nicholas' actions. He was not acting as a rogue vigilante but on his authority as bishop and spiritual commander of the Lycian territory when he personally oversaw the destruction of the temple: "He went himself inside the abominable places of the temple, not only destroying the building and its elements, but shooing away the demons that lurked there."[70] The demons inside "were compelled by God to leave their home" and go into exile, vowing revenge on the man of God who had expelled them.[71]

The dramatic tale of Nicholas' attack on the Artemis cult was told not only by Michael, but by countless preachers, monks, clerics, and laypeople. It grew larger with time. By the tenth century, Symeon Metaphrastes described the holy man as a regular crusader, traveling from town to town sledge-hammering local temples: "Wherever he found a pagan shrine, he knocked it down, reducing it to rubble. In this manner, he evicted the resident demons and ushered in a peace for all to enjoy."[72] Like Michael, Symeon relayed the demolition of Myra's great shrine of Artemis, but, true to his nickname, Metaphrastes—one who abridges, elaborates, and embellishes—he enhanced the story with rich details:

> [Nicholas] did not abstain from the shrine of Artemis, but advanced against it as well, doing what he had done earlier to other temples. The temple was more admirable and beautiful than any other, surpassing all in magnitude, and was a delightful habitation for demons. For this reason, he went up against this temple and attacked it vigorously and fiercely. Not only did he tear down everything that had been raised high, throwing it down to the ground, he also tore up everything to the foundation itself. Indeed, what was highest on

the temple was plowed into the dirt and what was on the ground now protruded into the air. The evil demons were not able to stand fast at the arrival of the saint, but emitted loud screeches and fled. And they complained because they had been greatly injured and ejected against their will from their property.[73]

The story of Nicholas' holy assault continued to grow. The Old English version of the *Life of St. Nicholas,* dating to the eleventh century, states that "after he was ordained as bishop, he would not permit any idolatry to take place" anywhere in the province of Lycia, but drove out heathen gods and goddesses, sorcerers and witches, and all things demonic.[74] Before long, new legends circulated. The *Vita Lycio-Alexandrina,* a fifteenth-century text, reports that one of the devils expelled by Nicholas entered a bronze statue in Alexandria and refused to leave. The saint had to be summoned, but before he arrived the slippery spirit decided it best to avoid confrontation and disappeared, causing the statue to crash to the ground.[75]

Nicholas was certainly not alone in his zealous attacks on paganism. In the town of Ancyra, Christians were instructed by church officials to cast out and avoid "those who foretell the future, and follow pagan customs, or admit into their houses people in order to discover magical remedies, or to perform expiations."[76] In the countryside, St. Hypatius of Rufinianea (d. 446) cut down and burned a venerated tree thought to be associated with Artemis.[77] Sacred groves and venerated cypress trees dotted the landscape of Asia Minor. The sanctuary of Apollo in Antioch was famed for its laurel trees and cypresses of enormous height. Christians spared none of them. Sanctuaries were desecrated, trees chopped. Like St. Martin before the sacred pine tree and St. Boniface before the oak of Geismar, each had to be cut down and destroyed. A coin from third-century Myra shows a tree with the goddess Artemis crouched in its branches. Two men stand below with raised axes.[78] St. Nicholas of Sion expelled a local spirit of Artemis from a water-spring at Arnabanda and challenged an enchanted cypress near the village of Plakoma. Inhabitants of the village warned him that the last person who tried the tree had been slaughtered with his own axe by the demon within. Disregarding the caution, Nicholas charged the men to cut it. "A shiver ran through all those who were standing around holy Nicholas, and no one dared so much as to look at the tree."[79] When it was apparent that no one would touch the sacred tree, Nicholas of Sion called for the blade and declared that he would rid them of the foul thing by chopping the tree down himself. Making the sign of the cross, he struck the cypress seven times. He ordered the people to move around and assemble on the north slope of the hill, as he expected the tree to fall to the west. The spirit inside the tree had other plans and made the tree lean toward the north slope where everyone had gathered, causing them to scream and cry out, "Servant of God, the tree is coming down on top of us, and we will perish."[80] Nicholas of Sion made the sign of the cross, put both hands on the tree, and pushed it back while shouting, "In the name of my Lord Jesus Christ I command you: turn back and go down where God has ordained you."[81] These acts, as we have seen, were later attributed to the homonymous saint from Myra. For this reason, medieval church frescoes sometimes depict Nicholas of Myra, red in the face with holy anger, toppling temple columns with his bare hands and then swinging an axe into the base of a sacred cypress.[82]

Holy men went to battle against the wiles of the evil one, expelling demons and protecting themselves by the sign of the cross. Martin of Tours, like Nicholas of Sion, once halted a sacred tree from falling on top of him by making the "sign of salvation," that is, the sign of the cross.[83] Cyril of Jerusalem called the sign "a badge of the faithful, and a terror to devils."[84] Friardus, while in the field cutting corn, repelled wasps with the same sign.[85] Theodoret reports that even the apostate and unbelieving Julian made recourse to it in order to rid himself of a demon.[86] And so, Christians claimed the victory over "false gods" of tradition and ancestry. They fervently quoted James 4:7, "Resist the devil, and he will flee from you."

123

Artemis, it was said, did not possess divine power to aid and protect but only a "daimonic" power to injure and deceive. An inscription found in Ephesus and dating to the fifth century reads: "Having torn down the beguiling image of the *daimon* Artemis, Demeas set up this marker of the truth in honor of God, the expeller of idols, and the cross, the deathless victory-bearing symbol of Christ."[87] Demeas, perhaps a provincial official or town councilor, commissioned the marker. Artemis, it should be observed, was no deity but a *daimon*, that is to say, a "spirit" or "phantom" or "demon." She was a death-dealing spirit who tempted and deceived citizens with her "beguiling image." According to Demeas she had been expelled from the city by the true power, the cross, the "deathless victory-bearing symbol of Christ."

It is not surprising, given this history of open religious warfare between the devotees of Christ and Artemis, that Christians claimed responsibility, retrospectively, for the destruction of the Ephesian temple of Artemis. Although actually it was wrecked by the Goths in 262, legends began to surface within a generation or two that it had fallen at the hands of Christian saints. The *Acts of John*, possibly composed in the late third century, related the adventures of St. John the apostle in Ephesus. On the birthday of Artemis, so the narrative reads, everybody came to the temple dressed in white garments, but John wore black.[88] The people were offended by his lack of respect; some grabbed him and threatened him with death. Unfazed, John challenged the power of Artemis in front of everyone. He closed his eyes and prayed in a loud voice, at which the altar dutifully split into many pieces along with seven of its idols. But then something else happened: the roof of the temple suddenly collapsed, and one priest was crushed underneath. Some people ran about hysterically while others fell to their knees, tore their garments, and cried out, "There is only one God, that of John, only one God who has compassion for us. . . . Have mercy upon us, God, according to your will, and deliver us from our great error."[89] The scene, though imaginary, is terrifying.

Bishop Nicholas' attacks were just as intense, owing to the fact that Artemis and her demons would not go quietly. Michael reports that after Nicholas' own demise a demon bent on retribution approached pilgrims boarding a ship destined for Myra.[90] She disguised herself as an old hag and carried with her a small flask of oil. She asked the pilgrims to take the oil to the tomb of St. Nicholas at Myra as an offering of devotion. The oil was to be used to light the lamps of the church and to sprinkle about the altar and the tomb. But it was revealed in a dream to one of the passengers that the flask was not what it appeared and should be cast immediately into the sea. This was done, and the flask of oil proved to be a bomb. Flames spewed forth, polluting the air with smoke and stench.[91] The description of the device bears similarities to "Greek fire," a military invention of the seventh century that the guardians of Constantinople came to employ with deadly efficiency. Packed in clay casings, the explosives could be hurled down from high city walls or launched at approaching enemy vessels.[92] The passengers and crew on board the ship destined for Myra gave themselves up for lost as the waters shook and the ship wrenched about violently. Suddenly, the luminous spirit of Nicholas intervened and restored calm to the turbulent sea. The pilgrims, being able to continue on their way, gave thanks to God and to his servant, the great Nicholas.[93] The tale is worth reproducing in its entirety.

125

> It happened that there gathered a variety of pilgrims from distant places. They prepared to make a visit to this health-giving place where the beloved Saint rested, and receive his grace, known to be illuminating, as well as his flowing oil. However all of this came to the attention of an infamous and tortuous demon, who once inhabited the Temple of Artemis, from whence the Saint and Wonderworker, our Father Nicholas, had completely expelled her. Since she could not come near the metropolis of Myra, she assumed the form of a little old woman, and appeared to the pilgrims and held out in her

hand a jar that appeared to be full of oil, which in truth was not that, although it seemed to be oil. But it was full of a powerful concoction able to cause great evil.

"Take this," the demon said, "I ask you, friends, as it is a votive offering from me for the Saint. And I certainly understand that this is not a small matter for you, but it is something easily carried. You, then, when you reach the desired and venerable place, light the lamps for me with this, that they might burn with a bright flame for my soul."

After [Nicholas] had expelled the demons once and for all from the altar of Artemis, they had not been able to penetrate that region for the remainder of the Saint's life, nor inflict any evil upon him. Since she was full of ill-will, as soon as the Saint departed from this life she began to plot destruction, so that her ill-will might produce works against his most glorious Sanctuary where from his body flows out oil. As soon as the travelers accepted the jar from the evil spirit and agreed to take it to Myra, they set sail, navigating well throughout the first day. That night, when darkness fell all around, the servant Nicholas appeared as if glowing to the one who was storing the diabolical jar. He said to him: "Immediately when you rise in the morning, throw that strange jar you have into the waves of the sea."

When the person rose in the morning, he did without delay what he had been told in his sleep. In the place it landed huge flames flew up high in the air, and everything was covered in darkness. Pungent odors and dense smoke emitted from the sea. In addition, the waves came in and out, crashing with tremendous force, splashing water and discharging something like sparks. Fear gripped all those sailing. And indeed the entire ship was stirred up in the sea. To be sure, the darkness and strong wind caused them to fear, so that they despaired of directing the ship. As they discussed from every point of view the need to drive back, their cause of salvation appeared in order to save: he himself appeared in order to help out. Quickly bounding down he freed them from the harm and danger of the demonic trick she had tried to pull off by means of that satanic thing which she had given them, wanting them to pour out what she had delivered to them.

Once the people's fear had lifted, and as the light of day returned, a divine wind blew on them, so that, little by little, the ship came to a place to land. They began to understand the evil scheme of the jar: that it was full of a certain kind of matter that was thrown into the sea, which the demon had crafted to be released in the sacred Sanctuary. On account of what happened, and for their special rescue from calamity, they returned thanks to God, and to Nicholas.[94]

Full of high-seas adventures, treachery, explosions, disguises, dreams, and miraculous activity, the narrative acts as a warning to pilgrims and pious Christians to take care; Michael cautions his reader to be aware that the evil one "prowls around like a roaring lion, seeking someone to devour" (1 Pet 5:8).

Stories of supernatural conflict became commonplace. In Apamea, a troublesome "black demon" hid within its shrine, refusing to depart or allow workers to demolish it; bishop Marcellus ordered holy water to be sprinkled on the base and columns of the shrine, and the demon fled.[95] Since they no longer received veneration in the open and since they were hounded by holy men and driven out by prayer, the spirits began to hide and even disguise themselves. For this reason, the saints always had to be on guard. During a Basket of Artemis festival, Artemis appeared to St. Hypatius on a country road cloaked as an old woman. Hypatius was not fooled, however, owing to the fact that the old woman stood as tall as ten men.[96] The demons learned to conceal themselves in secret, masking their forms so as not to be discovered. Because they assumed different shapes, diligent inquiry needed to be made at every dubious encounter. St. Martin of Tours investigated a supposed tomb of a venerated martyr on the hunch that it was the shrine of a demon; on another occasion he forced a funeral procession to halt on suspicion that it was a pagan sacrificial rite.[97] Both of his suspicions proved incorrect, but the stories nevertheless give glimpses into the fearful and uncertain times.

The struggle with the shadowy powers tested the resolve of the Christian community. But after years of vigilance and toil, the new Christian faith carried the day. Nicholas and his church triumphed over Artemis and the demons. Near the Gulf of Patras in Aitolia a chapel of St. Nicholas covers the spot where once stood a temple to Artemis. A similar configuration can be seen near Chalcis, once called Aulis.[98] People were taught to invoke the name of the holy St. Nicholas instead of Artemis for the protection of sailors and their cargoes as well as the provision of grains, produce, and food supplies.[99]

Other Conflicts

The name of Nicholas was associated with other interreligious conflicts through the ages. One medieval Albanian folktale puts the saint in an entertaining and comical contest with Mohammed, founder and prophet of Islam. As the story goes, Mohammed dined at the house of St. Nicholas. When it came time to eat, Mohammed expected a waitstaff to appear with plates of food, but saw no one. Nicholas explained that servants were not needed. When he spoke the word, anything he wanted to eat and drink appeared instantaneously on the table, hot and ready. Duly impressed, Mohammed invited Nicholas to come to his house and dine. Not to be outdone, he planned to repeat Nicholas' miracle by means of his own craftiness, installing a moveable wall next to his dining table so that, with a light knock, someone behind the wall could push out a table of food. Everything went according to plan until Mohammed surreptitiously knocked, and then knocked louder, to no response. The servant was deaf! Nicholas himself got up and pulled the table of food through the hidden door in the wall, much to his host's embarrassment. On the following day, Mohammed tried to redeem himself by causing thunder. The trick involved the following: at a signal, a cannon would fire and pots and dishes would be sent crashing down a nearby hill. Mohammed raised his hand to give the signal, but nothing happened. The hidden cannon did not go off, and the dishes were not released. Equally frustrated and humiliated, Mohammed turned to Nicholas, who simply clapped his hands. Lightning and thunder exploded across the blue sky. Mohammed left shaken and amazed.[100]

In Poland, the legend is told of young Zelechy, son of a Polish prince, who out of curiosity followed the wizened and gray-bearded Nicholas deep into the forest of Bjaloviez. Coming to a clearing in the forest, they discovered an ancient pagan gathering. Shadowy figures circled a gnarled and massive oak tree, listening to the hooded priest explain that the blood of the tribal chief's son must be offered as a sacrifice to the spirit Svjatowid, who dwelt within the tree. Zelechy watched in horror as the boy was forced to place his head on the sacred stone. A sword flashed. Suddenly Nicholas stepped forward and grabbed the weapon from the priest's hand. He turned and began to hack the great oak until it fell with a crash. Nicholas then preached the gospel to those gathered.

129

Russians in particular adored the good saint and claimed him as their own, erecting countless shrines and churches in his honor. He was incorporated into a number of their folktales. The tale of Sadko and the King of the Sea, put to music by Rimskij Korsakov, relates how penniless Sadko sat by Lake Ilmen and played a guitar-like instrument called the *gusli*. Suddenly there arose from the waters the Sea Tsar, King of the Sea, who praised Sadko for his beautiful playing. He offered to reward the talented musician: he should go into the city of Novgorod and "strike a great wager," betting that he could pull from the lake a fish with golden fins. Sadko of course won the bet with the help of the Sea King. He became a wealthy businessman and prominent citizen in Novgorod, sailing the sea with thirty ships of merchandise. But he forgot to pay tribute to the god of the lake, the Sea King. For this he was recalled to the ocean floor and made to play his gusli before the King and his Queen. The music pleased the King, and he began to dance. The more he danced the more the sea's surface above foamed and churned.

> Many ships were being smashed on the blue sea,
> Much property was being destroyed,
> Many pious people were being drowned.
> Then people prayed to Mikola Mozhaisky.
> Then someone touched Sadko on the right shoulder,
> "Hail to you, Sadko of Novgorod!
> That's enough playing on your maple gusli!"
> Sadko of Novgorod turned around and looked.
> Behold, there stood a gray old man.[101]

Mikola Mozhaisky is the shade of St. Nicholas. He has been reduced to little more than a stock character, the traditional patron of sailors, a gray old man. Yet it is possible to make out the faded lines of his former self and, more importantly, of an old conflict between the God of Jesus and the spirits of the natural world.[102] Sadko, meanwhile, could not stop playing because the king would not allow it. Mikola suggested he break the strings and the peg of his instrument. This he did, and the music and dancing came to a halt. Mikola, it should be noted, did not have the power to stop the music or soothe the waters of the sea. Thoroughly tamed by the folklore format, he could only scheme a solution. He retained little more than the power of suggestion.

These three short tales represent a small sample of the legends and folktales that collected like snowflakes on a rooftop to the memory of Nicholas. Many of them involved confrontation with natural and supernatural powers, and in this way remembered the rivalry between Artemis and the saint. But as individual snowflakes lose their distinctiveness when they merge to form a single blanket of white, so the legacy of Nicholas softened and blurred with time. The hints of history turned into the stuff of legend, the heritage of folklore, and the free-for-all of fairytale.

5

Riots, Beheadings, and Other Near Misfortunes

B etween the years 330 and 332, bad weather forced a convoy of military ships to land at Andriake, the port of Myra. The ships were destined for Phrygia Adaifalorum, where the Romans intended to put down a Gothic revolt on the border. The Gothic tribe known as the Taifales was once again wreaking havoc.[1] Upon landing, the commanding officers gave the troops permission to fan out across the city in search of food and entertainment. Some local hooligans, seeing an opportunity, seized upon the clever idea of disguising themselves in soldier's clothing in order to stir up trouble by looting and pilfering. The imposters were arrested, but the local citizens, unaware of what had really happened, began to wrongly accuse the soldiers of the mischief. A riot broke out, and the city was thrust into turmoil. Someone ran to get Bishop Nicholas, who was now near the age of seventy. A respected pastor of the church and patron of the city, he was not intimidated by the rioters or the military personnel. He descended into the tumultuous Placomatus plaza, quieted the mob, and then made peace with the soldiers by holding a conference with the commanding officers, whose names were Nepotianus, Ursus, and Eupoleonis.[2]

Immediate Actions and Distant Dreams

As Nicholas was clearing up the confusion, a panicked report reached his ears that Eustathius, the provincial governor of the region, was about to execute three innocent men—presumably for the crimes of impersonating Roman soldiers and for stealing, though the criminal charges are not specified in the text. Nicholas set off at a brisk pace for the Praetorium, or palace, to speak with Eustathius. Nicholas suspected foul play as Eustathius, so the text suggests, was known to be corrupt and easily bribed. One can imagine Nicholas' dark robes stirring the dust beneath him as he walked with briskness and determination. The three commanding officers tagged along behind him. While en route, Nicholas was stopped and informed of yet a new development: the convicts had already been moved to "the place of the beheading" known as Byrra. The concerned bishop wheeled around and took off at dead run in the opposite direction. He burst into the plaza of Byrra to find the condemned men on their knees, hands tied behind their backs, and faces covered with linen cloths. Like the three Hebrews—Shadrach, Meshach, and Abednego—about to be tossed into the fiery furnace, the men had given themselves up for dead. Nicholas forced his way through the crowd of wide-eyed gawkers, yanked the sword from the executioner, and threw it to the ground. Dramatically, he untied the prisoners' hands and set them free. Then he marched off to find the governor, Eustathius, in order to chastise him for his miscarriage of justice—condemning innocent citizens without a proper trial. The basis of Nicholas' legal right to confront and challenge the ruling of a civil judge is found in the Sirmondian Constitutions issued by Constantine himself.[3] One such constitution specified that either party in a civil case could appeal over and above the protests of the other to a bishop, whose verdict was binding and incontestable. Even Ablabius, Constantine's Praetorian prefect (who will soon be introduced in the story), wondered in a letter if Constantine had truly intended bishops to have this unprecedented privilege. He had.

Back at the Praetorium, Nicholas "broke down the door."[4] He burst inside, and a sentinel hurried off to inform the governor of his arrival. Eustathius, trying to maintain his composure, greeted Nicholas with deference and compliments. Bishop Nicholas was not amused; he stopped the governor in mid-sentence and accused him of being a "thief" and an "enemy of God," calling him "sacrilegious and bloodthirsty and unjust." According to the text, Nicholas raised his voice and castigated Eustathius in the harshest terms, saying,

> "And you even dare to come before me, you who do not fear God! You who had the cruel intention to kill innocent people! Since you committed this kind of wickedness I cannot have any respect for you. God is reserving for the unjust a tortured life. The most pious emperor knows your faults. He knows how your government works and how this province allows looting and killing men against the law and without trial for deadly greed and gain."[5]

Eustathius wilted under the assault. He fell to his knees and begged pardon. He admitted guilt but then added that the principals of the city, Eudoxius and Simonides, were the ones most to blame. They were the first to make the false accusations. Nicholas would not be fooled or distracted. Eustathius had accepted a bribe of two hundred pieces of gold to accept their false testimonies. Nicholas deduced the real cause and said, "It was not Eudoxius and Simonides, but Gold and Silver that bribed you and made you commit these atrocities."[6] There is a word-play in the Greek between the words for gold and silver and the names of the two principals of the city. In the end, Nicholas prayed a long prayer and pardoned the guilty governor. The three Roman officers, Nepotianus, Ursus, and Eupoleonis, had witnessed the entire event.

A number of things about this story stand out, most important among them the fact that Nicholas was not a saint ready

133

to die quietly in the arena as a martyr. He defended the innocent, freed the captive, and challenged the authorities. In the
new and Christianized world, a bishop could rebuff a local
judge and speak face to face with military officers. People who
were wrongfully incarcerated in jail could count on Nicholas. It is no surprise that he was soon known as the patron
saint of prisoners. The earliest known dedication to St. Nicholas in the city of Rome was a church adjacent to a municipal
prison.[7] In this regard, it is interesting to compare Nicholas'
nail-biting rescue of three innocent men with a similar story
told in the *Ecclesiastical History* of Theodoret of Cyrrhus
(c. 393–460). According to Theodoret, Emperor Julian, known
as the Apostate since he was the last non-Christian to rule
the Roman Empire, tried his best to reverse the Christianization of the Empire set in motion by his uncle, the former
Emperor Constantine. Julian wanted to expel Christians
from military service, so he made his men throw a pinch of
incense upon an altar in order to get paid. The soldiers went
through the motions and only later realized they had been
tricked into "sacrificing to the gods." Certain Christian soldiers, discovering the ruse, "ran through the Forum exclaiming that they were Christians, that they had been tricked by
the emperor's contrivances, that they retracted their apostasy,
and were ready to try to undo the defeat which had befallen
them unwittingly."[8] They asked that their bodies be committed to the flames so that their burning flesh might atone for
the idolatrous incense they had unwittingly burned. Emperor
Julian ordered them beheaded. The men were led to the spot
for executing criminals. They knelt down and exposed their
necks to the executioner. At that moment, a messenger ran
up announcing a reprieve and shouting for the executioner
to halt. Just as in the Nicholas story, the innocent men were
saved from the sword at the last minute. Unconventionally,
though, the tale does not end with rejoicing. The men were
dismayed and disappointed at losing the chance to make the
ultimate witness for Christ and so gain the glory of becoming

martyrs. "Ah," one of them cried out, "[I am] not worthy of being called Christ's martyr!"[9]

The difference between these two similar stories is startling. Whereas Theodoret commended the soldiers because they proved their loyalty to Christ by exposing themselves to death, even to the point of showing regret when their lives were spared, Nicholas proved his zeal for the preservation of life. He made clear that life—all life—was precious and worth saving. Not that Nicholas' loyalty to Christ was in question; he had already demonstrated his courage and his willingness to die for the gospel when he faced the terrors of Diocletian's persecution some years earlier. He was not afraid of death, but he did not have an unnatural desire to die or be party to death. "Sacrifice and offering you did not desire" (Ps 40:6).

The bishop's bravery, boldness, and sharp sense of justice made an impression on the three Roman officers, Nepotianus, Ursus, and Eupoleonis. And, not long after this episode, they found themselves in a predicament eerily similar to that of the three innocent men of Myra. When they returned to Constantinople victorious in their dealings with the Gothic uprisings in Phrygia, they discovered to their surprise that their jealous peers greeted their return not with acclamations but accusations against their integrity and loyalty. Nepotianus and his comrades, they said, did not squelch a rebellion—they plotted an even greater coup. The officers were charged with making alliances with the Phrygian Goths to overthrow Constantine himself. The allegations were brought to Ablabius, who conveyed them to the emperor with these words:

> "My lord the Emperor, because you govern the Empire with Christian piety and because the whole world lives in peace under your command, the devil has envied all the good you have brought and given rise to enemies against us at home. Indeed, he has penetrated into the heart of the generals who have gone and returned from Phrygia. So they are devising a plot against your power and plan to rise up against your

peaceful kingdom. They have collaborated with others among your friends, using promises and advance payments, the lure of donations and an abundance of riches."[10]

Ablabius reassured Constantine that he had come to him as soon as he discovered the plot, and, what was more, that God's hand was at work, foiling the plans of the evildoers. The God who "loves humankind and is the Lord of your godly kingdom" had spurred some informants to find him immediately and tell him what was afoot.[11] The advance warning strategically positioned Constantine and Ablabius to take decisive action, and they had the men imprisoned. Soon after, friends of the accused officers began to petition for their release or at least a hearing. In response, the jealous peers applied pressure to Ablabius, bribing him, so the text says, with money and political favor if he helped them. Ablabius called for the immediate execution of Nepotianus, Urus, and Eupoleonis, saying he had learned that they conspired not only to overthrow the government but to assassinate the emperor. On the basis of this charge, it was decided that the men should be put to death at sunrise.

—*The Role of Flavius Ablabius*—

What would make Ablabius listen to such unfounded charges? Why would he accept bribes for the execution of these three men? Flavius Ablabius is one of history's ambiguous and amorphous characters. Born in Crete, where he served in his first administrative capacity as a lowly clerk, he converted to Christianity and quickly rose in the ranks of Constantine's officers, attaining the status of Praetorian prefect over Asia for about ten years, between 329 and 338, during which time he held the consulship for the year 331. Gerardo Cioffari believes that, if the story of the military officers has any historical merit to it, its events most likely occurred during Ablabius' year of consulship.[12] During that year, he would have had close and personal contact with the emperor. Anyone bringing a case of high treason would have addressed themselves to the consul. Because the accusers went to Ablabius, it stands to reason that he must have been serving as consul at that time, and the year must have been 331. Nicholas would have been near the age of seventy. Furthermore, the ancient historians Socrates and Theodoret record rumor of an assassination and usurpation plot during the same year. They insinuate that it involved one of Constantine's own guards, perhaps a man named Philumenus.[13] Constantine survived the threat to his power, as he had many others, by swift and brutal action. Although a Christian by devotion, experience had made him a hard-edged political realist. He did not hesitate to put to death his rival Licinius despite Licinius being married to his sister Constantia. Nor did he spare his own wife Fausta or his able-bodied and competent son Crispus.[14] He rooted out and eliminated trouble wherever it was found.

137

Historians have difficulty discerning Ablabius' intentions and motives. On the one hand, he was a defender of Athanasius and orthodox Christians. Between the years of 331 and 333 he helped clarify the rights of bishops, especially with regards to courts of law. He sided with Athanasius in a dispute with the Meletian bishops in the year 337, which ultimately brought him into conflict with the Emperor Constantius II, Constantine's son and successor. Either that year or the next, Ablabius was put to death on charges that were said to be false. If he was executed for defending Athanasius and the cause of orthodox Christianity, he should be celebrated as a martyr. On the other hand, he may have been a supreme politician and power-player. Some ancient historians suspected Ablabius of using his

Christian faith to promote himself through the ranks of imperial office. A relevant and infamous incident involves the Neoplatonic philosopher, Sopater of Apamea, who served Constantine as assessor of the court. Sozomenus, the ecclesiastical historian, gives evidence that Sopater may have been critical of the morals of the Emperor Constantine and his prefect Ablabius.[15] Ablabius, so the story goes, soon found his opportunity for revenge on the philosopher. He blamed a grain shortage on Sopater, whom he accused of casting a spell, and had him dispatched.[16] Seen from this angle, he was not so much a humble servant of God as a shrewd power-politician.

Ablabius' motives in the story of the military officers are difficult to discern. It is possible that what motivated Ablabius was not concern for the welfare of the emperor, but position, authority, wealth, and influence. If true, it explains Ablabius' actions, but not those of the accusers who conspired with him. We must ask what reason they had to present a false case to Ablabius and press it with bribes and promises. Cioffari speculates that the accusers were primarily targeting Nepotianus.[17] He was the one they wanted to get rid of. Cioffari reasons that the Nepotianus of the story of the military officers is none other than an actual distant relative of Constantine, and thus might have been a threat to certain powerful men in Constantinople. Constantine's father, Constantius, had a daughter by Theodora named Eutropia, who married a powerful man named Virius Nepotianus in 314. Together they had a son, Iulius Nepotianus. It is presumed that this son is the Nepotianus of our story. And so, it might be the case that the accusers, acting through Ablabius, were trying to dispose of a potential rival to the throne when they imprisoned Nepotianus.

Conversely, Ablabius may have had good reason to suspect Nepotianus of treachery. Perhaps it was not savvy politics but sound information and discernment that led him to imprison the officers. Nepotianus had military experience, powerful allies, and troops at his disposal—and of course he could also claim legitimate family ties to the emperor. Here was as likely a candidate as any to instigate a rebellion. This is in fact what happened. In the year 350, Nepotianus made a bid for the throne. Zosimus relates how it happened: "Nepotianus, nephew to Constantius, by his sister Eutropia, collected a band of persons addicted to robbery and all kinds of debauchery, with whom he came to Rome, and appeared in an imperial dress."[18] Once admitted into the city, Nepotianus seized the reins of government, slaughtered those who opposed him, and let his bandits run riot. For a few days, fear gripped everyone under his unpredictable military rule, but his takeover did not last long. An army was sent to liberate Rome and put Nepotianus to the sword. Thus ended his story in ignominy.

In 331, did Nepotianus exhibit ambitions to put on the purple? Or was he innocent? Did Ablabius act on a clear conscience and good information? Or did he scheme to dispose of a potential rival and gain favor with the men who brought charges against Nepotianus? We can only speculate. The anonymous author of the story of the military officers, it is true, sides with Nepotianus and says that he was the unsuspecting victim of false accusations. The text exonerates him of any wrongdoing and presents Ablabius as weak and easily manipulated. But what was the truth of the matter? Most likely it is found somewhere in between.

Nepotianus, Ursus, and Eupoleonis were informed that they would be killed the following morning. Like Daniel, who was ensnared in a plot by his conniving peers, so the three Roman officers found themselves entrapped by their peers. They wondered if there would be any escape from this lion's den. They despaired and gave themselves up for dead. "What did we do that we should be so wretchedly snuffed out?"[19] But then, remembering the events they had witnessed in Myra, Nepotianus called out to the God of Nicholas and pleaded: "Just as You saved the three men in Lycia who were wrongfully and shamefully condemned to death, please now save us!"[20] That night, Nicholas appeared in a vision to the slumbering Emperor Constantine, chided him for his rash judgment, and demanded the release of Nepotianus and the other officers.

> By the grace of God who always raises up those who glorify Him and redeems the humble in spirit, Saint Nicholas (in the same way that he shows compassion for all those who seek him in desperation and ask for his protection) that night appeared to the emperor and said: "Constantine, Rise up and free the three generals who are kept in prison, because they were unjustly thrown there. If you do not do as I tell you I will bring war in the region of Durres and I will reduce your men to food for animals and give your remains to the vultures. I have conferred with Christ against you, the King of kings."
>
> The emperor said, "Who are you, and how did you get into my palace?"
>
> The voice said, "I am Bishop Nicholas, a sinner, who lives in a city of Lycia." Having said this, he disappeared.[21]

Constantine, now fully awake, called for his prefect, Ablabius, and told him what happened. Ablabius turned white as a bedsheet. He had just had the same dream. Dreams and visions were by no means uncommon in late antiquity. They were highly valued and their messages trusted. As recorded in the New Testament, Peter, Paul, John, and Mary received visions; the mystical Shepherd of Hermas transcribed an elaborate string of them; Antony, the famous monk of Egypt, fought the devil in his dreams; Martin of Tours was visited by Saints Mary, Agnes, and Thecla in visions; Constantine confided in Eusebius of Caesarea about his vision of the labarum, the

Chi-Rho insignia that he took to be a sign of Christ; Augustine and his mother, Monica, shared a tearful vision at Ostia, the port of Rome. Dreams carried the weight of truth, visions portended future events, and angelic visitations revealed hidden meaning. On the basis of his dream, Emperor Constantine summoned the three prisoners to his presence. What dark spell had they cast over his sleep? What kind of foul magic had they beckoned? The emperor charged the men to answer him, but they did not know what to say. Dumbfounded, Nepotianus spoke on behalf of the men: "Most pious Lord, your servants have no knowledge of magic. But if we had any such thought, or if we have done any wrong against the honor of your pious Emperor's person, may your gracious arm put us under the most terrible torments and wracks of torture."[22]

When it became obvious that the condemned officers had no idea what the emperor or Ablabius were talking about, Constantine asked them if they knew anyone named "Nicholas." Overjoyed at the mention of the name, they related what they had seen in Myra and how they had called out to the God of Nicholas in their distress. Constantine perceived the hand of Almighty Providence at work, repented of his ignorance and arrogance, and released the prisoners. In humble gratitude to God, the men shaved their heads and donned the simple garments of pilgrims, then made their way back to Myra with gifts of gold, silver, and costly clothing to thank God and venerate the blessed Nicholas.

Bold as a Lion

The best known anecdote from the life of St. Nicholas is undoubtedly the story of the three poor daughters to whom Nicholas anonymously delivered bags of gold. It provides a historical link to the Santa Claus tradition of gift-giving and is much more agreeable to modern sensibilities than some of the other stories. This has not always been the case, however. At one time, the episode recounted just above, called the *praxis de stratelatis* or "The Story of the Military Officers," was by far the most widely known. More significant still, it is the oldest known story about Nicholas, in circulation long before Michael wrote his biography. Gustav Anrich identifies three recensions, or versions, of this narrative dating from the early 500s.[23] All three recensions appear prior to and independent of Michael the Archimandrite's biography of Nicholas. In addition, the story is referenced in the *Encomium* of Proclus (390–446), patriarch of Constantinople, and in a fragment from the sixth-century Eustratios of Constantinople.[24] On the walls of ancient Byzantine churches, where scenes from the life of Nicholas are depicted in frescoes, it is interesting to note that the story of the military officers receives on average three frames of action, whereas every other episode (birth, ordination, sea rescue, death) is allotted only one frame of action.[25] These diverse pieces of evidence testify to the story's antiquity and widespread popularity. The episode is mentioned in an important seventh-century roll call of the martyrs and saints, the *Martyrologium Romanum*.[26] This reference is significant because it indicates that the story was known even among Latin speakers at a very early date.[27] Karl Meisen speculates that the story probably arose in Myra itself, within fifty to one hundred years after the saint's death, for the glorification of a local hero. He and Gustav Anrich extrapolate from this that the story was put into writing in the mid-500s (during the reign of Justinian).[28] Gerardo Cioffari believes the story may have existed in written form as early as 350–400.[29]

The story of the military officers most tantalizes historians because of its use of proper names. Proper names provide points of reference that can be tested against other historical sources, and so they lend credibility to the story. The narrative provides the names of three Roman generals, a local judge, two leading citizens of Myra, the emperor, and his trusted advisor. It supplies the names of places, including Andriake, Phrygia, Constantinople, and Myra. The story also identifies various locations within the city of Myra, such as the Placomatus plaza, the Byrra, the Leonti, the Praetorium, and the Dios-corus.[30] The specificity supports the narrative's authenticity. And so, here it is, more than halfway through this biography of Nicholas, that we examine one of the most reliable witnesses to his existence.

Perhaps because it was so well known, Michael the Archi-mandrite simply summarizes the story in his own account without providing much detail. He assumes that his readers are familiar with the basic plotline and indicates that they "already know and have read what is written concerning these works that inspire divine joy."[31] Ironically, in the first biogra-phy of Nicholas, one of the most popular and exciting stories about him gets condensed into a few short lines.

Even so, the story of the military officers presents us with a tournament of virtues and values. Like some of the other epi-sodes recounted in Michael's *Life of St. Nicholas*, it was chosen to show the superiority of Christian devotion to the ways of the world. Christianity outperformed the pagan gods, the worldly authorities, and the misfortunes of nature. In the story of the military officers, the Christian bishop was shown to be more effective at crowd control than the army, not as easily cor-rupted as the local governor who condemned three innocent men to beheading, and more capable of seeing through intrigue and lies than even the emperor and his aide.[32] Compared to the holy man, the agents of the world appeared incompetent and blind. The historian Socrates shares an episode from the life of Eutychian, a Novatian monk who dwelled at Olympus, that is strikingly similar in content and message to the story of the military officers. Socrates says he heard the account from Auxanon, who witnessed it personally as a young man. One of Constantine's "military attendants," left unnamed in Socrates' account, was accused of treasonous activities. Fearing for his life, he fled to the hills only to be caught near Olympus in the region of Bithynia and imprisoned in heavy chains. Eutychian went to visit the man and asked the guards to relieve him of his unbearable shackles. They refused, but

143

the chains miraculously fell off the man's body anyway. After speaking with the condemned prisoner, he and Auxanon traveled to the imperial palace in Constantinople where Eutychian pleaded the man's case and saved his life.[33] Whereas the official authorities knew only brutal justice and unflinching judgment, the Christian holy man sought the truth and defended the innocent.

The story of the military officers teaches a related lesson: the civil authorities, even the professedly Christian ones, were not to be trusted. Lavish shrines to martyrs reminded local residents of fellow believers who had fallen at the hands of the authorities. The blood of the martyrs would not soon be forgotten. Although Christianity was now legal and the emperor identified himself as a Christian, the memory of the martyrs caused old-timers to keep up their vigilance. The witness of St. Leo from Patara as well as Myra's martyrs Crescentem, Dioscorides, and Themistocles, killed by anti-Christian overlords, served as warnings: the authorities could turn violent at any time.[34] This context should be kept in mind when reading the story of the military officers. The episode questioned the legitimacy of the civil powers to judge, to enact, and to rule. It challenged the very institutions of government and demanded that these too be Christianized. It was not enough that individuals be baptized—the powers that regulated their lives must be redeemed as well. Old governments must give way to new ones just as old values must be replaced by Christian ones and old injustices rectified by righteousness. Destroying the shrines of Artemis had been the easy work. The hard work was negotiating everyday life, the treatment of major illnesses and minor ailments, the arrangement of hearth and home, the behavior of public administrators, the management of money, the governance of society, and the proper care of the dead.

In the story of the military officers, Nicholas acted as a true protector of his diocese; he was the *patronus*, the big man in town (fig. 8). The people turned to him in their moments of civil crisis: when a riot broke out in the plaza against the

144

Roman soldiers and when three innocent men were about to be beheaded. He stood up to a frenzied mob and to an over-zealous civic judge. Nicholas' sphere of influence was not limited to the province of Myra, either. His protection extended to everyone he touched, including the three Roman officers with whom he dealt.[35] When they were arrested in far-away Constantinople, their defender had not abandoned them.[36]

145

FIGURE 8
Russian statue of St. Nicholas with sword and church

There is almost nothing in the story of the military officers that reminds us of his connection to Santa Claus. It is not the kind of tale one would expect to find in a book of holiday cheer and Christmas memories. But it does bring into focus two characteristics of Nicholas the man: his courage and his concern for justice. Nicholas showed true bravery in the face of danger. Because of his courage, the early and anonymous author of the story of the military officers quotes Proverbs 28:1, "The righteous are bold as a lion."[37] Nicholas' zeal for justice resulted in swift and authoritative action before executioners, judges, governors, and military men. Later generations of Christians read this story with rapt attention, hoping that in their most distressing dilemmas, whether they were falsely accused by their neighbors or bound and shackled to the executioner's bench, God Almighty would send St. Nicholas to their side. In a homily delivered at the high church of Constantinople, the metropolitan bishop Methodius (d. 847) recognized no limit to the power of Nicholas' protection: "Those who suffer injustice he liberates; those who are attacked with false charges he aids; let those who sing his praises confirm that he converts sinners."[38] He was a true "helper," a loyal "defender," and a prudential "overseer."[39] The power of God worked through the hands of the saints.

The saints not only rescued those in legal distress, but assisted individuals in need of healing and miraculous intervention. Their divinely infused power was equal to that of the magicians, augers, soothsayers, and traditional healers who operated in the shadows and wayside places. These practitioners of the old ways were collectively referred to as *arioli*. The *arioli* were unchristian holy men. Gregory of Tours (538–594) related an anecdote in which a youth named Aquilinus fell into a frenzied seizure while out hunting with his father in Gaul, modern-day France. His family immediately called for the *arioli* who came and applied various remedies but to no avail. Aquilinus had to be carried to the shrine of St. Martin to be healed.[40] For Gregory, it was a matter of common sense: "A bit of dust from the church [of Martin] is more powerful than those men with their foolish medicines."[41] Richard Fletcher makes the observation that this story, though it celebrates the power and victory of the Christian God, reveals the influence that the old country healers still held over the people. The people sought out the *arioli* first, though there is no indication that they themselves were pagans, and consulted the Christian God only when traditional remedies failed. Despite being outlawed by the civil authorities and shunned by preachers like Caesarius of Arles and Martin of Braga, the wonder-working *arioli* continued to be relied on by people in dire situations; even priests, deacons, and bishops resorted to their aid on occasion.[42] On account of lingering suspicions and superstitions, it was important for hagiographers and preachers to emphasize a saint's ability to perform the same works as the traditional *arioli*. Methodius' homily celebrated St. Nicholas as a holy man imbued with divine power and purpose, able to "put to flight sickness and demons also."[43] "No one can deny his faithfulness; he is truly admired by all."[44] The blessed Nicholas was capable of doing by the power of Christ all that the pagans did by magic. From the sands of India to the shores of Britain, so Methodius declared, his assistance was "available to all, so that all might be saved."[45] Nicholas' biographer Michael concurs: "There are not, I think, any believers in the world who have not found him a help in danger and the defender of those living in various tribulations."[46]

Barrel of Trouble

The often illiterate and unsophisticated believers of the early Middle Ages were drawn to the lives of the saints because in them they found hope, courage, faith, and wonder. The saints were men and women who had rubbed shoulders with ordinary folk in the real world. They were knowable, relatable, and approachable in ways that the Almighty, in his divine omnipotence and transcendence, often was not. The stories of the saints were thus told and retold to the delight of the listeners who knew them by heart. With each retelling, new elements were added, while others were elaborated. And so, the stories began to drift from biography to lore. Like the soft accumulation of leaves under a tree or the gentle fall of snow on the earth, small accretions of detail began to form on the lives of saints. Almost imperceptibly, narratives once rooted in fact slid into fantasy, farce, and formula.

A Latin manuscript, now housed in London which dates back to the eleventh century, contains some student grammatical exercises composed by the Bavarian schoolmaster Godehard (d. 960), or someone else from his Hildesheim school located in Lower Saxony, Germany, near present-day Hanover.[47] In one of those exercises, a suspiciously new tale makes an appearance. Three "clerks" (*klúros* in Greek, *clericus* in Latin), or young clergymen, perhaps subdeacons or seminarians, decided to take up lodging at an inn one night. The proprietor and his wife, seeing that the youngsters were alone and that their bags jingled with coin, hatched a plan to murder them and take their money. The deed was done, but no sooner than the bodies were disposed of, there came a knock at the door. It was St. Nicholas, disguised as a poor traveler. The innkeepers opened the door to their new guest with warm smiles and invited him in. When the weary traveler asked for some fresh meat to eat, they told him they had none to give. St. Nicholas erupted:

> Falsum refers atque mendacium
> nuper enim per infortunium
> peregisti opus nefarium
> clericorum fundens exitium
> per corpora.

Notice the overt rhyming scheme in the Latin. We are reminded that this is a simple school exercise. Translated into English, Nicholas' speech is rendered as follows:

"You tender falsehoods and lies
About a very recent travesty!
You have carried out a nefarious deed,
Inflicting bodily death on the clerks."[48]

The author does not say how the husband and wife responded to the accusation; it can be inferred that they confessed their guilt and begged for forgiveness. St. Nicholas prayed for their pardon and asked the Lord that the clerks be restored to life.[49] This being done, the drama ends with a chorus of angelic praise to God and his faithful servant Nicholas.

Soon theatrical troops were performing variations of this drama all over Europe, especially as part of the merrymaking on St. Nicholas Day. It has been credited as one of the first nonliturgical, nonbiblical plays to be performed in the Middle Ages. It is significant that the drama first appeared in a collection of school exercises because it very well could have arisen within the classroom, as part of school lore, or, most likely, on the school stage. School boys and convent girls readily identified with Nicholas, the Boy Bishop, whose feast day coincided with the winter festivals and Christmas. According to Meisen, the older students and teachers staged performances on the eve of St. Nicholas Day for the whole school to enjoy. The plays were instructive for the younger children, to be sure, but were also filled with humor and merriment.[50]

The imagination which gave birth to the theatrical production of the three clerks and the evil innkeepers inspired other changes and amendments. New versions of the story simplified some aspects and embellished others. No longer were the victims clerks; they were three boys—making their roles more generic and easy to fill. No longer was the offense of the innkeeper and his wife a mere triple homicide; the boys were dismembered, cut up, and salted in a tub or a pickle barrel. This gruesome addition caused some storytellers to change the murderers from innkeepers to a knife-wielding butcher. The outcome was the same; St. Nicholas raised the boys back to life and punished the evildoer. Here is one rendition of the traditional ballad, loosely translated from old French by the eminent nineteenth-century folklore scholar James Henry Dixon:

> Three little children sought the plain
> Gleaners of the golden grain.
>
> They lingered past the angel-song,
> And dewy shadows swept along.
>
> 'Mid the silence of the wood
> The butcher's lonely cottage stood,
>
> "Butcher! lodge us for the night,
> Lodge us till the morning light."
>
> "Enter in, ye children small,
> I can find a place for all."
>
> The butcher seized a knife straightway,
> And did the little creatures slay.
>
> He put them in his tub of brine,
> In pieces small as they were swine.
>
> St. Nicholas, at seven years end,
> His way did to the forest wend.[51]

The saintly detective asked to stay the night, as had the children. The butcher granted him entrance and inquired what he would like for supper. Ham? Veal? St. Nicholas requested swine cured seven years in brine. Stunned, the man stumbled back and tried to flee, but the holy man stopped him. He then approached the barrel and spoke to the children within, raising them from their horrid fate.

It is no surprise that Dixon's rhymed version of the legend resembles the fables of Hansel and Gretel and Little Red Riding Hood. Dark woods, scared children, murderous adults, and hints of magic conformed to the fairytale pattern of the day, as dictated by the Grimm brothers. In its late nineteenth-century form, the episode of the pickled lads seems to have no obvious relationship to the narrative of the three military officers. How could the one possibly be the source for the other? To answer this question, we should return to Godehard and his Hildesheim schoolmen and ask where they got the idea of St. Nicholas restoring to life three murdered clerks.

We might learn first that the homicidal innkeeper was a stock character in medieval storytelling. Many tales circulated of murder in the tavern and death at the inn. Secondly, the three clerks are connected to Nicholas at least superficially by the number three. Sets of three are standard devices in the Nicholas cycles. Thirdly, we find that the typical artistic rendering of the story of the military officers seen throughout Europe at the time may have inadvertently given rise to the story. The story of the military officers was regularly depicted in cathedral stained glass, in the artwork of the chanceries, and on the frescoes of monastery chapels.[52] A strong argument could be made that the tale of the three murder victims disposed in a barrel arose from misunderstandings of these pictures. Artists often painted the story in multiple frames of action: one frame of Nicholas halting the beheadings, one of the officers languishing in prison, one of Nicholas' nighttime appearance to Constantine and Ablabius, one of the liberated officers paying homage to the good bishop. Sometimes, however, the story was condensed to a single iconic image: the three officers, Nepotianus, Ursus, and Eupoleonis, stretching their hands out the prison window toward Nicholas, calling upon his succor. To give more artistic prominence to the main figure, the saint, the three men were depicted in miniature form, which made them look like small boys. In addition, the jail cell was standardized into its iconic form: the prison tower. The overall impression, to those who did not know the story, was that three tiny children were standing inside a wooden barrel and reaching up to Nicholas so that he might lift them out. Some then interpreted the image as Nicholas christening

151

three babies in a baptismal font. Others saw "three men in a tub." Inquisitive youngsters pointed and innocently asked their parents to tell them about the children in the pickle barrel. In that way, one thing could have led to another and a new story was born. Or perhaps the order was reverse. Perhaps the frescoes were created to reinforce the new stories that were already being told of Nicholas. It is hard if not impossible to reconstruct the order of evolution.[53] The misperception was not helped by the fact that, in the standard Latin text, the three imprisoned men were called "innocent ones," *innocentes*. The term was often used as a euphemism for "children," *pueri*. And in some versions of the story from the tenth century, the word *innocentes* was in fact replaced by *pueri*, with the result that St. Nicholas seemed to be saving three children, from death.[54] In conclusion, multiple misunderstandings and miscommunications could have contributed to the distortion of the story of the military officers and the creation of an entirely new Nicholas fable.

To Protect and Provide

Again and again Nicholas' life testified to God's gracious hand protecting and providing. In the fierce contest of Christianity against its religious rivals, this testimony proved crucial. The honor and reverence once due to the Great Mother Artemis was now due to the Great Creator and Redeemer of all. The fear and respect once owed to traditional deities now belonged to the God revealed in Jesus of Nazareth. As St. Paul reminded the Galatians, "Formerly, when you did not know God, you were slaves to those who by nature are not gods. But now . . . you know God—or rather are known by God" (Gal 4:8-9). The Christian God the people were coming to know could be counted on to save the lost and the dying. Michael included in his biography of Nicholas one episode in which distressed sailors called upon the aid of the divinely empowered bishop of Myra to smooth out the raging waves.

Once some sailors, while navigating the seas, found themselves, by demonic design, in the midst of a violent wind
storm that caused giant waves. They realized that they were
surrounded on all sides by threats of death. They remembered then Saint Nicholas and invoked his aid, calling him
by name. The holy father and quick help to those who call
upon him with trust in the midst of adversity, according
to the will of God, appeared among them in their moment
of greatest distress and said, "Behold, I heard the call, and
rushed to help."[55]

Nicholas did more than comfort the sailors by his presence; he
assisted them with the boat. He shouted out encouragements
and "began to work with them to move and direct the ship as
needed, using the ropes and poles."[56] As soon as the weather-
beaten sailors hit dry land, they rushed up the hill to the near-
est church to give thanks to God and make votive offerings.
When they saw the good bishop Nicholas standing there performing his regular duties, they rushed forward and prostrated
themselves. Nicholas was taken aback. Like the apostle Peter
who reprimanded the inhabitants of Cornelius' house for falling down in worship before him, Nicholas instructed the men
to rise. He did not seem to be aware that he had been in the
boat helping them. That was not important anyway. God had
saved them, not him. God was the one at work.[57]

With stories like these, it is no wonder that the temple of
Poseidon was replaced with a church of St. Nicholas on the
island of Eleusa. Nautical maps of the Adriatic, the Ionian,
and the Aegean became punctuated with St. Nicholas quay-
sides and isles. Where once fearful travelers had begged Apollonius of Tyana to join them on their sea voyages, thinking
him "superior to storm, fire, and the greatest obstacles,"[58] they
now said to one another: "May St. Nicholas hold your tiller."[59]
Ships were often fitted with small shrines to Nicholas; a guid-
ing star was named after him. Little wonder that the American author Washington Irving equipped the Goede Vrouw,
the matronly Dutch ship known as the "Good Woman"

that supposedly carried emigrants from Amsterdam to New Amsterdam, with the figurehead of St. Nicholas, which he comically described as wearing "a low, broad brimmed hat, a huge pair of Flemish trunk hose, and a pipe that reached to the end of the bowsprit."[60] The ever-watchful saint sailed to the New World with intrepid seamen, first the Vikings, who knew and revered Nicholas, and then Christopher Columbus, who christened a port in Haiti with the name of Nicholas on his first voyage. Nicholas' aiding hand was invoked where once the names of Poseidon and—especially in the Aegean—Artemis were heard.

Provision during Famine

Artemis of Ephesus, it was true, had not only protected sailors and their cargoes, but had guaranteed fertility to the soil. She provided produce, grain, and harvest. Was Nicholas also up to the task of provision as well as protection? Material scarcity, attended by its twin companions, hunger and cold, preyed relentlessly upon people in the ancient world. The poor citizens of the city of Rome huddled close together in enormous, multi-storied warrens known as "islands" and were sustained only by regular corn doles, which, according to the lists, went out to well over two hundred thousand dependents. Emperor Nerva, in the last years of the first century, offered loan money to Italian estates at a rate of 5 percent and pooled the interest into a communal fund for poor children. In the late second century, Emperor Marcus Aurelius, acting in memory of his deceased wife Faustina, distributed enough money to support five thousand needy children. Leading citizens in town often patronized individuals in need. Grateful clients waited on their patrons at sunrise for handouts, always ready to run errands or perform small tasks for payment. Because a widespread, efficient welfare system did not exist in Nicholas' era, people counted on donatives, municipal gifts, and acts of generosity for their very existence.

Michael the Archimandrite records an episode in which Nicholas embraced his role as civic provider. A terrible famine had gripped the countryside and depleted Myra's inhabitants of their resources. For those on the edges of society, starvation had set in already. Bishop Nicholas intervened to convince a grain ship to part with some of its precious cargo and save the city. Told in a simple and straightforward way, the episode is free of the stylistic flourishes and decorative phrases that generally accompany Michael's writing, suggesting that he did no more than copy it from another source.

Once there was a severe lack of the wheat in the land of Lycia. It so happened that an Alexandrian ship, loaded with grain, landed in the port of Andriake to resupply. The merchants came and told Saint Nicholas. The godly man came to Andriake from the city of Myra and ordered the sailors to unload some of the contents from each vessel, "so that we don't die of famine," he said. They said that the wheat was destined for the people in the capital and therefore they could not acquiesce to his request. The holy man replied, "Take out from each ship one hundred bushels of your load and let me worry about how to deal with your masters in Constantinople."

The captains were won over by his words and gave him grain as he had asked. And so, with a favorable wind blowing at their sails, they reached Byzantium [Constantinople]. They went to have the grain measured and found that its weight corresponded to the amount registered when they embarked at Alexandria. Then they were astonished by this prodigy, and began to tell the receivers at the docks the extraordinary miracles of Saint Nicholas. And they all glorified God who always gives the grace to those who love him.

Meanwhile, the holy man took the grain, measured it out, and distributed it to all. So, everyone thanked God because the grain that they had received as a gift from him was enough to last them two years. In fact, since they kept back a part for re-planting, they sowed their land with the excess and thus enjoyed the benefits of God through the intercession of his servant Nicholas.[61]

Nicholas proved himself to be not only a protector but a provider for his people. Like the ideal civic patron, he brokered a deal to acquire the essentials of life, grain for food.[62] The reader is not told where he got his earnest money to secure the deal. Possibly it came out of his own pocket. It is also possible that there is more than meets the eye to Nicholas' comment, "and let me worry about how to deal with your masters in Constantinople." Emperor Constantine allocated a regular corn supply to the churches for their own consumption and for distribution to the poor. He also gave them annual stipends of cash. Perhaps Nicholas intended to claim this cargo as his duly deserved supply of sustenance, the allotment guaranteed by the emperor. Whatever the case may be, in return for his leadership and noble action, Nicholas accrued honor, respect, and "status" (*status, honos*). Michael says that "everyone thanked God," but Symeon Metaphrastes adds that the people thanked not only God but also Nicholas: "Residents there attribute the relief of the famine to God and to the great Nicholas—as they do for many other things."[63] The Christian bishop did for the city what Artemis, the town council, and the *decurions* failed to do. Reasonably, he should be revered above them. The victory of Christianity is the victory of saintly provision and protection.

—*The Miracle of the Wine*—

Similar to the holy man from Myra, St. Nicholas of Sion showed himself capable of supplying even the smallest needs. Once, he hosted a group of clerics for a meal.

When they saw the pitifully meager offerings being produced, they whispered among themselves, saying of the pitcher of wine, "We will not find in it enough to rinse our mouths."[64] Their host overheard their ungrateful murmurings but instead of chastising his guests, Nicholas defused the embarrassing situation with goodwill and a pinch of the miraculous. He went out to them and said, "Today, my children, it is my turn to pour for you."[65] He picked up the pitcher from the table and began pouring wine, filling and refilling cups, as much as anyone wanted. The guests, now slightly inebriated, raised a toast, "Glory be to God, who gave such grace to the servant of God Nicholas. Let no one disbelieve him from this day on. For God does many signs and miracles through him."[66]

Protection from Empire

The people of Myra had need of protection from the wiles of demons and the woes of famine. Nicholas of Myra met both of those needs. As will be seen, they also needed protection from the ravenous appetite of the imperial government. The *pax romana* ("Peace of Rome") did not exist merely on the goodwill of the people; it had to be forcibly extracted from their hide, sweat, and blood. Taxes were levied across the empire for the maintenance of the military and the infrastructure of the government. The demand for payment did not take into account economic fluctuations, the devaluation of currency, drought, famine, and other unforeseen circumstances. It mattered not that a family who had been able to pay last year did not have the money this year. Payment was due. Nonpayment was nonnegotiable. It was their "liturgy"—"the work of the people" (*leiturgia* in Greek). Local procurators and governors were held responsible for delivering payment to the emperor and so resorted to brutal tactics and blunt force in their collection efforts. Those efforts were often influenced by the fact that the officials were at liberty to keep for themselves anything collected above the required amount owed to the emperor.

"At the time of our most pious Emperor Constantine there came an order in which it was determined by the tax collectors that the city of Myra had to pay ten-thousand denarii."[67] So begins an anonymously authored text known as the *praxis de tributo*, or "Story of the Reduction of Tribute." It first surfaced in written form in the seventh century, perhaps as much as a century before Michael wrote his *Life of St. Nicholas*, and clues suggest it might be older than that.[68] The episode narrates a crisis that was precipitated by an increase in taxes. The citizens of Myra were told they must remit ten thousand denarii to the imperial treasury. The text does not say how much they had been paying, but the new amount was seen by the people as exorbitant and impossible to meet. It was simply too much for the humble denizens of Myra. Economic crisis ensued. The people turned to bishop Nicholas, now a trusted patron and minister of the city, for help. They fell to their knees and begged him to write a letter to the emperor to inform him of the misery brought on by the new tribute.[69] Nicholas saw the anguish in their faces and promised to do more than write a letter to Constantine. "My beloved children, not only will I help you with letters, but I will go in person to the august Emperor with your case." He vowed, "I will continue to implore him with sweet words and convince him to put an end to his order, which has resulted in disaster and created hatred and envy."[70]

The people's plea to Nicholas for relief was not out of line, and Nicholas, as bishop, was indeed in a position to help them, as can be seen in other cases from history. Germanus (378–447), the bishop of Auxerre, was commended for protecting the people from unbearable taxation. Germanus, like a good public patron, not only looked out for the economic welfare of the people, he restrained the king of the Alans from vandalizing the land, led a British army in battle, and traveled to the imperial court at Ravenna to plead his people's case. It is worth noting that before accepting the position of bishop, Germanus had worked as a lawyer and served as a governor of Armorica, in Gaul.[71] More and more people began to look to the bishops for leadership in public projects, assistance for the sick and the imprisoned, legal negotiations, and even banking. As legacies, endowments, and donations were left to churches, bishops suddenly found themselves managing large amounts of money and sizable tracts of land. In 580, Masona, bishop of the Spanish town of Mérida, opened a bank that made loans to the public.[72] Sometimes the practice got out of hand. The Council of Nicaea, for instance, learned that some priests were charging 1 percent interest per month on loans and 50 percent upon repayment. The council ordered the usury to stop immediately.[73]

Nicholas was not looking for profit when he packed his things and traveled north. Using the same route he once used to journey to Nicaea, he continued on to Constantinople until he came to a Christian temple in Blachernis dedicated to Mother Mary. There he stayed, celebrated the Eucharist, and shared his woes with the good people of the church, who prayed for him.[74] With his heart strengthened and his courage renewed, he continued on his mission. It is tantalizing to wonder if he met with Athanasius, who was in the metropolis of Constantinople and in regular contact with the emperor, or with any of the infamous Melitian bishops from Africa. We are not told those details, but we are given access to his meeting with the emperor.

> At daybreak, he went to the palace of our most pious Emperor. He went up and this miracle occurred: the sun's rays came through the windows where the Augustus [Constantine] sat and he [Nicholas] threw his sacred cloak [*pallium*] on the sunbeam, and there it remained, as if being worn, raised and suspended on it. The Emperor saw the miracle of the cloak, and that it was left hanging without anyone supporting it,

and he got up in terror and made demonstrations of affection to our Holy Father Nicholas.[75]

Like Moses in the court of the Pharaoh, Nicholas used a miraculous demonstration to get the emperor's attention. Mission accomplished, the good bishop explained that the people of his town, though they were loyal and faithful citizens and supporters, could not possibly muster the ten thousand denarii expected of them. Still wonderstruck, Constantine called his notary, Theodosius, to come to his side. Quill and parchment at the ready, he asked Nicholas: "How much do you want me to take as a tribute, father?"[76] Brashly, Nicholas suggested a mere one hundred denarii. The new and reduced amount was written down, certified with the royal seal, and handed to the bishop. On leaving the palace, Nicholas quickly found a stick, tied it to the official document, and threw it in the sea. Back at the port of Myra, the parchment was spotted bobbing in the water by some fishermen, who retrieved it and delivered it to the chiefs of the city. After much inspection and discussion of the curious and miraculous document, they showed it to the governor, who acknowledged the seal and declared the edict legitimate.[77]

Meanwhile, Emperor Constantine was experiencing a change of heart. His advisors expressed their shock and dismay that he had acquiesced so readily to Nicholas' ridiculously low tribute sum. It set a bad precedent and gave the impression that tax amounts could be negotiated and lowered upon request. The emperor's courts would be flooded with whining excuses and sniveling pleas. And so, Constantine recalled Nicholas to his court.

> The emperor was very pleased to see him and invited him to sit next to him, then said: "Give us back the paper, father, so that we might adjust the tribute tax. I overstated the amount of reduction that will be allowed to the city."
>
> The saint said: "My Lord, long live your majesty! Three days have passed since your order arrived in the city."

Upon hearing this, the emperor was astonished and said: "Nicholas, how can you say such a thing, since it has been just three days since I wrote it?"

The saint replied: "Lord Emperor, send a messenger to town with your order, and if he does not find it as I have said, may your royal majesty do with me as he pleases."[78]

Nicholas' instincts had been to send word of the imperial order immediately, and so wasted no time in forwarding the emperor's settlement to Myra. Certainly he wanted to relieve the anxious people of the city as soon as he could, but perhaps he also anticipated the emperor's change of mind. When Constantine did in fact reconsider the matter, Nicholas could only apologize: the edict was already in effect. It could not be rescinded without causing the emperor to lose face.

Behind the bright bursts of miracle—Nicholas' cloak suspended on a sunbeam and the parchment thrown into the sea at Constantinople and retrieved at Myra—it is possible to detect the fingerprint of historical fact. The main issue addressed, overtaxation, was a common thorn and complaint. Zosimus, a Byzantine of the late fifth century, worked in the imperial treasury and had insider information on such matters. He wrote about a *collatio lustralis*, that is, an "atoning" or "ceremonial" tribute instituted by Constantine: "He also laid a tax of gold and silver on all merchants and tradesmen, even to the lowest classes, nor did he even spare the poorest prostitute."[79] The new tax on urban tradesmen (and women!) was collected every five years and, although it was not unreasonable in itself, the tax proved a fearful burden on those unprepared for it. Zosimus described the scene with bitterness: "When the tax was to be paid, nothing could be heard through the whole city but lamentations and complaints."[80] Children were ripped from their mothers, fathers prostituted their daughters, and the poorest were whipped until they found the money—surely an exaggeration from Zosimus but perhaps not far from the truth.[81] It is highly possible that the announcement of a *collatio lustralis*

161

caused such a crisis in Myra.[82] The merchants and traders of the city were caught off guard by this new tribute and likely came to Nicholas for advice and assistance.

Nicholas' request on behalf of his city for a reduction is not out of line either, but certainly was within the parameters of a bishop's prerogative. Constantine was known to have given favors and exemptions to entire villages and cities when he learned of their fervent Christian devotion, as happened at Gaza's port of Maiuma, at Antaradus, a community on the island of Aradus, and at Orcistus, a Phrygian city in the district of Nacoleia.[83] Additionally, because other bishops like Athanasius, Arius, Hosios, and Eusebius enjoyed occasional audiences with Emperor Constantine, it is conceivable that Nicholas did likewise. One other minor detail, the mention of the name of the notary, Theodosius, also lends a certain degree of credibility to the story. Even so, good judgment will flinch at the idea of giving credence to this episode.[84] Michael, the primary biographer we have been following, does not include the tale, indicating that he either did not know the story or that he could not verify it.

Regardless of the final verdict about this episode's historicity, there is something to be learned reflexively; even if it does not represent historical fact, it reflects a common impression people had of the saint. The story of the reduction of tribute depicts Nicolas as a patron of the city, a devout believer who put his faith in God's care even in a time of crisis, a man unafraid to take bold action and travel to the capital in person to make a request, and someone who could command an audience with the emperor himself. We learn what virtues people saw in him and what characteristics they had come to admire. Interestingly, Nicholas was celebrated for negotiating economic relief at a time when saints were increasingly being recognized and admired for their disdain of money and material possessions.[85] The desert monk Hyperichius said that poverty was the monk's treasure; the monks of Scetis would not touch the bags of gold that had been donated to their commune—the giver ultimately had to take them back and distribute them to the poor himself; a destitute but devout widow who lived with her daughters in Ostracinus refused to accept the charity of alms, saying she trusted God for her needs. Even books of the Gospels and the Psalter should be given away or sold, if need be, for the sake of the poor.[86] The ascetic spirituality of the monastic movement was growing fast and affecting Christianity's discussions about money. More and more the mark of true holiness was the ability to sever all ties with possessions and remain unconcerned with money. Gregory of Tours told the tragic tale of a custodian whose job it was to collect alms on behalf of the church and distribute them to the poor. Not only did the man keep back some of the money for himself, he lied about it, so that when he finally confessed his wrongdoing, he died immediately. Gregory laments, "He was trapped by his evil desire and died in such a way that he lost the reward of life"; just as greediness hanged Judas for the sale of his master (Matt 27:5) and incited jealousy at the widow who purchased heaven for the price of two mites (Mark 12:42-44), so it killed the sad custodian for one coin.[87] Money makes monsters of good people. In another instance, a gardener who kept a small pot of coins in case he got sick or injured was punished for his greed by a nasty case of gangrene.[88] The message of the preachers was that all must try, by God's mercy, to free themselves from the grip of greed. Somehow Nicholas did this; he defied the odds and avoided the perversion that comes with any attachment to money. Nicholas was one of the few, so it would seem, able to work for economic justice and deal with the gritty problems of finance without becoming entangled in them. He was involved yet remained pure. His character was untainted by greed because he worked not for his own wealth but for the provision of his people.

6

Death Is Only the Beginning

"After living for some time in the city of Myra and perfuming all with the sweetly fragrant and piously scented conduct of his life and pastoral duties, he left his mortal life to enter eternal rest."[1] Thus reads the humble entry of Michael the Archimandrite on the death of the saint. Michael uses the sense of smell to communicate the delightful effect the good pastor had on everyone around him. Like a strongly scented bouquet that fragrances the entire house and is enjoyed by all who enter, so Nicholas' life touched everyone in Myra and bettered the lives of all. Michael adds that "his precious body, with the fragrant odor of virtue, was buried in his church."[2] Even in the coldness of death, the warm aroma of Nicholas' works lingered. And as the people tearfully interred his body in a specially constructed church built in his memory beyond the walls of the city, they hoped he would still look out for them and, if possible, intercede before God himself on their behalf. Indeed, Michael crosses the threshold between earth and heaven to reassure his readers that in death Nicholas "was cheered by the choirs of angels and joyfully with the multitude of patriarchs began to intercede unceasingly for those who called upon him in the joy of faith, especially for those who were oppressed and found themselves in misfortune and misery."[3]

Michael's record of Nicholas' death is poignant, but legend would not leave the story so plain and unornamented. Writing in the high Middle Ages, Jacobus de Voragine re-creates Nicholas' final moments before death. "When the Lord wished to call Nicholas to Himself, the saint prayed that He would send His angels."[4] Nicholas looked up from his deathbed and saw their misty forms materializing before his eyes. "And when he saw them coming, he bowed his head and recited the Psalm *In Te Domine, speravi*."[5] Nicholas recited, so Jacobus says, Psalm 31, which begins with the words, "In you, LORD, I have taken refuge; let me never be put to shame." According to Jacobus, "when he came to the words *in manus tuas*, which means 'into Thy hands I commit my spirit,' he breathed forth his soul to the sound of heavenly music."[6] Setting aside the theatrics of Jacobus' account, there are two important facts to be gleaned: the fact that Nicholas died in faith and that the cause of death was old age. Jacobus de Voragine, Michael, and other relevant sources testify to these facts. Bishop Nicholas of Myra had not suffered the martyr's fate, though he had endured the torments of persecution. He suffered no major illness or wrongdoing at the end; his breath simply gave out. His gentle death was to be celebrated; his life had overlapped with some of the brightest lights in church history: the controversial theologian of orthodoxy Athanasius; Athanasius' mentor Alexander of Alexandria; the chronicler and biographer Eusebius of Caesarea; Arius the arch-heretic; the first Christian emperor Constantine and his devout mother Helena; Lactantius, a Christian author and personal tutor to the imperial family; Antony of Egypt, the famously long-lived monk; and Pachomius, the father of all monastic communes.[7] These figures cumulatively represent a golden age in Christian history. Throughout the halcyon days of the mid-fourth century, anything was possible. God's Spirit was sweeping the land, and the doors of the church could not be closed because of the people streaming in. The air swirled with strange and bold ideas, novel lifestyles, new construction projects, and original ways of instituting and organizing.

Nicholas could not have lived at a more critical moment in church history.

The real question is, when did he die? In what year? If it is correct that Nicholas' birth was around the year 260, he would have been sixty-five at the Council of Nicaea in 325. This conforms to the general impression that Nicholas was one of the more elderly at the great council. Contemporary scholars put the year of his death between 333 and 335, making him roughly seventy-five years old.[8] This is just a conjecture. Jacobus de Voragine locates his death in the precise year of 343, for reasons unknown. A wide range of dates can be compiled from the documentary evidence, beginning with an early date of A.D. 287 and ending with Goffredo of Bussero's late date of A.D. 365. A list of proposed death dates include the years 287, 312, 325, 333, 334, 335, 341, 342, 343, 345, 350, 351, 352, and 365.[9] Perhaps for this reason *The Oxford Dictionary of Saints* does not attempt to assign him any life-dates beyond the "4th century."[10]

Despite uncertainty regarding the year of his passing, the feast day of Nicholas' death from the earliest times has been celebrated on December 6. Why this date? The simplest explanation is that December 6 was the day on which he actually died. But there is more to consider. The sixth day of December was a special day in the calendar; it marked the symbolic start of winter and called for additional prayers and offerings to Artemis and Poseidon on behalf of those who dared venture onto the high seas in the winter months. Many sailors docked their boats during those months, although a few braved the unpredictable storms and weather. All agreed that the winter sea was a terrible and cruel thing, demanding special reverence and honor to the gods who controlled them. The sixth day of each month, and December in particular, was dedicated to Artemis, who enjoyed a very large sanctuary in Myra until Nicholas closed it down. The annual remembrance of Nicholas on the sixth of December carried a clear message: the God of Nicholas had usurped Artemis. The God of Jesus Christ, whom Nicholas had worshipped, had defeated the goddess of Greek lore. The old calendar had been wiped clean, and a new calendar was in effect. The dating of Christmas shares a similar story. Once celebrated on March 25 in some places and on January 6 in others, the commemoration of the birth of Jesus was moved to December 25 in the early to mid-300s. The date was well-chosen: not only was it exactly nine months from Jesus' miraculous conception in the womb of Mary (celebrated on March 25), it was also the winter solstice in the Julian calendar and the birthday of the Sun in the imperial cult of the Unconquered Sun (*Sol Invictus*). The Persian religions of Manichaeanism and Zoroastrianism likewise commemorated on that day the birth of the sun god, known to them as Mithras. Celebrating the birth of Jesus on December 25 offered an opportunity for Christians to rival the cults of the Unconquered Sun and Mithras and the debaucheries that attended them.

Wise men and women realized that in this struggle between the new religion and the old ones, it was not reasonable to expect people simply to give up their long-held pagan festivals. The ordinary housewives, sailors, merchants, children, and laborers were not self-denying monks who could live without feasts and special days. In the late 300s, Gregory of Nazianzus (330–390) delivered a sermon in Constantinople in which he compared God to "a schoolmaster or doctor, taking away some ancestral customs, allowing others." Tenderly, Gregory explained, "He yields on some trifles which make for happiness, just as physicians do with the sick to get the medicine taken along with the sweeter ingredients artfully blended in. A departure from time-honored, customary ways is, after all, not easy."[11] The Christian calendar took into account this innate human need by gradually replacing pagan holidays with Christian ones, pagan memorials with Christian ones, and pagan rituals with Christian ones. The memory of Nicholas could purify the sixth of December in the waters of faith and advance the cause of Christian virtue. On this point, Gregory I (540–604), the much-beloved and celebrated bishop of Rome, put forth some sensible guidelines. Writing with a pastor's heart to his missionary representative in Canterbury, England, on how to handle Anglo-Saxon customs and traditions, Gregory I warned against austerity and extreme measures. The Anglo-Saxon heritage should be treated delicate care. "The temples of the idols in that nation ought not to be destroyed; but let the idols that are in them be destroyed."[12] It was enough to clear the idols; the temples themselves need not be torn down. If they were well built, the sensible thing to do would be to reuse them. Gregory lauded the actions of St. Benedict.[13] When he arrived at Monte Cassino, Benedict found a temple of Apollo; he smashed its statues and cut down the surrounding sacred grove, but repurposed the temple itself for God by installing shrines to St. Martin and St. John inside.

If the people were given a chance to see the cross of Christ in place of the old idols or to celebrate the Christian virtues of Nicholas in place of Artemis, they might find the process of conversion a little less painful and a little more possible. Sometimes the attempts of the bishops and missionaries were crass and manipulative. In about the year 500, a well-meaning bishop of Javols, France, built a church near a sacred lake, where locals often went to throw in libation offerings of linen cloths, pelts of wool, cheese, wax, and bread.[14] The bishop placed relics from St. Hilary of Poitiers in the church and said to the people, "Do not, my sons, sin before God! For there is no religious piety to a lake. Do not stain your hearts with these empty rituals, but rather acknowledge God and direct your devotion to His friends. Respect St Hilary, a bishop of God whose relics are located here."[15] This unnamed bishop of Javols tried to transfer the allegiance of the rustic people from the lake to the God of Jesus Christ by means of the physical relics of St. Hilary. It was a simple trade of one for the other. This example illustrates a subtle and unavoidable danger in following the advice of either Gregory of Nazianzus or Gregory I—that evangelism becomes a matter of marketing to people's expectations and adapting Christianity to local custom for the sake of gaining adherents.

History reveals that the memories of the saints, and Nicholas in particular, have been misused in these and other ways—one need only think of the annual exploitation of Nicholas in the Christmas season by marketers, movies, and malls.

The Myrrh of Myra

Here at the tail-end of our story, as Michael's narrative drifts off into a peaceful revelry, we are aroused from our slumber by the announcement of something very strange. "Immediately it [the tomb] began to ooze pleasant and aromatic oil," Michael says, "that removed every curse and was useful for providing a saving remedy that repels evil, for the glory of Christ, our true God who is glorified."[16] From the edges and underside of the tomb's marble and cement came the gentle drip of a liquid—it was variously described as myrrh (*múrra* in Greek), oil (*oleum* in Latin), balm, unguent, or ointment (*unguentum* in Latin).[17] In addition to the "odor of sanctity" that Nicholas exuded while alive, his body gave off in death the fragrant oil of healing—used, in Symeon Metaphrastes' words, "for the elevation of souls and the health of bodies."[18] To those in need it was a teardrop from heaven, a trickle from the river of life. Pilgrims thronged to the sanctuary like bees to nectar; they paid homage and collected vials of ointment for loved ones who were sick. The myrrh of Myra was swallowed, rubbed on injuries, sprinkled on the tops of heads, and treasured as a precious relic. It had beneficial effects on those unable to walk or see or hear or speak, as well as those who were plagued by demons.[19] While Roman Catholics preferred it mixed in pure water, Orthodox Russians added it to anointing oil. The liquid was also referred to by pious pilgrims as manna—the name of the flaky white substance that miraculously fed the Israelites in the desert (Exod 16:31; Num 11:7-8). According to Gregory, the sixth-century bishop of Tours, the tombs of John of Ephesus and the apostle Andrew each separately produced manna, which Gregory described as having the texture of flour or dust and a strong fragrance.[20] The substance had healing powers and was consumed by the sick and infirm. Eventually, the term "manna" came to be applied generally to any miraculous excretions, be they solid, liquid, or vapor.

Michael the Archimandrite reports healings, deliverances, and cures attributed to the medicinal myrrh. To the healthy it provided a shield of blessing. The miraculous liqueur was not a bizarre-but-true curiosity to amaze tourists, nor was it a sensational aberration of nature to puzzle scientists; it was a source of pride and a proof of Nicholas' piety. It was confirmation that, while he was alive, God's shadow had hovered over Nicholas and that God's hand had guided him. While Nicholas was on earth, righteousness seeped out of his words and actions; now it continued out of his physical shell. In a sense, his presence had not departed at death. His merit might still be approached, and his goodness might benefit those in desperate need. The *praesentia* or presence of a saint did not evaporate, disappear, or disintegrate with the corruption of the grave. Sulpicius Severus, the biographer of St. Martin, assured the deacon Aurelius in a letter that "[Martin] will not forsake us, believe me, he will not forsake us, but will be present with us as we talk about him and near to us as we pray."[21] An ancient Greek hymn praised the blessing of St. Nicholas' holy manna, saying that it served as armor to protect the innocent against the wiles of the devil without and the temptation of the passions within.

171

> Your sacred body rests in holiness in Myra,
> Emanating fragrant myrrh in perpetuity.
> It is sprinkled on those who approach
> In order to drive out the ugly stench of the passions,
> O Nicholas,
> And to put to flight the host of demons.[22]

The twelfth-century Adam of St. Victor likewise expressed joy over the holy oil (*unctionis*), which healed the sick, relieved pain, and gave triumph to righteous crusaders battling sin.[23] Theofrid (1040–1110), abbot of Echternach, included Nicholas' miraculous myrrh in his encyclopedic *Flores Epitaphii Sanctorum*, a romp through natural and interconnected curiosities, as part of his entry on holy water, wine, and oil.[24] Though he was a naturalist, Theofrid did not investigate the properties of the stuff. Modern readers want to know exactly what substance leaked from the tomb. An organic, chemical, or biological description was finally performed in 1925 when the University of Bari, Italy, conducted a chemical analysis and revealed the liquid was, basically, water. Even so, the liquid is still ceremoniously collected from the concrete slab sarcophagus on one day of the year—May 9—diluted in anointed water or golden oil, bottled, and sold to pilgrims who visit the basilica.

Because of this phenomenon, Nicholas was given the title of "myroblyte," one whose relics secreted liquid. The phenomenon was not entirely unknown in late antiquity. Hot springs and mineral waters bubbled up and overflowed with holy ointment, attracting the sick and lame and injured, as happened at the miracle-granting pool of Bethesda in John 5:1-15.[25] The tombs of St. Catherine and St. Matthew exuded myrrh and became major pilgrimage destinations. A factory was set up thirty miles outside Alexandria to fashion and produce cruets, figurines, and lamps for the oil of St. Menas. Whether the substance leaking from Nicholas' tomb came from the embalming fluids, the condensation of water on porous rock, or was in fact a singularly miraculous marvel, the effect was the same: pilgrims and devotees from all over Asia Minor, Greece, Italy, and Europe entered the tiny town of Myra to see the wonder. An anonymous tenth-century author described how the myrrh was collected at Myra. He watched as four custodians stood in the atrium and at regular intervals went to extract liquid from the tomb with a sponge.[26] The saint's tomb became an international destination as well as a popular stopoff for those pilgrimaging to the Holy Land.

Bread upon the Water

One of the earliest references to St. Nicholas in the historical record, significant because it can be dated with precision, connects him to the sea and to the patronage of sailors. It comes from the imperial historian Procopius in the year 555. Procopius reports that the Emperor Justinian (527–565) "established a shrine to St. Priscus and St. Nicholas, an entirely new creation of his own, at a spot where the Byzantines love especially to tarry."[27] The shrine was built on a picturesque piece of land that jutted out from the shore and, except for its walkway, was surrounded by water. Procopius observes that some people went out to venerate the saints while others simply enjoyed the charm of the place. Either way, his remarks reveal at least two things. First, that the fame of Nicholas reached Constantinople, the capital of the eastern Roman Empire, by the mid-sixth century if not earlier. It also suggests that Nicholas' importance at that time was connected not with gift-giving or Christmas but with seafaring. The shrine protruded over the Sea of Marmara as a beacon of hope to all who traversed its waters. One can imagine the comfort and assurance afforded to sailors who looked up after a long voyage and saw the Church of Priscus and Nicholas rising above the waters of the Golden Horn, nodding a blessing to the vessels that approached. Eventually the church dropped the name of Priscus and was dedicated exclusively to Nicholas—it was his blessing and protection that the crowds came for every year on December 6.[28]

The sea was the life-blood of the Mediterranean world, and its significance can scarcely be overstated. In an age before airplanes, trains, automobiles, cell phones, and the Internet, navigation of the waterways was essential to commerce, military success, politics, news, and transportation. So, the fact that Nicholas' name was invoked for safety on the turbulent waters shows the high degree of respect, honor, and power accorded to him. Spaces for little shrines were included in boats; niches were carved into docks and wharves so that icons, miniature golden-robed statues of the saint, waxy candles, flowers, and little offering boxes could be placed there. A sailor or captain rattled by a close call on the high seas would make his way quickly to the shrine to pay his respects and give thanks to the patron and protector of seamen. Nicholas loaves were kept on board so they could be tossed into the churning waters at the first sign of bad weather; some sailors did not bother to wait for trouble but threw out three small loaves upon embarkation to ensure safe travels. These small details testify to the enormously important role Nicholas played in the lives of sailors, captains, fishermen, and sea-merchants. Reciprocally, Nicholas' nautical connection helped spread his own fame. Merchants carried more than cargo across the choppy waters; they carried tales of good St. Nicholas. As sailors of the fifth century onward swapped stories, secrets, tricks, and trades, they were sure to drop the name of Nicholas in the conversation.

Here again, Nicholas of Myra is linked to St. Nicholas of Sion. In his *Life* are multiple references to the sea and multiple stories of nautical deliverance. When he journeyed to see the holy sites in Palestine and Egypt during his second pilgrimage, a fierce storm overtook the vessel. Nicholas of Sion had experienced a bad premonition about the trip, and now his fears were being realized. Nevertheless, he bravely led the sailors in prayer during their time of distress. "And bending his knee once again, the servant of God Nicholas prayed for long hours. And at the end of the prayer they all responded to him with the 'Amen.' And the wind and the waves stilled, and there was a great calm at sea."[29] The crew and passengers survived the night; in the morning they inventoried the damage brought about by the storm and found that the spar of the mast had come unfastened and hung limply from its beam. A certain young Egyptian, Ammonios by name, climbed up the mast to fix it but fell and died upon impact. His companions lost their composure and wailed over the dead body, but Nicholas of Sion said, "Weep not, but rather let us beseech God our Master. My Lord Jesus Christ will raise him, even though he be dead."[30] He prayed, made the sign of the cross, and reassured the grieving sailors that God's will would be done. Then he reached down and took Ammonios by the hand and raised him to life. To the amazed sailors he said, "Receive your shipmate safe and sound and grieve not."[31] Nicholas of Sion's presence had the effect of a talisman and a good luck charm. Understandably, ship captains and skippers welcomed him on board. The presence of the holy man was sure to bring about "favorable winds."[32] But blessings were guaranteed on condition of honest dealing. On their return trip after the second pilgrimage, Nicholas and company met a captain piloting a carrier to Constantinople. He promised to drop Nicholas and his companions at a convenient Lycian port, like Phoinix (present-day Finike) or Andriake or Tristomon (present-day Ucagiz). However, the ship caught a miraculously favorable wind and the captain could not risk losing it to dock in Lycia. Nicholas was distraught and "broke into tears." When he and his comrades regained themselves, they prayed, ate their supper, and went to sleep. The next morning, as they were about to pass by Tristomon, a violent wind whipped up from the west, halting the carrier's progress. The skipper was compelled to drop anchor and send the monks of Sion to shore in a dinghy.[33]

These and other anecdotes compounded and reinforced the belief that St. Nicholas, referred to simply as the Wonderworker, afforded special protection and provision to sailors. Men facing the watery jaws of death at sea cared little if it was St. Nicholas of Sion or St. Nicholas of Myra who came; they pleaded for God to send to their aid St. Nicholas, wherever he was and whoever he was. St. Nicholas held the tiller, and that was all that mattered. Over strong drinks, men of the wharf sat in dimly lit taverns spinning yarns. In one, St. Nicholas fell asleep at a rowdy party of his heavenly companions. The saints had gathered to talk, laugh, and share wine, but when the cup passed to him he let it slip from his hand. St. Elias nudged him awake. Nicholas apologized and explained that he had just returned from helping three hundred ships weather a storm.[34]

Another tale, recorded in both Greek and Latin variations, describes a barbarian invasion of Calabria on Italy's southern shores. An icon of St. Nicholas was among the plunder. Following John the Deacon's Latin edition, the substance of the story is reproduced here.

Coming from the region of Africa, the Guandalorum army invaded the land of Calabria, and set the whole land on fire; a barbarian discovered there in the home of a Christian an image of Saint Nicholas depicted meticulously on a wood panel. In an instant he stealthily hid it under the fold of his garment, even though he had no idea what it was. When he had come back to the others who were guarding the Christian captives in chains, he questioned one from among them. "Let me ask you something," he said. "Tell me whose image is this that has been so beautifully depicted on this panel." Saying this, he showed him the Icon.

When the Christians looked upon it, they replied with tears and weeping: "The image that we see is called Saint Nicholas. His many miracles and mighty works, before God and before humans, clearly prove that he shows himself to be manifestly alive, even beyond the grave."

When the barbarian understood what he heard, he kept the icon hidden, so that no news of it spread to anyone. When the Guandalorum army returned to Africa, loaded with captives and many spoils, the barbarian returned also, and placed the Saint Nicholas Icon in his house. The barbarian was also himself a customs officer. One day the barbarian brought out the Icon and put it in front of his collection of goods, where there was everything he owned: gold, silver, even clothes. And he spoke to the Icon, saying, "Nicholas, watch over this collection, for I have to go away."

With these words to the Image, he departed, leaving behind all his treasures, free for anyone to see. He was as secure when he set out as if he had put in place a whole gang of guards. But, some thieves happened to walk by and saw everything uncovered with no one watching things.

They said that they would come again by night and steal everything of value in the house. And that is what they did. Returning at night, they took everything—the gold, the silver, the clothes, and so on—and left with it. Only the Icon hanging in front remained. These things happened, however, by the dispensation of God, so that this occasion might clearly show and teach throughout the regions of Africa what kind of great merit Nicholas possesses.

But when the barbarian, whose treasure it was, came back and found his house empty, nothing being left inside except his Saint Nicholas Icon, he cried aloud and wept, emitting bitter hisses and groans. Turning to the Icon, he looked in the face of the blessed Nicholas and spoke to it as if it were a living and rational person, saying, "O Nicholas, I left you as a good guard of my treasure! What did you do? Return my things to me or else I will whip you badly." And with this said, he took a whip and beat the Image of Saint Nicholas. When he wore himself out beating the image, he said, "Know for certain that I will throw you in the fire if you don't return what is mine."

The most pious confessor, the most blessed Nicholas, greatly moved by the thought of his Icon suffering, as if he himself were being whipped, went quickly to a place close by where the thieves were dividing up the goods they had stolen from the Saracen's treasury. Then Saint Nicholas said to them, "O unhappy and miserable men, what are you doing? Do you not know that I myself was there when you committed this crime? My eyes were watching when you stole these and those things."

Then relating one by one the value and worth of everything that was taken from the treasury, he added these words, "Understand that this theft of yours, which you perpetrated, if you don't make it right and return the loot you stole, I will publicly declare what happened. All that stuff is under my care and because of your crime I was wrongfully beaten with a whip. Believe me that I will in no way spare you if you do not follow my advice. By tomorrow you will be handed over to die."

Then the robbers, realizing they'd been caught and assuming that he [Nicholas] was a citizen that had found them out, were not a little concerned, and in fact were more terrified than you'd think. Drawn up short by the fear of death, they returned everything in the dark of night, putting it back in the treasury.[35]

Needless to say, when the barbarian discovered the next morning that everything had been returned to its rightful place, he acknowledged God. He submitted to the Christian faith and was baptized. He also made a donation toward the building of a new church in honor of St. Nicholas. John the Deacon concludes by saying, "This was the first occasion by which the blessed Nicholas became known among the regions of Africa, and little by little his name grew among the barbarians, as likewise great shows of obsequiousness were continually performed by these people, who were without baptism."[36]

It is symptomatic of the times that the episode recounted by John the Deacon involves a barbarian. Invaders from foreign lands were on the minds of everyone. After the fourth century, the threat of barbarian incursion increasingly became a preoccupation of those living in what was left of the old Roman Empire. Whether the Huns, Visigoths, Ostrogoths, Vandals, Alemanni, or Saxons, and then later the Lombards, Normans, Arabic Saracens, and the Seljuk Turks, the anxiety of invasion, pillage, rape, and captivity crept into politics, commerce, religion, and even storytelling. Nor were these idle fears. Beginning shortly after the year 630, Arabic armies raided Asia Minor and other provinces regularly. The chronicler Theophanes reported that the infamous Caliph Haroun-al-Rashid had once sent a fleet of ships to attack Rhodes in the year 808. On the way, the admiral in charge, Koumeid, ordered a detachment to break off from the main body and demolish the tomb at Myra. According to Theophanes, an all-consuming storm erupted from the sea, wrecking the fleet before the deed could be done. In another version of this same story, related by Landulf Sagax, Haroun-al-Rashid himself led an expedition to vandalize the tomb. By the saving hand of Providence, he destroyed the wrong one.[37] It is impossible to determine the historical merit of these stories. Even if they are complete fabrications, though, they provide us with a valuable glimpse into the fearful mood of the day. As early as the seventh century, Arab invaders off the shores of Asia Minor destroyed a St. Nicholas basilica on an island known today as Gemiler Island.

In 1065 a new menace appeared on the eastern horizon, fiercer and crueler than the Arabic Saracens. From the ancient lands of Persia, the independent and religiously intolerant Seljuk Turks swarmed the eastern borders and conquered Jerusalem. Zealously attached to their Islamic faith, the new Turkish regime closed off Jerusalem and the Holy Land sites to pilgrims, harassed Christian pilgrims in the area, and demolished or desecrated Christian churches. No longer would devotees be allowed access to the Jordan River, Bethlehem, or the garden of Gethsemane. No longer would Christian chapels, cathedrals, and martyriums be respected and left alone. The Seljuk Turks continued their advance west and north into Asia Minor, reducing Nicaea in 1080 and Antioch in 1084, ravishing the countryside of Lycia, and knocking at the gates of Constantinople. Alexius Comnenus dispatched desperate letters pleading for aid for the besieged city. None came. The Turks made clear their intentions about Constantinople by naming Nicaea, just across the Bosphorus from Constantinople, their new capital city. They planted themselves firmly against the West. Tensions mounted until 1096 when a tide of fear-driven anger and righteous indignation broke loose across Europe. Waves of unorganized pilgrims marched forth, barely waiting for armies of trained soldiers to equip and assemble. The red cross of Christ was painted on shields, stitched on flags, and sewed onto white tunics. Crusaders converged en masse on Nicaea, Antioch, and finally Jerusalem, bringing the carnage of war with them.

In the midst of all this chaos, a much smaller crusading party docked in Andriake, the port of Myra, in 1087. The company, made up of sailors from Bari, Italy, had come to liberate the body of St. Nicholas from Turkish captivity. In 1087, although Christian monks still controlled and maintained the church at Myra, everyone knew it was only a matter of time before a Seljuk Turk raiding party blew through town, demolished the shrine, and desecrated the tomb. Bloodthirsty gangs of armed Seljuk warriors prowled the region. The times were uncertain and confused; prospects were grim. Because the perceived threat to the beloved saint's sanctity was real, it is not surprising that concerned Christians made designs to remove St. Nicholas' bones to a more secure location.

The "translation of relics," as it was piously called, was a common occurrence in late antiquity and the Middle Ages.[38] St. Catherine's body was transferred from Alexandria to the monastery at Mt. Sinai; St. Mark's from Alexandria to Venice; St. Clement's to Rome; St. Marcellinus' from Rome to Seligenstadt. The trafficking of relics and bodies quickly became big business. The presence of a saint, or part of a saint, or something the saint owned, was a powerful and effective blessing. Cathedrals and monasteries kept detailed inventories of relics they possessed.

Ornate boxes and containers of gold, silver, and glass were fashioned to house the treasures. These "reliquaries" are counted as important historical artifacts and works of art in their own right; a tooth might be placed inside an elaborately sculpted ark or tabernacle, complete with singing cherubim and paneled scenes; an arm bone might be set inside a silver forearm with hand raised in two-finger blessing; a skull might be enclosed in a bust of a saint, carefully molded and painted. The translated relic was carefully preserved and displayed.

Of course, fraud and misrepresentation ran rampant. Erasmus and other Reformation satirists could only laugh at the great many heads of St. John the Baptist, arm bones of St. Elisha, splinters from the wood of the cross, and vials of milk from Mary's breasts found in cathedrals and shrines across Europe.

The true bones of a saint as popular and respected as Nicholas lured the most adventuresome and daring of them all: the seafaring Venetians and Barians. Venice and Bari, both situated on the eastern shores of Italy, were at this time major maritime ports. Anyone needing transportation across the Adriatic, Ionian, or Mediterranean came into or left from these docks. At various times, the Byzantines and the Normans had laid claim to them. The cities had grown ferociously competitive as their businesses had expanded. Civic pride had swollen with wealth and respectability. The bones of Nicholas would increase that pride and were sure to bring business from pilgrims and interest from church authorities. New monasteries and basilicas would be erected. In the early spring of 1087, the ever-watchful Barians caught wind of a Venetian raid on Myra. If the Barians wanted the bones of Nicholas, they would have to act fast. A contemporary witness named Nicephorus, who identifies himself as a Barian clerk, documents in robust detail what happened next. A commercial vessel on its return trip from Antioch dropped anchor at Andriake. Two pilgrims who had joined the crew in Antioch scouted out the church of St. Nicholas, which was located outside the walls of the old town of Myra. The Barians wanted to avoid a confrontation with any Seljuk Turks that might be in the area. The pilgrims hurried back to report that they had seen none, at which point forty-seven sailors disembarked, leaving fifteen behind to tend the ship. An authenticated parchment located in the Basilica di San Nicola archives lists the names of sixty-two sailors involved in the expedition.[39] Some of those names can even be seen etched in stone on the outside walls of the basilica.

The men entered the church dressed as humble pilgrims. They asked to see the tomb of the blessed saint and collect a small amount of myrrh, but the monks serving in that place quickly grew suspicious. They confronted the group: "Why do you ask such things? Do you plan to take the saint? You know that we can't let you do that: in truth we would rather die than permit you to take him!"[40]

The Barians wasted no time; they acknowledged their intentions and revealed their weapons, picks, and shovels from underneath their cloaks. They quickly overpowered the monks and posted guards at all entrances so the townspeople could not be alerted as to what they were doing. The monks bemoaned their situation and warned the sailors, begging them not to do something so abominable and violent. The resolve of the sailors had begun to waver when something unexpected happened: a vial of Nicholas' holy myrrh rolled off a column and crashed on the marble floor. It should have shattered, but did not. The sailors took it as a sign to steady their nerves. The monks, realizing that the cause was lost, confirmed the sign and admitted to the sailors that a year earlier Nicholas had told them in a vision his body would be moved. Divine providence was at work. Nicephorus relates what transpired next.

182

Then the youth already mentioned, Matthew, after discussing what had been said, sheathed his sword and picked up an iron mallet. He struck with vigor the marble paneled pavement covering the body of the saint and chipped out little pieces from it. He had not dug very deeply when his associates set about working with him. They discovered a marble tomb, intensely radiant, which they uncovered. They were very afraid to strike it, not wanting any harm to come of it. Then he [Matthew], being more daring than the others, could not endure the heat of the moment. Disregarding whatsoever evil might come, he struck the coffin lid boldly, breaking it bit by bit. When opened, the holy body found inside the tomb was saturated in holy liquid, nearly half-way full, [and was seen by] both the priests who had ordered the breaking and their assistants, as well as some of the sailors and their associates who had taken part in doing it. At once, moreover, such a fragrant odor came forth that everyone thought that they were standing in the paradise

of God. Not only to all those present, but the scent in truth
blended with the breezes in the air all the way to the sea,
which was almost three miles away, so that it spread to the
others. From what they smelled, all were immediately full
of joy and realized that the holy confessor of Christ had consented to their associates.[41]

Nicephorus states that the whole place filled with the aroma of
holiness; Gregory of Tours and Lucianus both report a similar
phenomenon accompanying the discovery of saintly tombs.[42]
The presence of the aroma signified two things. First, it confirmed God's will that the bones be taken, and when the sailors
who had remained on the boat caught wind of the scent, they
took it as a sign of such. Second, it confirmed to the Barians
that they had located the right tomb. They must have anticipated that the custodians of the crypt would try to stall or mis-
direct them. But the aromatic fragrance gave away the prize
and guaranteed its authenticity.

Standing before the open coffin and seeing its contents, the
men hesitated. A proper fear of the holy gripped them, and they
dared not move. Once again, the brave (and perhaps foolhardy)
Matthew took charge and plunged ahead.

> At this, he became rash, throwing himself fearlessly upon
> the Saint, stopping at nothing, so to speak. Faltering but full
> of holy ardor, he descended into the tomb in his clothes and
> shoes. Once in, he submerged his hands in the liquid. He
> found the holy relics floating, and the sweetness of the scent
> filled the vicinity like an insatiable kiss reaching out to the
> venerable priests. From this it was made clear that the true
> confessor of Christ was freely joining the Barians.[43]

Nicephorus specifies that the Barian sailors took nothing
from the church other than the bones. They were not con-
ducting a greedy raid for resalable treasures, but a preordained
rescue of blessed relics. Matthew wrapped the body and lifted
it out. With chants and hymns of praise, the Barian sailors

made their way back to the boat. The denizens of Myra slowly began to understand what was taking place; they raced down to the shore, waded out into the waves, and begged the Barians not to take their patron saint. They pleaded for even a small part of the body to be left behind. The sun began to set and, deaf to the Myran laments, the sailors caught a gentle puff of wind that pushed them out to sea and over the horizon. During the voyage the sailors pledged not to touch or pilfer any of the bones from the corpse; one sailor had a vision that they would reach the safety of Bari in twenty days; a small bird sang and circled the boat as a sign that Providence was with them. Then, on the ninth of May 1087, the much-anticipated cargo docked at Bari's wharf. The same day a new pope (Victor III) was being consecrated in Rome after a nearly two-year interregnum. To this day, May 9 is commemorated in Bari with parades, red and white flags, and reenactments of the translation and holy procession of the body from a boat to the basilica.[44]

St. Nicholas thus came to be honored two times each year: once on his death day, December 6, and once on the day of his translation, May 9. His memory was cheered in the deep cold of winter and in the warming green of spring. A delightful Russian folktale provides an entertaining, alternative explanation for the double celebration. Once, the cart of a peasant became mired in the thick mud of a country road. St. Cassian passed by, and the peasant called out to him for help. The saint refused, saying that he could not sully his robes. Not long afterward, St. Nicholas passed by, and again the peasant called out for help. Without hesitation, Nicholas stepped into the tar-like muck and pushed the cart out. Later the two saints reported back to heaven. Cassian admitted to having seen the poor man stuck in the mud, but he assured the Lord that he had acted responsibly and not soiled his heavenly garments. Nicholas' clothes, on the other hand, were caked in mud and completely ruined. To the astonishment of both saints, God did not berate Nicholas for his dirty robes but instead commended him. And, because Cassian did not stop to help the stranded peasant, his memory would be honored only once every four years, on February 29 (a date occurring only in leap years), but St. Nicholas would be remembered twice a year, once on December 6 and once on May 9.

When the boat arrived in Bari on May 9, 1087, the buzz of excitement was equaled only by a strain of tension that was growing between the townspeople and the church authorities. The townspeople wanted the body to become the crowning jewel of the city and be laid in a specially constructed crypt. Church officials demanded that the body be moved to the episcopal see, the bishop's palace or the cathedral, which was also in town. From there it might be moved to an even more prominent location, perhaps Rome. Abbot Elias (d. 1105) temporarily settled the question by placing the bones in his monastery, the monastery of Saint Benedict. Nicephorus added a scandalous detail: the archbishop of Bari, the Lord Ursus,

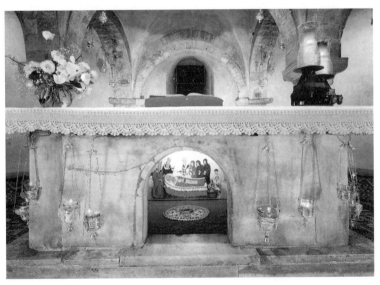

FIGURE 9
Tomb of St. Nicholas, Basilica di San Nicola, Bari, Italy

was not present for the landing of the boat. He was at Canosa, *pro causa sanctitatis implenda*—"fulfilling holy responsibilities."[45] Not long after the publication of Nicephorus' account, a certain archdeacon named John complained that it did injustice to the archbishop. John supplied Lord Ursus a more pious alibi. He was not dithering about in Canosa; he was in Trani awaiting transport to Jerusalem. The Lord Ursus was preparing for sanctified pilgrimage.[46] Whatever version we choose to believe, both John and Nicephorus agreed that the archbishop Ursus hastily returned to Bari where he paid his respects to the body. But then—as the Barians must have surely expected—he ordered that the relics be transferred to his custody. The sailors and the leaders of the city objected: the bones must stay with the people. The citizens of Bari realized that to contravene the command of Ursus, whose very name meant "the Bear," was something done at great peril. Representatives from the archbishop and the citizens met to negotiate. Hot words were exchanged, and weapons were drawn. Fighting broke out, and two youth died, one from each party.[47]

Eventually, Abbot Elias and the citizens of Bari prevailed, with the blessing of the church authorities and even the pope. The body remained in the city, and a stout Romanesque basilica was built for the occasion: the Basilica di San Nicola. Ten years later, in 1098, the new site was inaugurated by a major church conference of 183 bishops held under the protective shadow of Nicholas. As a destination of holy pilgrimage, Bari rivaled Santiago de Compostela in Spain and the eternal city of Rome herself.

The bones were laid in a reinforced concrete tomb in a low-ceilinged crypt located directly beneath the tabernacle and altar of the basilica. The remains safely interred, Nicephorus could declare with confidence that Nicholas had escaped the hammer of the Muslims. But he did not escape the chisel. In an ironic twist of history, Muslim artisans were commissioned to lay the tile work around the altar and throne of the new basilica. A repeating design borders the raised platform.

On close inspection, the design, which can be seen by visitors to this day, reveals itself to be an artistically crafted Arabic monogram: *Allah is great.*[48]

About 75 percent of Nicholas' skeleton is present and accounted for at Bari. Owing to the fact that it was taken from the church at Myra by force and in a rush, it is not surprising that the Bari skeleton is incomplete. In 1099, sailors from Venice landed at Myra and confiscated the remainder of the bones, along with those of St. Theodore. These were deposited in Venice's island monastery, San Nicoló del Lido. Soon after, a finger bone appeared in the province of Lorraine, France. As early as 1101, Richer de Senones reported that "a certain knight who had been born in these parts . . . brought a jointed finger bone that is said to be stored at the place of the Port."[49] The timing of this reference suggests that the knight in question was someone on return from either the First Crusade launched in 1096 or the Crusade of 1101. The finger seems not to have come from the original tomb in Myra, but from Bari, which served as a popular crusaders' port. A name of the knight responsible for donating the finger was learned in 1163: Aubert du Neufchâtel.[50] Legend eventually supplied him with a story: Aubert was returning from the First Crusade by way of Bari and decided to visit the shrine of Nicholas. There he met a guardian of the crypt who happened to be a relative. After much pleading, the guard granted Aubert access to the tomb itself. A finger's worth of bone was removed and taken to his homeland. Aubert presented the remarkable treasure to the St. Nicholas chapel on the banks of the Meurthe River, Saint-Nicolas-de-Port. People flocked from all parts of Europe to Saint-Nicolas-de-Port in order to view the relic; they also came to see the chains donated by liberated prisoners and captives of war, especially those of Cuno, a crusading knight of Réchicourt. These were proof that God answered prayers and that Nicholas kept a special eye on those bound against their will and imprisoned unjustly.[51] Other bones described as those of Nicholas surfaced elsewhere. The scholar Charles Jones found seventeen teeth purportedly from Nicholas scattered in churches from Spain to Constantinople.[52] Miscellaneous bones attributed to Nicholas are on display to this day in Turkey's Antalya Museum. Some bones said to be his were given to the St. Nicholas Greek Orthodox Church located in New York. Tragically, those relics were destroyed in the collapse of the World Trade Center on September 11, 2001.[53] The church is slated to be rebuilt, but its relics are irreplaceable.

On a visit to Demre, modern-day Myra, one can see the mouths of tombs cut into the face of a hill, the rounded bowl of an amphitheater with its stair-step rows of bench-seats where Nicholas once sat, and the fragmentary remains of a once-bustling and energetic metropolis where Nicholas walked. The tourist can step inside the excavated and restored church of St. Nicholas where he or she will discover a side chapel with what was presumably the original resting place of the saint—an ornate sarcophagus that clearly has been smashed open. There is a gentle bronze statue in the garden that depicts Nicholas standing straight, as if posing for a picture, while holding a bag of toys on one shoulder. A second statue was added in the year 2000 as a gift from Moscow (fig. 10); it was a formidable Greek icon of Nicholas, complete with liturgical vestments, a Bible, a halo, and a hand raised in blessing. The bronze figure was perched atop a globe of the earth, which rested on a white plinth in the middle of the town's square. Carol Myers reports that Russian pilgrims regularly knelt before the statue in reverence.[54] Five years later, however, the town council of Demre decided to remove the gift and in its place put something just as astonishing as the priestly Nicholas for a country that is nearly 100 percent Muslim—a brightly colored, American-style Santa Claus (fig. 11). The Santa holds a bulging sack of goodies over his left shoulder and a large bell in his right hand, giving the impression of a Salvation Army ringer. The image played on the international commercial potential and tourist appeal of the man dressed in red fur. At the same time, a small group of Muslim Turks formed the Santa Claus Foundation and

FIGURE 10
Russian statue in Demre, Turkey
(Photograph courtesy of Albert Zuurveld)

FIGURE 11
American Santa Claus, Demre, Turkey
(Photograph courtesy of Carol Myers)

requested that the Roman Catholic Church return the bones of St. Nicholas to their original resting place.[55] Ultimately, however, the commercial fervor gave way to national pride. On Christmas Day 2008, an entirely new statue was unveiled. This one, which is still in place today, features a Turkish man with a trimmed beard, dressed in traditional Turkish clothing (fig. 12). He wears a patterned jacket and rounded Seljuk styled cap, or *boerk*, and carries on his shoulder not a bag of goodies but a young child. Behind him appears a slightly older boy dressed in a simple tunic.

The debacle at Demre provides a fitting illustration of just how difficult it is to fix the image of this amorphous, Protean character. In the quest for the real Santa Claus, what is discovered more often than not is that he can assume any shape. He

190

FIGURE 12
Turkish statue in Demre, Turkey
(Photograph courtesy of Carol Myers)

can accommodate anyone. William J. Bennett is correct to call him a sort of "every-saint, one for all people and all causes."[56] In the mid-nineteenth century Anna Jameson, a notable saint scholar, expressed a similar opinion, calling Nicholas of Myra "the most universally popular and interesting" of all saints.[57] Guardian of the orphan, provider for the needy, and defender of the defenseless, the name of this every-saint could be "invoked by the peaceable citizen, by the labourer who toiled for his daily bread, by the merchant who traded from shore to shore, by the mariner struggling with the stormy ocean."[58] On one occasion he might be the patron of children, smiling kindly on them with his gifts; on another he was the disciplinarian who carried a whip and put switches in the stockings of naughty girls and boys. Through the ages the persona of Nicholas has been illusive, transitory, and accommodating to any need.

On account of the miraculous conception and birth of baby Nicholas, barren women sought his help. Amata, a middle-aged Italian woman who traveled to Bari in 1244 asking for a child, conceived and gave birth to a boy whom she named Nicholas. He became a noteworthy saint in his own right and is remembered today as St. Nicholas of Tolentino (1245–1305). Nicholas of Myra's famous nighttime gifts of gold to the three maidens elicited all manner of patronages: unwed girls, newlyweds, gift-givers, pawnbrokers, bankers, and loan-dealers, and traders of almost any type. The unemployed and destitute also looked to him because he aided the poor family in their hour of need. The battle with the bomb on the high seas brought under his care not only pilgrims, voyagers, and navigators, but also firemen. Because of his quick-fingered dealing to procure grain for the famished metropolis of Myra, grain dealers, merchants, and millers claimed the saint. Stories of Nicholas rescuing ships caught in storms caused sailors, mariners, boatmen, and dock workers to venerate his memory. The story of the military officers inspired soldiers and knights to call upon him, as well as prisoners and captives of any sort. The legend of the three murdered children stuffed into barrels brought more patronages: meat-butchers, children, seminarians, and brewers (because of the barrels)—the late medieval tradition of brewing Samichlaus beer once a year on December 6 continues to this day in Austria. Because Nicholas showed, in all these, a zeal for justice and fairness, he became the patron of law students, lawyers, judges, and clerks of the court. Because of the fragrant myrrh which flowed from his tomb, perfumers, florists, and embalmers named him their patron. A guild of pharmacists and apothecaries likewise adopted his patronage, as demonstrated by a stained glass window they donated to the Chartres Cathedral. The name of Nicholas spread far and wide, from popes and tsars to inventors and scholars. It is borne by fourteen additional individuals who have been officially recognized as "saints," plus five "blessed" Nicholai and one Saint Colette. Thousands of churches, chapels, cloisters, cemeteries, and hospices throughout Europe and the world carry Nicholas' name.[59] Cities, regions, and even countries (Greece and Russia) have dedicated themselves to him. To be sure, he has been one of history's most beloved individuals, and his story will continue to be told for generations to come.

Notes

Chapter 1

1 The icon is known as *Agios Nikolaos o Streidas*—St. Nicholas of the Oyster. Martin Ebon, *Saint Nicholas: Life and Legend* (New York: Harper & Row, 1975), 19.

2 Luigi Martino, "Ricognizione anatomica e studio antropometico delle reliquie ossee di San Nicola di Bari," *Bollettino di san Nicola*, numero speciale (April–December 1957); accessed online at Cripte e Santi website, http://www.enec.it/Cripte/reliquie.htm.

3 Quoted in Ian Sample, "How Do You Reconstruct Santa's Face?" *The Guardian*, December 16, 2004, http://www.guardian.co.uk/science/2004/dec/16/thisweekssciencequestions1.

4 Maurice Chittenden, "Revealed: The Real Santa, A Saint with a Broken Nose," *The Sunday Times*, Dec. 12, 2004, http://www.timesonline.co.uk/tol/news/uk/article402170.ece.

5 Quoted in Sample, "How Do You Reconstruct?"

6 Gerry Bowler, *Santa Claus: A Biography* (Toronto: McClelland & Stewart, 2005), 121–24.

7 Edward Clare, *St. Nicholas: His Legends and Iconography* (Florence: Leo S. Olschki, 1985), 22.

8 This image can be found in Clare, *St. Nicholas*, 23. Photograph by Kurt Weitzmann. Used with permission of the publisher.

9 Clare cites Otto Demus to say that less than 1 percent of all Byzantine art survived the Western crusade of 1204. Clare, *St. Nicholas*, 21.

10   Marianna Mayer, *The Real Santa Claus* (New York: Dial, 2001); Louise Carus, *The Real St. Nicholas* (Wheaton: Theosophical Publishing, 2002).

11   Gerardo Cioffari, "St. Nicholas: Documentary Evidence in Literature and Archeology," *Bollettino di San Nicola* 66, nos. 11 and 12 (1997): 12.

12   Ihor Ševčenko and Nancy Patterson Ševčenko, "Introduction," in *The Life of Saint Nicholas of Sion* (Brookline, Mass.: Hellenic College Press, 1984), 13.

13   Symeon Metaphrastes, *Bios kai Politeia*, in *Patrologia Graeca*, ed. J.-P. Migne (Paris, 1857–1866), 116:317–56.

14   Gustav Anrich, *Hagios Nikolaos: Der heilige Nikolaus in der griechischen Kirche*, 2 vols. (Leipzig: Teubner, 1913–1917), 2:514.

15   Charles Jones, *Saint Nicholas of Myra, Bari, and Manhattan* (Chicago: University of Chicago Press, 1978), 7.

16   See, e.g., Peter Brown's works, *The Cult of the Saints* (Chicago: University of Chicago Press, 1981); *Authority and the Sacred* (New York: Cambridge University Press, 1995); and *The Rise of Western Christendom*, 2nd ed. (Malden: Blackwell, 2003).

17   Nicholas was almost an exact contemporary of Antony.

18   A. G. Gibson, "St. Nicholas of Myra," in *New Catholic Encyclopedia* (New York: McGraw-Hill, 1967), 10:454.

19   Walter Nigg, *Great Saints* (Hinsdale: Regnery, 1946; trans. William Stirling, London: Francis Aldor, 1948).

20   *The Oxford Dictionary of Saints*, ed. David Farmer, 3rd ed., s.v. "Nicholas."

21   Aviad Kleinberg, *Flesh Made Word: Saints' Stories and the Western Imagination* (Cambridge, Mass.: Harvard University Press, 2008).

22   Thomas Craughwell, *Saints Preserved: An Encyclopedia of Relics* (New York: Image Books, 2011), 220.

23   Gerardo Cioffari, *Saint Nicholas: His Life, Miracles and Legends*, trans. Victoria Sportelli (Bari: Centro Studi Nicolaiani, 2008), 9, 41.

24   Jones, *Saint Nicholas of Myra*, 12–13.

25   Procopius, *De aedificiis* 1.6, in *Procopius*, trans. H. B. Dewing, Loeb Classical Library 7 (Cambridge, Mass.: Harvard University Press, 1935), 62–63.

26   Proclus, *Proclus of Constantinople and the Cult of the Virgin in Late Antiquity: Homilies 1–5, Text and Translations*, ed. Nicholas Constas (New York: Brill, 2002).

27 Cioffari, "St. Nicholas: Documentary Evidence," 9. Also see Cioffari, *S. Nicola nella Critica Storica* (Bari: Centro Studi Nicolaiani, 1987), 17–21.
28 Cioffari, *S. Nicola*, 17–45. Anrich, *Hagios Nikolaos*, 1:67–91.
29 Anrich, *Hagios Nikolaos*, 2:452, 468.
30 *Oxford Dictionary of Saints*, 354–55.
31 Anrich, *Hagios Nikolaos*, 2:301–2.
32 T. G. Elliot, *The Christianity of Constantine the Great* (Scranton, Pa.: University of Scranton Press, 1996), 195.
33 Eduard Schwartz, *Über die Bischofslisten der Synoden von Chalkedon, Nicaea, und Konstantinopel* (München: Verlag der Bayerischen Akademie der Wissenschaften, 1937), 63. Günther C. Hansen, *Theodoros Anagnostes Kierchengeschichte* (Berlin: Akademie-Verlag, 1971), xi.
34 (1) List of 221 names; (2) Alexandrian Reworking of 225 names; (3) Corpus Canonum of Antioch (before 381); (4–8) Latin Lists I, II, III, IV and V; (9) Syriac List of the year 501; (10) Coptic List of 162 names. Cioffari, *Saint Nicholas*, 22.
35 (1) *Historia Tripartita* of Theodore the Lector (c. 515); (2) Vat. Gr, saec. XIV; (3) Sinaiticus 1117; (4) Hierosolymitanus Metoch, 2; (5) Hierosolymitanus Patr., 167; (6) Arabicus, saec. XIV. Cioffari, *Saint Nicholas*, 22. In support of the authenticity and accuracy of the later and longer lists, Cioffari cites Beneševič, Lebedev, Leclercq, Honigmann, and Schwartz. Cioffari, *S. Nicola*, 23–29.
36 Günther C. Hansen has compiled the extant fragments of this work, *Theodoros Anagnostes Kierchengeschichte* (Berlin: Akademie-Verlag, 1971).
37 Theodore the Lector, *Tripartite History*, fragmentary pages reproduced from the Codex Marcianus gr. 344 in Hansen, *Theodoros*. Cioffari, *Saint Nicholas*, 22; *S. Nicola*, 23–29.
38 Eduard Schwartz has tentatively validated the legitimacy of the document; see *Über die Bischofslisten*, 63. Hansen maintains certain reservations, *Theodoros*, xi.
39 Aart Blom, *Nikolaas van Myra en zijn tijd* (Hilversum: Verloren, 1998).
40 Jona Lendering, "Saint Nicholas, Sinterklaas, Santa Claus," *Livius: Articles on Ancient History*, last modified April 30, 2008, accessed January 18, 2011, http://www.livius.org/ne-nn/nicholas/nicholas_of_myra1.html.
41 Symeon Metaphrastes, *Bios kai Politeia* 16, in Migne, *Patrologia Graeca*, 116:337A.

Chapter 2

1 John Turtle Wood, *Discoveries at Ephesus, Including the Site and Remains of the Great Temple of Diana* (London: Longmans & Green, 1877), 155.

2 Philostratus, *The Life of Apollonius of Tyana* 4.2, in *Apollonius of Tyana*, vol. 1, trans. Christopher P. Jones (Cambridge, Mass.: Harvard University Press, 2005).

3 Robert Fleischer, *Artemis von Ephesos und verwandte Kulstatuen aus Anatolien und Syrien* (Leiden: Brill, 1973).

4 Richard Oster, "Ephesus as a Religious Center under the Principate I: Paganism Before Constantine," *Aufstieg und Niedergang der römischen Welt*, vol. 2, no. 18.3 (1990): 1700–1706; Lynn R. LiDonnici, "The Images of Artemis Ephesia and Greco-Roman Worship: A Reconsideration," *Harvard Theological Review* 85, no. 4 (1992): 389–415, esp. 394.

5 Cited by Rick Strelan, *Paul, Artemis and the Jews* (New York: de Gruyter, 1996), 46.

6 It was said that the goddess of the moon and her brother Apollo, the god of the sun, emerged from their mother's womb as twins, born of the illicit union of Zeus and Leto; Hesiod, *Theogony* 918–20, in *Theogony and Works of Days*, trans. M. L. West (New York: Oxford University Press, 2009). Artemis came into the world first and in time to help her mother, Leto, deliver her younger brother—already indicating her calling to aid women through life's rites of passage: puberty, marriage, childbirth, and death.

7 *The Gothic History of Jordanes* 20.107, in *The Gothic History of Jordanes*, trans. Charles C. Mierow (Princeton: Princeton University Press, 1915), 81.

8 Michael the Archimandrite, *Vita per Michaelem* 1; this work is divided into paragraphs, and citations throughout the notes will refer to the paragraph number. Greek text in Gustav Anrich, *Hagios Nikolaos: Der heilige Nikolaus in der griechischen Kirche*, 2 vols. (Leipzig: Teubner, 1913–1917), 1:111–39; Greek-Latin parallel text in Niccolò Carminio Falconi, ed., *Sancti Confessoris Pontificis et Celeberrimi Thaumaturgi Nicolai Acta Primigenia* (Naples, 1751), 39–55; Maria Teresa Bruno, *S. Nicola nelle fonti narrative greche* (Bari: Centro Studi Nicolaiani, 1985), 15–49.

9 Michael, *Vita per Michaelem* 1.

10 Michael, *Vita per Michaelem* 1.

11 Michael, *Vita per Michaelem* 1.

12 Frank Trombley, "Christianity and Paganism, II: Asia Minor," in *The Cambridge History of Christianity* (New York: Cambridge University Press, 2007), 2:192–93.

13 Michael, *Vita per Michaelem* 2.

14 Lothar Heiser, *Nikolaus von Myra; Heiliger der ungeteilten Christenheit* (Berlin: Paulinus-Verlag Trier, 1978), 55–79.

15 Ambrose, *Epistle* 22.9-10, in *Patrologia Latina*, ed. J.-P. Migne (Paris, 1844–1855), 16:874–880.

16 Sulpicius Severus, *Vita S. Martini* 1.1-6, in *Early Christian Lives*, trans. Carolinne White (New York: Penguin, 1998), 135.

17 Severus, *Vita S. Martini* 1.6, in White, *Early Christian Lives*, 135.

18 Severus, *Vita S. Martini* 1.6, in White, *Early Christian Lives*, 135.

19 Severus, *Vita S. Martini* 1.6, in White, *Early Christian Lives*, 135.

20 Michael, *Vita per Michaelem* 2.

21 See Ivan Illich, *In the Vineyard of the Text* (Chicago: University of Chicago Press, 1993), 88–89.

22 The dating of this text is by no means certain. Niccolò Carminio Falconi, the eighteenth-century archbishop of Santa Severina, argued for a date of 840, based on his conclusion that Michael was none other than a certain Methodius, patriarch of Constantinople; Niccolò Carminio Falconi, *Sancti Confessoris Pontificis et Celeberrimi Thaumaturgi Nicolai Acta Primigenia* (Naples, 1751), 39. Gustav Anrich accepts Falconi's basic dating with a range between 814–842, while rejecting his authorship hypothesis; see Anrich, *Hagios Nikolaos*, 2:264–65. Gerardo Cioffari presents a compelling case for a much earlier date, 700–710, although his evidence admittedly allows for a wider range, sometime between 648 and 847; Gerardo Cioffari, *S. Nicola nella Critica Storica* (Bari: Centro Studi Nicolaiani, 1987), 59.

23 The twelve sections, with the addition of preface and conclusion, are divided as follows: Preface (1–2); Nicholas' birth to noble and rich parents (3); His mother's infertility and his disciplined lactation habits (4–5); Education, youthful virtue, and death of his parents (6–9); Story of three dowries (10–18); Nicholas ordained by divine revelation (19–24); Pastoral abilities and orthodoxy (25–28); Destruction of the Temple of Artemis (29); Story of the military officers (30–33); Sailors miraculously

saved (34–36); Relief from famine (37–39); Nicholas' death and the miracle of the manna/myrrh (41–42); Pilgrims saved from the demon's firebomb (44–48); Final invocation (50–52).

24 Michael, *Vita per Michaelem* 4.

25 Origen, *Homilies on Luke* 14 (Luke 2:22); *Commentary on Romans* 5.9 (Rom 6:57); *Homilies on Leviticus* 8.3 (Lev 12:2). See Joachim Jeremias, *Infant Baptism in the First Four Centuries* (Philadelphia: Westminster, 1960), 65–66.

26 Michael, *Vita per Michaelem* 4.

27 Michael, *Vita per Michaelem* 4.

28 Michael, *Vita per Michaelem* 4.

29 Quoted in Charles Jones, *Saint Nicholas of Myra, Bari, and Manhattan* (Chicago: University of Chicago Press, 1978), 51. Jones notes that about the same time this sermon was being preached, Wace was composing his versification of Nicholas' life and would devote some thirty-five lines of poetry to this lactation miracle.

30 This story was first attributed to Nicholas of Sion. *Bios tou hagiou Nikolaou* 2, in *The Life of Saint Nicholas of Sion*, trans. Ihor Ševčenko and Nancy Patterson Ševčenko (Brookline, Mass.: Hellenic College Press, 1984), 23. For a truly strange derivative of this story involving an infant seven days old standing and pronouncing a liberating blessing on John Chrysostom, see Anna Jameson, *Sacred and Legendary Art* (London: Longeman, Brown, Green, and Longmans, 1848), 1:315–22.

31 Christian Høgel, *Symeon Metaphrastes: Rewriting and Canonization* (Copenhagen: Museum Tusculanum, 2002), 20–21.

32 Gregory of Tours, *Glory of the Confessors*, trans. Raymond Van Dam (Liverpool: Liverpool University Press, 1989), 1–2.

33 Athanasius, "Preface," to *Vita Antoni*, in White, *Early Christian Lives*, 8.

34 Hippolyte Delehaye, *The Legends of the Saints*, trans. Donald Attwater (New York: Fordham University Press, 1962), 8–9.

35 Raymond Van Dam, "Introduction," in *Glory of the Martyrs* (Liverpool: Liverpool University Press, 1988), 15.

36 Michael, *Vita per Michaelem* 2; Heb 11:1-40.

37 Bryan Spinks, "The Growth of Liturgy and the Church Year," in *Cambridge History of Christianity*, 2:616.

38 Georgia Frank, "Lay Devotion in Context," in *Cambridge History of Christianity*, 2:541.

39 Augustine, Sermon 273.9, in *The Works of Saint Augustine* III/8, trans. Edmund Hill (Hyde Park: New City Press, 1994), 21. Sermons 273–305 deal with the veneration of saints.

40 "General Introduction," in Basil of Caesarea, *Let us die that we may live": Greek Homilies on Christian Martyrs from Asia Minor, Palestine and Syria,* trans. and ed. Johan Leemans et al. (New York: Routledge, 2003), 19.

41 Basil, "General Introduction," in Leemans et al., *"Let us die,"* 19.

42 Georgia Frank, "Lay Devotion in Context," in *Cambridge History of Christianity,* 2:538.

43 Anselm, "Prayer to St. Nicholas," in *The Prayers and Meditations of Saint Anselm,* trans. Benedicta Ward (New York: Penguin, 1973), 184–85.

44 Thomas Naogeorg, *The Popish Kingdome, or Reigne of the Anti-Christ,* trans. Barnabe Googe (London, 1570), pt. 4, lines 825–32.

45 Martin Luther deplored the idea that saints mediated grace to believers from their celestial treasury; he lamented the accretion of miraculous deeds and outlandish claims made of saints; he even lashed out against the "Nicholas Bishop" custom, saying that God does not recognize the spiritual value of the *"Larvenvolk und Niclas Bischoffe."* Martin Luther, qtd. in Karl Meisen, *Nikolauskult und Nikolausbrauch im Abendlande* (Düsseldorf, 1931), 469. Luther opposed the cult of the saints in all its forms yet he could still write, "Next to Holy Scripture, there certainly is no more useful book for Christians than the lives of the saints, especially when unadulterated and authentic." Martin Luther, qtd. in Kenneth Woodward, *Making Saints* (New York: Simon and Schuster, 1990), 75.

46 Richard McBrien, *Lives of the Saints* (New York: HarperCollins, 2001), 6.

47 Christian Høgel, *Symeon Metaphrastes: Rewriting and Canonization* (Copenhagen: Museum Tusculanum, 2002), 61.

48 Symeon Metaphrastes, *Passio S. Luciani, Vita Sactorum Mensis 01, Januaris,* in *Patrologia Graeca,* ed. J.-P. Migne (Paris, 1857–1866), 114:398–416.

49 A similar story can be found in *The Golden Legend,* which reports the case of a certain St. Hippolytus, who, on the orders of Emperor Valerian, was dragged to death by horses for converting to Christianity. This character unfortunately has no historical basis. He is none other than the mythological Greek hero and consort of Diana. According to the myth, Hippolytus was dragged to death behind his chariot at the provocation of Poseidon. In the early Middle Ages, the story of Hippolytus

was simply baptized into the Christian canon of saints' lives. Jacobus de Voragine, *The Golden Legend*, trans. Granger Ryan and Helmut Ripperger (New York: Arno, 1969), 446–49; James Frazer, *The Golden Bough* (New York: Collier, 1922, 1950), 6.

50 Symeon Metaphrastes, *Barbara*, in Migne, *Patrologia Graeca*, 116:301–16.

51 "For this reason, his life should be narrated and the speech contemplated for its strengths. Even if it is already known to you, so that you don't need a history lesson repeated or your memories refreshed, then read to cheer your souls, which love virtue." Symeon Metaphrastes, *Bios kai Politeia* 1, in Migne, *Patrologia Graeca*, 116:317A–B.

52 Michael, *Vita per Michaelem* 2.

53 John Chrysostom, *De virginitate* 14.1, qtd. in Peter Brown, *The Body and Society* (New York: Columbia University Press, 1988), 6.

54 John Boswell, *The Kindness of Strangers: The Abandonment of Children in Western Europe from Late Antiquity to the Renaissance* (New York: Vintage, 1990), 57–68, 100–110. Tim Parkin, *Demography and Roman Society* (Baltimore: Johns Hopkins University Press, 1992), 96.

55 J. N. Hays, *Epidemics and Pandemics* (Santa Barbara: ABC-CLIO, 2005), 20.

56 Barbara Tuchman, *A Distant Mirror: The Calamitous 14th Century* (Knopf: New York, 1984), 49.

57 Other manuscripts call them Theophanes and Joanna. For instance, see de Voragine, *Golden Legend*, 17.

58 *Bios tou hagiou Nikolaou* 2, in Ševčenko and Ševčenko, *Life of Saint Nicholas*, 23.

59 Peter Cobb, "The Liturgy of the Word in the Early Church," in *The Study of the Liturgy*, rev. ed. (New York: Oxford University Press, 1992), 219–29; E. J. Yarnold, "The Liturgy of the Faithful in the Fourth and Early Fifth Centuries," in *Study of the Liturgy*, ed. Cheslyn Jones et al., 230–44.

60 Ignatius of Antioch, *Ad Ephesios* 20, in *Patrologia Graeca*, ed. J.-P. Migne, 5:661A.

61 Richard Fletcher, *The Barbarian Conversion from Paganism to Christianity* (New York: Holt, 1997), 36.

62 Many of Gregory's own writings have been preserved in *Patrologia Graeca*, ed. J.-P. Migne, 10:963–1048.

63 James Ermatinger, *Daily Life of Christians in Ancient Rome*

(Santa Barbara: Greenwood, 2006), 145. See also Stephen Mitchell, *Anatolia: Land, Men and Gods in Asia Minor* (New York: Oxford University Press, 1993), 2:63.

64 All three images are discussed in *1 Clement* 24–25, in *The Apostolic Fathers*, ed. Bart D. Ehrman (Cambridge, Mass.: Harvard University Press, 2003), vol. 1.

65 *Encomium Andreae Cretensis* 7, in Falconi, *Acta Primigenia*, 80.

66 *Acta Sanctorum, Februarii, III* (Venice, 1736), 57–59; Cioffari, *S. Nicola*, 134.

67 Michael, *Vita per Michaelem* 5.

68 See André Vauchez, *Sainthood in the Later Middle Ages* (New York: Cambridge University Press, 1997), 433–39.

69 Michael, *Vita per Michaelem* 5.

70 Michael, *Vita per Michaelem* 5.

71 Michael, *Vita per Michaelem* 5.

72 Michael, *Vita per Michaelem* 5.

73 Michael, *Vita per Michaelem* 5.

74 The seven-day week was of Semitic origin and not followed at this time by the Greeks and Romans. Sacha Stern, *Calendar and Community: A History of the Jewish Calendar* (Oxford: Oxford University Press, 2001); Eviatar Zerubavel, *The Seven Day Circle: The History and Meaning of the Week* (Chicago: University of Chicago Press, 1989), 6.

75 For more on classical education, see H. I. Marrou, *A History of Education in Antiquity*, trans. George Lamb (Madison: University of Wisconsin Press, 1982).

76 E. M. Treharne, *The Old English Life of St Nicholas with the Old English Life of St Giles* (Leeds: Leeds Texts and Monographs, 1997), 34.

77 Reginold, "Vita beati Nicolai episcopi," *Sanctuarium seu Vitae Sanctorum*, ed. Boninus Mombritius (Hildesheim: Georg Olms Verlag, 1479, 1978), 2:307–9.

78 In the Greek versions of this story, the boy is named Basilion, or Basil. See *Encomium Methodii* 4–9, in Falconi, *Acta Primigenia*, 58–65. Also see Bruno, *S. Nicola nelle fonti narrative greche*, 129–33.

79 Reginold, "Vita beati," 309.

80 Martin Ebon, *Saint Nicholas: Life and Legend* (New York: Harper & Row, 1975), 52.

Chapter 3

1   Michael the Archimandrite, *Vita per Michaelem* 9, in Gustav Anrich, *Hagios Nikolaos: Der heilige Nikolaus in der griechischen Kirche*, 2 vols. (Leipzig: Teubner, 1913–1917), 1:117; and in Niccolò Carminio Falconi, ed., *Sancti Confessoris Pontificis et Celeberrimi Thaumaturgi Nicolai Acta Primigenia* (Naples, 1751), 42–43.

2   Michael, *Vita per Michaelem* 9.

3   Michael, *Vita per Michaelem* 9.

4   Michael, *Vita per Michaelem* 9.

5   Michael, *Vita per Michaelem* 9. Michael also quotes Prov 3:3: "Let almsgiving and faithfulness never leave you, but bind them around your neck and you will find mercy."

6   Tertullian, *Apologia* 39, in *The Ante-Nicene Fathers* (hereafter ANF), ed. Alexander Roberts and James Donaldson (Peabody: Hendrickson, 1885, 2004), 3:46.

7   Tertullian, *Apologia* 39, ANF 3:46. Tertullian details how the church's funds were distributed:

> For they are not taken thence and spent on feasts, and drinking-bouts, and eating-houses, but to support and bury poor people, to supply the wants of boys and girls destitute of means and parents, and of old persons confined now to the house; such, too, as have suffered shipwreck; and if there happen to be any in the mines, or banished to the islands, or shut up in the prisons, for nothing but their fidelity to the cause of God's Church, they become the nurslings of their confession.

8   Michael, *Vita per Michaelem* 11.

9   Michael, *Vita per Michaelem* 10.

10 Michael, *Vita per Michaelem* 10.

11 Michael, *Vita per Michaelem* 10.

12 Zosimus, *Historia nova* (London: Green & Chaplin, 1814), bk. 2, 56.

13 Arnold H. M. Jones, *Constantine and the Conversion of Europe*, rev. ed. (New York: Collier, 1962), 188.

14 Basil, *Homilia Illud Lucae, Destruam* 4, in *Patrologia Graeca*, ed. J.-P. Migne (Paris, 1857–1866), 31:268–69.

15 Ambrose, *De Nabuthae* 5, in vol. 32/2 of the Corpus scriptorum ecclesiasticorum latinorum (CSEL) series, vol. ed. C. Schenkl (Vienna: Hoelder, Pichler, Tempsky, 1897), 478.

16 Ambrose, *De Nabuthae* 5, in Schenkl, *Corpus scriptorum* 32.2, 479.
17 Ambrose, *De Nabuthae* 5, in Schenkl, *Corpus scriptorum* 32.2, 479.
18 Canons of the Council of Elvira, 15–17, trans. in Samuel Laeuchli, *Power and Sexuality: The Emergence of Canon Law at the Synod of Elvira* (Philadelphia: Temple University Press, 1972).
19 For further ecclesial protections for women in marriage, see *Constitutions of the Holy Apostles: Ecclesiastical Canons* 6, 48, 67, ANF 7:500–505.
20 Michael, *Vita per Michaelem* 11.
21 Michael, *Vita per Michaelem* 11. "He considered in his mind the counsel of Solomon who says: 'God loves a cheerful and giving person' [Prov 22:8] and also, 'The one who cares for the poor cares for himself' [Prov 22:9], and again, 'Do good things for God and humanity' [Prov 3:4] and especially this one is most fitting: 'Snatch up those who are in danger of being led away to death' [Prov 24:11]."
22 Michael, *Vita per Michaelem* 11.
23 Michael, *Vita per Michaelem* 13–15.
24 On the other hand, Michael is vague and unspecific concerning details of the story, leaving the reader with many questions. What are the names of the father and the girls? Who did they marry? What is the timeline of events? The reader imagines that weeks or perhaps months elapsed between each mysterious gift of gold, but the text gives the impression that the gifts might have come in quick succession. There are few details that support the episode's claim to historicity. Gerardo Cioffari, *S. Nicola nella Critica Storica* (Bari: Centro Studi Nicolaiani, 1987), 149.
25 Michael, *Vita per Michaelem* 16–17. Symeon Metaphrastes elaborates the poor man's words to Nicholas:

> If the Lord—great in his kindness—had not caused you to pity us, then, it scares me to think, long before now my three daughters and I would have surely died. But look! Through you God has saved us and freed us from the unhappy plight of sin and woe: He lifts the beggars from the miry pit and from the earth he raises the poor.

Symeon Metaphrastes, *Bios kai Politeia* 8, in *Patrologia Graeca*, ed. J.-P. Migne (Paris, 1857–1866), 116:328A. It should also be

203

noted that Falconi's Latin edition of Michael's *Life* expands the father's speech. In it he says,

> What was able to raise me up if not your kindness and our common Lord, Jesus Christ? For a long time I was living disreputably under sin, resulting in my life now. Today, however, O blessed one, because of you God saved us. Both from the pit of need and greed he rescued us. Out of gratitude to you, we must offer on this day all of our lives, on behalf of the one whose hand provided our defense, raising the weak off the ground and lifting the poor out of their filth. It was by your generosity, your truly merciful liberality.

Vita per Michaelem 17, in Falconi, *Acta Primigenia*, 43.

26   Jacobus de Voragine, *Golden Legend*, trans. William Caxton, 1483. Manuscript reproduced in *Nicolaus Studi Storici* 18.1 (Bari: Centro Studi Nicolaiani, 2007), 216.

27   Michael, *Vita per Michaelem* 17.

28   Symeon Metaphrastes, *Bios kai Politeia* 9, in Migne, *Patrologia Graeca*, 116:328A.

29   Philostratus, *The Life of Apollonius of Tyana* 1.3, in *Philostratus: Apollonius of Tyana*, trans. Christopher P. Jones, Loeb Classical Library 16 (Cambridge, Mass.: Harvard University Press, 2005), vol. 1.

30   Simon Swain, "Defending Hellenism: Philostratus, *In Honour of Apollonius*," in *Apologetics in the Roman Empire*, ed. Mark Edwards, Martin Goodman, and Simon Price (New York: Oxford University Press, 1999), 157–96.

31   Macarius, *Apocriticus* 3.1, 4.5, in *The Apocriticus of Macarius Magnes*, trans. T. W. Crafer (New York: Macmillan, 1919), 52, 128.

32   Tradition attributed *Against Hierocles* to Eusebius of Caesarea, but this has been discredited. Tomas Hägg, "Hierocles the Lover of Truth and Eusebius the Sophist," *Symbolae Osloenses* 67 (1992): 138–50.

33   This is certainly not the only instance of rivalry. Symeon the Fool might also be considered a Christian version of the philosopher Diogenes of Sinope. Derek Kueger, *Symeon the Holy Fool* (Berkeley: University of California Press, 1996), 72.

34   Philostratus, *Life of Apollonius* 1.13, in Jones, *Philostratus*.

35   Philostratus, *Life of Apollonius* 5.24, in Jones, *Philostratus*.

36   Philostratus, *Life of Apollonius* 6.39, in Jones, *Philostratus*.

37 Philostratus, *Life of Apollonius* 6.39, in Jones, *Philostratus.*
38 Michael, *Vita per Michaelem* 16.
39 Michael, *Vita per Michaelem* 11–13, and Symeon Meta-phrastes, *Bios kai Politeia* 5–6, in Migne, *Patrologia Graeca*, 116:321C–324C.
40 It is a tenth-century version of *Vita Nicolai Sionitae.* Anrich, *Hagios Nikolaos*, 1:56–57.
41 Athanasius, *Vita Antonii* 1.2, in *Early Christian Lives*, trans. Carolinne White (New York: Penguin, 1998), 9.
42 *Verba Seniorum*, in *The Desert Fathers: Sayings of the Early Christian Monks*, trans. Benedicta Ward (New York: Penguin, 2003), 53.
43 *Verba Seniorum*, in Ward, *Desert Fathers*, 53.
44 *Didache* 1.6; text reproduced and translated in Bart Ehrman, *Lost Scriptures: Books That Did Not Make It into the Old Testament* (New York: Oxford University Press, 2003), 212.
45 A woman has no need of "conjugal intercourse with a temporary husband" as long as she is "united to the true husband," that is, Christ. *Acts of Thomas* 14, text reproduced and translated in Ehrman, *Lost Scriptures*, 127.
46 de Voragine, *Golden Legend*, 90–91.
47 Gregory the Great, *Life of Benedict* 2.1-2, in White, *Early Christian Lives*, 168.
48 Jerome, *Life of Paul of Thebes* 1, in White, *Early Christian Lives*, 76.
49 Canons of Nicaea, Canon 1, *Nicene and Post-Nicene Fathers: Second Series* (hereafter NPNF2), ed. Henry Wace and Philip Schaff (Peabody: Hendrickson, 1994), 14:8.
50 Socrates, *Historia ecclesiastica* 1.11, NPNF2 2:18.
51 One motion that did pass was Canon 3: "The great Council has stringently forbidden any bishop, priest, deacon, or any of the clergy, to have a woman living with him, except a mother, sister, aunt, or some such person who is beyond all suspicion." Canons of Nicaea, NPNF2 14:11.
52 *Acts of Peter* 13; *Acts of Paul* 8. Texts in *The Apocryphal New Testament*, ed. J. K. Elliott (New York: Oxford University Press, 1993), 350–430.
53 One illustrative example: "The Passion of the Scillitan Martyrs," ANF 9:285.
54 Gregory of Nyssa, "The Life of St. Macrina," *Saint Gregory of Nyssa: Ascetical Works*, The Fathers of the Church (Washington, D.C.: Catholic University of America, 1967), 58:176.

55 Theodoret of Cyrrhus, *A History of the Monks of Syria*, 2nd ed., trans. R. M. Price (Collegeville, Minn.: Cistercian Publications, 1985), 26.11–12.

56 Hyperichius, in Ward, *Desert Fathers*, 106.

57 Jerome, *Life of Hilarion* 14, in White, *Early Christian Lives*, 94–95.

58 Thomas Aquinas, *Summa Theologiae*, Secunda Secundae, Question 107, Article 1.

59 Seneca, *De benef.* 2. See Aquinas, *Summa Theologiae*, Secunda Secundae, Question 107, Article 1.

60 Aquinas, *Summa Theologiae*, Secunda Secundae, Question 107, Article 1.

61 Aquinas, *Summa Theologiae*, Secunda Secundae, Question 107, Article 1.

62 Michael, *Vita per Michaelem* 13.

63 Michael, *Vita per Michaelem* 18. Michael continues his praise of Nicholas with these words:

> Helping the needy, he brilliantly showed us the good soul. He manifested to us the image of the merciful Savior, that we, even though the sickliness of our pastoral office is clear to all, might yet attain the dignity of the High Priest [*Archieraticam*].

64 James Henry Dixon, "Contributions from Foreign Ballad Literature: The Provençal Ballad of St. Nicholas and the Butcher," *Notes and Queries: A Medium of Inter-Communication for Literary Men, General Readers, Etc.*, 3rd ser. (January 15, 1866), 9:31.

65 Dixon, "Contributions from Foreign Ballad Literature," 31.

66 de Voragine, *Golden Legend*, 22.

67 Michael, *Vita per Michaelem* 9.

68 Michael, *Vita per Michaelem* 9.

69 Michael, *Vita per Michaelem* 9.

70 Symeon Metaphrastes, *Bios kai Politeia* 10, in in Migne, *Patrologia Graeca*, 116:352C–D. Gerardo Cioffari, "St. Nicholas: Documentary Evidence in Literature and Archeology," *Bollettino di San Nicola* 66, nos. 11 and 12 (1997): 5–19.

71 This detail about location is given in the next paragraph.

72 *Bios tou hagiou Nikolaou* 5, in *The Life of Saint Nicholas of Sion*, trans. Ihor Ševčenko and Nancy Patterson Ševčenko (Brookline, Mass.: Hellenic College Press, 1984), 25. The bracketed remarks are mine.

73 See, e.g., Symeon Metaphrastes, *Bios kai Politeia* 14–15, in

Migne, *Patrologia Graeca*, 116:353–56; or Tryphologio Rutheno, *Brevis narratio de translatione sacri corporis*, in Falconi, *Acta Primigenia*, 139.

74 *Bios tou hagiou Nikolaou* 8, in Ševčenko and Ševčenko, *Life of Saint Nicholas*, 29.

75 *Bios tou hagiou Nikolaou* 9, in Ševčenko and Ševčenko, *Life of Saint Nicholas*, 31.

76 *Bios tou hagiou Nikolaou* 9, in Ševčenko and Ševčenko, *Life of Saint Nicholas*, 31.

77 Cyril of Jerusalem dates the discovery of the cross to the reign of Constantine, though not necessarily during the visit of Constantine's mother, Helena, to the Holy Lands. Cyril of Jerusalem, "Letter to Constantius II" 3–5, in *Cyril of Jerusalem*, trans. Leo McCauley and Anthony Stephenson, The Fathers of the Church (Washington, D.C.: Catholic University of America Press, 1970), 64:232–33.

78 Celsus provides the most thorough condemnation of the early Christians, as recorded in sections 1.28, 1.62, 4.14, 6.78 of Origen, *Contra Celsum*, trans. Henry Chadwick (Cambridge: Cambridge University Press, 1953); also see Justin Martyr, *Apologia 1*, 8–9, 24–25, in Migne, *Patrologia Graeca*, 6:337B–339B, 364–365B; Aristides, *Apologia*, ANF 9:263–79.

79 *Epistle to Diognetus* 5, ANF 1:26–27.

80 *Historia Augusta: Life of Hadrian* 1.14.2, in *Historia Augusta*, trans. David Magie, Loeb Classical Library 139 (Cambridge, Mass.: Harvard University Press, 1921, 1991), 43–44.

81 Eusebius, *Historia ecclesiastica* 4.6, NPNF2 1:177.

82 Eusebius, *Historia ecclesiastica* 4.6, NPNF2 1:177.

83 Lactantius, *De mortibus* 10, in Migne, *Patrologia Latina*, 7:210–211A.

84 Lactantius, *De mortibus* 13, in Migne, *Patrologia Latina*, 7:214B.

85 Eusebius, *Historia ecclesiastica* 8.6, NPNF2 1:328.

86 The edict stated "that every suit at law should be received against them; while, on the other hand, they were debarred from being plaintiffs in questions of wrong, adultery, or theft." Lactantius, *De mortibus* 13, in Migne, *Patrologia Latina*, 7:214B.

87 Michael, *Vita per Michaelem* 22.

88 Michael, *Vita per Michaelem* 23.

89 Timothy Barnes, *Athanasius and Constantius: Theology and Politics in the Constantinian Empire* (Cambridge, Mass.: Harvard University Press, 2001), 21.

90 Monk Ekkehard, qtd. in Charles M. Gayley, *Plays of Our Fore-fathers, and Some of the Traditions upon Which They Were Founded* (New York: Duffield, 1907), 55.

91 Charles Jones, *Saint Nicholas of Myra, Bari, and Manhattan* (Chicago: University of Chicago Press, 1978), 303–4.

92 Karl Meisen, *Nikolauskult und Nikolausbrauch im Abend-lande* (Düsseldorf: Schwann, 1931), 307–8.

93 Michael, *Vita per Michaelem* 24.

94 Plutarch, *Parallel Lives*, Loeb Classical Library (Cambridge, Mass.: Harvard University Press, 1919), 7:273.

95 *Acts of Thecla* 42; see Ehrman, *Lost Scriptures*, 118.

96 Sulpicius Severus, *Vita Martini* 9, in White, *Early Christian Lives*, 143.

97 Possidius, *Sancti Augustini vita* 4, in Migne, *Patrologia Latina* 32:37.

98 Ignatius of Antioch, *Ad Ephesios* 6, in Migne, *Patrologia Graeca*, 5:649B.

99 *Ancient Statutes of the Church*, Canons 1–10, reprinted in *Pagans and Christians in Late Antiquity*, ed. A. D. Lee (New York: Routledge, 2000), 218.

100 Michael, *Vita per Michaelem* 24.

101 See Claudia Rapp, *Holy Bishops in Late Antiquity: The Nature of Christian Leadership in an Age of Transition* (Berkeley: University of California Press, 2005).

102 Michael, *Vita per Michaelem* 24.

103 Nicephorus Kallistos Xanthopoulos, qtd. in Gerardo Cioffari, *Saint Nicholas* (Bari: Centro Studi Nicolaiani, 2008), 17. See Nicephorus Kallistos Xanthopoulos, *Historia Ecclesiastica* 8.42, in Migne, *Patrologia Graeca*, 146:167.

104 Nicephorus Kallistos Xanthopoulos, *Historia Ecclesiastica* 8.42, in Migne, *Patrologia Graeca*, 146:167.

105 Eusebius, *Historia ecclesiastica* 8.2, NPNF2 1:324.

106 Michael, *Vita per Michaelem* 25.

107 Michael, *Vita per Michaelem* 25.

108 Eusebius, *Vita Constantini* 2.1-18, in *Über das Leben des Kaiser Konstantins*, ed. F. Winkelmann, *Eusebius' Werke: Band 1*, 2nd ed. (Berlin: Akademie-Verlag, 1975).

109 Eusebius, *Vita Constantini* 2.1, in Winkelmann, *Über das Leben*; Barnes, *Athanasius and Constantius*, 71.

110 Constantine's letter in which these privileges and provisions are outlined is reproduced by Eusebius, *Vita Constantini* 2.24–42, in Winkelmann, *Über das Leben*.

Chapter 4

1   Eusebius, *A New Eusebius*, trans. J. Stevenson and W. H. C. Frend (London: SPCK, 1963, 1987), 338.

2   Eusebius, *Vita Constantini* 3.7, in *Über das Leben des Kaiser Konstantins*, ed. F. Winkelmann, *Eusebius' Werke: Band 1*, 2nd ed. (Berlin: Akademie-Verlag, 1975).

3   Eusebius, *Vita Constantini* 3.10–11, in Winkelmann, *Über das Leben*; Gelasius of Cyzicus, *Historia consilii Nicaeni* 2.7.1–41, in *Patrologia Graeca*, ed. J.-P. Migne (Paris, 1857–1866), 85:1231–44.

4   Eusebius, *Vita Constantini* 3.18, in Winkelmann, *Über das Leben*; Arnold H. M. Jones, *Constantine and the Conversion of Europe*, rev. ed. (New York: Collier, 1962), 140.

5   Arius to Eusebius of Nicomedia, reproduced in Theodoret, *Historia ecclesiastica* 1.4, NPNF2 3:41.

6   There are many good surveys of the Arian controversy. See, for instance, R. P. C. Hanson, *The Search for the Christian Doctrine of God: The Arian Controversy* (Edinburgh: T&T Clark, 1988); Lewis Ayres, *Nicaea and Its Legacy* (New York: Oxford University Press, 2006); Leo D. Davis, *The First Seven Ecumenical Councils (325–787): Their History and Theology* (Collegeville, Minn.: Liturgical Press, 1990); Rowan Williams, *Arius: Heresy and Tradition*, rev. ed. (Grand Rapids: Eerdmans, 2002).

7   "Epistle Catholic" of Alexander and the presbyters of Alexandria, ANF 6:297. For discussion, see Timothy Barnes, *Constantine and Eusebius* (Cambridge, Mass.: Harvard University Press, 1981), 202–3.

8   For a precedent of this argument, see Novatian, *De Trinitate* 31, in *Patrologia Latina*, ed. J.-P. Migne (Paris, 1844–1855), 3:949B–950C.

9   Hanson, *Search for the Christian Doctrine*, 146–51.

10   C. Luibhéid, "The Arianism of Eusebius of Nicomedia," *Irish Theological Quarterly* 43, no. 1 (1976): 8–9; Elliot, *Christianity of Constantine*, 223–24.

11   Eusebius of Caesarea quoted by Socrates, *Historia ecclesiastica* 1.7, NPNF2 2:11.

12   *The Creeds of Christendom*, ed. Philip Schaff (New York: Harper & Brothers, 1877, 1919), 1:29.

13   Schaff, *Creeds of Christendom*, 1:29.

14   Eusebius, *Vita Constantini* 2.12, in Winkelmann, *Über das Leben*.

15   Michael the Archimandrite, *Vita per Michaelem* 25, in Gustav

Anrich, *Hagios Nikolaos: Der heilige Nikolaus in der griechischen Kirche*, 2 vols. (Leipzig: Teubner, 1913–1917), 1:126; and in Niccolò Carminio Falconi, ed., *Sancti Confessoris Pontificis et Celeberrimi Thaumaturgi Nicolai Acta Primigenia* (Naples, 1751), 45.

16 Michael, *Vita per Michaelem* 25.
17 Michael, *Vita per Michaelem* 25.
18 It should be said that the same miracle was reported of St. Spiridon, bishop of Trimithus in Cyprus. Gerardo Cioffari, *Saint Nicholas* (Bari: Centro Studi Nicolaiani, 2008), 20.
19 Arius' name does not appear in any of the lists of those who attended. In point of fact, he was a presbyter, not a bishop, and so had no official standing at the council. He may have been in the vicinity of Nicaea, lodging with his supporters, or he may have remained in Alexandria. But he did not take part in the proceedings.
20 Anrich, *Hagios Nikolaos*, 1:459.
21 Charles Rosa painted the ceiling in 1661. Gerardo Cioffari, *Basilica of Saint Nicholas* (Bari: Centro Studi Nicolaiani, 1997), 45.
22 Michael, *Vita per Michaelem* 40.
23 Lothar Heiser, *Nikolaus von Myra; Heiliger der ungeteilten Christenheit* (Berlin: Paulinus-Verlag Trier, 1978), 80–89.
24 See Socrates, *Historia ecclesiastica* 1.21, NPNF2 2:271–72; Theodoret, *Historia ecclesiastica* 5.7, NPNF2 3:135.
25 *Encomium* 2, in Falconi, *Acta Primigenia*, 76.
26 Two others were sent into exile for refusing to sign the Nicene Creed: Theonas of Marmarice and Secundus of Ptolemais. Philostorgius, *Historia ecclesiastica* 1.9–10, trans. E. Walford, *The Ecclesiastical History of Philostorgius as Epitomized by Photius* (London: Henry G. Bohn, 1855), 433–34.
27 As did St. Dominic to a certain heretic named Raymond. Jacobus de Voragine, *Golden Legend*, trans. Granger Ryan and Helmut Ripperger (New York: Arno, 1969), 423.
28 *Encomium* 6–7, in Falconi, *Acta Primigenia*, 79. The late first-century *1 Clement* also warned about strife and conflict between bishops. *1 Clement* 44, in *The Apostolic Fathers*, ed. Bart D. Ehrman (Cambridge, Mass.: Harvard University Press, 2003), vol. 1.
29 Philostorgius presents an altogether different scenario than the one given here, saying that Eusebius of Nicomedia, Maris, and Theognis were summoned to Constantine after three years

of exile, at which point they submitted a heretical creed in opposition of the Nicene, remaining obstinate in their errors. Philostorgius, *Historia ecclesiastica* 2.7, in Walford, *The Ecclesiastical History of Philostorgius*, 437. Elliot refutes Philostorgius' account as being a complete invention. Elliot, *Christianity of Constantine*, 218–19.

30   Reproduced in Socrates, *Historia Ecclesiastica* 1.14, NPNF2 2:20.

31   Socrates, *Historia Ecclesiastica* 1.14, NPNF2 2:20.

32   *Didache* 8:1, text reproduced and translated in Bart Ehrman, *Lost Scriptures: Books That Did Not Make It into the Old Testament* (New York: Oxford University Press, 2003), 214.

33   Pseudo-Dionysius, *Peri tes ouranias hierarchias* 3.1, in Migne, *Patrologia Graeca*, 3:425B–428A.

34   Peter Brown, "The Rise and Function of the Holy Man," *Journal of Roman Studies* 61 (1971): 80–101, reprinted in *Society and the Holy in Late Antiquity* (Berkeley: University of California Press, 1982), 103–52. On patronage, see Christopher Kelly, "Patronage," in *Late Antiquity: A Guide to the Postclassical World*, ed. G. W. Bowersock, Peter Brown, and Oleg Grabar (Cambridge, Mass.: Belknap Press, 1999), 637–38; Averil Cameron, *The Mediterranean World in Late Antiquity A.D. 395–600* (New York: Routledge, 1993), 85–102.

35   Peter Brown, *Rise of Western Christendom*, 2nd ed. (Malden, Mass.: Blackwell, 2003), 55. Also see Henry Chadwick, ed., *The Role of the Christian Bishop in Ancient Society* (Berkeley: Center for Hermeneutical Studies, 1979), 1.

36   Brown, *Rise of Western Christendom*, 55.

37   Jones, *Constantine and the Conversion*, 19.

38   J. B. Bury, *History of the Later Roman Empire* (New York: Dover, 1958), 1:59; Cameron, *Mediterranean World in Late Antiquity*, 94–101; J. Liebeschuetz, *The Decline and Fall of the Ancient City* (New York: Oxford University Press, 2001).

39   Brown, "Holy Man," 118.

40   Brown, "Holy Man," 118.

41   Brown, "Holy Man," 120.

42   Claudia Rapp, *Holy Bishops in Late Antiquity: The Nature of Christian Leadership in an Age of Transition* (Berkeley: University of California Press, 2005), 6.

43   John of Ephesus, *Lives of the Eastern Saints*, 1.9, qtd. in Susan Harvey, *Asceticism and Society in Crisis: John of Ephesus and*

"The Lives of the Eastern Saints" (Berkeley: University of California Press, 1990), 44.

44   Brown, "Holy Man," 135. Also see Peter Brown's 1976 article, "Town, Village and Holy Man: The Case of Syria," reprinted in *Society and the Holy in Late Antiquity*, 153–65. Peter Brown, *The Body and Society* (New York: Columbia University Press, 1988), 213–40.

45   Brown, "Holy Man," 122. John of Ephesus says that disobedience to Habib likewise brought curses and misfortunes. *Lives of the Eastern Saints* 1.15; see Harvey, *Asceticism and Society in Crisis*.

46   See Alba Maria Orselli, *L'idea e il culto del santo patrono cittadino nella letteratura latina Cristiana* (Bologna: Zanichelli, 1965).

47   Michael, *Vita per Michaelem* 2.

48   Justin, *Apologia 1* 24–26, in Migne, *Patrologia Graeca*, 6:364C–369A.

49   Peter Brown, *Authority and the Sacred* (New York: Cambridge University Press, 1995), xii–xiii.

50   Inscription on an Ephesian statue base, C. L. Brinks, "'Great is Artemis of the Ephesians': Acts 19:23-41 in Light of Goddess Worship in Ephesus," *The Catholic Biblical Quarterly* 71 (2009): 782.

51   Rick Strelan, *Paul, Artemis and the Jews* (New York: de Gruyter, 1996), 72.

52   Sozomenus, *Historia ecclesiastica* 2.5, NPNF2 2:261–62; Theodoret, *Historia ecclesiastica* 5.22, 29, NPNF2 3:148, 152.

53   "No person shall pollute himself with sacrificial animals; no person shall slaughter an innocent victim; no person shall approach the shrines, shall wander through the temples, or revere the images formed by mortal labor, lest he become guilty by divine and human laws." *The Theodosian Code and Novels and the Sirmondian Constitutions*, trans. Clyde Pharr (Princeton: Princeton University Press, 1952), 16.10.10.

54   Michele R. Salzman, "Christianity and Paganism, III: Italy," in *Cambridge History of Christianity* (New York: Cambridge University Press, 2007), 2:214.

55   Martin of Braga, *De correctione rusticorum* 8, in *Christianity and Paganism, 350–750: The Conversion of Western Europe*, ed. and trans. J. N. Hillgarth (Philadelphia: University of Pennsylvania Press, 1969; rpt. 1986), 59.

56 Martin of Braga, *De correctione rusticorum* 16, in Hillgarth, *Christianity and Paganism*, 62.

57 Brown, *Rise of Western Christendom*, 74.

58 Lactantius, *Divinae institutiones* 1.1, 2.16–19, and 3.9, in Migne, *Patrologia Latina*, 6:111–446B.

59 *Encomium Andreae Cretensis* 7, in Falconi, *Acta Primigenia*, 80.

60 Michael, *Vita per Michaelem* 28.

61 Michael, *Vita per Michaelem* 28.

62 Michael, *Vita per Michaelem* 28.

63 Mark the Deacon, *Vita Porphyrii* 65–70, in Migne, *Patrologia Graeca*, 65:1211–52.

64 *Life of St. Theodotus of Ancyra* 13–20, trans. Stephen Mitchell in "The Life of Saint Theodotus of Ancyra," *Anatolian Studies* 32 (1982): 106–7.

65 Michael, *Vita per Michaelem* 28.

66 Michael, *Vita per Michaelem* 28.

67 Michael, *Vita per Michaelem* 29.

68 Gerardo Cioffari, *S. Nicola nella Critica Storica* (Bari: Centro Studi Nicolaiani, 1987), 200.

69 Michael, *Vita per Michaelem* 29.

70 Michael, *Vita per Michaelem* 29.

71 Michael, *Vita per Michaelem* 29.

72 Symeon Metaphrastes, *Bios kai Politeia* 18, in Migne, *Patrologia Graeca*, 116:336D.

73 Symeon Metaphrastes, *Bios kai Politeia* 18, in Migne, *Patrologia Graeca*, 116:337A.

74 *Old English Life of St. Nicholas*, trans. E. M. Treharne (Leeds: Leeds Texts and Monographs, 1997), 108.

75 Anrich, *Hagios Nikolaos*, 1:301–11; 2:437–38.

76 Synod of Ancyra, Canon 24 and 4. See also the Synod of Gangra, Canon 2; Charles Hefele, *A History of the Councils from the Original Documents* (Edinburgh: T&T Clark, 1876), 1:221.

77 Callinicus, *De vita S. Hypatii* 30.1, in *Callinici De vita S. Hypatii liber*, ed. Philologisches Seminar of Bonn (Leipzig: Teubner, 1895), 35.

78 Anrich, *Hagios Nikolaos*, 2:225–26.

79 *Bios tou hagiou Nikolaou* 17, in *The Life of Saint Nicholas of Sion*, trans. Ihor Ševčenko and Nancy Patterson Ševčenko (Brookline, Mass.: Hellenic College Press, 1984), 37.

80 *Bios tou hagiou* 18, in Ševčenko and Ševčenko, *Life of Saint Nicholas*, 39.

81 *Bios tou hagiou* 18, in Ševčenko and Ševčenko, *Life of Saint Nicholas*, 39.

82 Cioffari, *Basilica of Saint Nicholas*, 45.

83 Sulpicius Severus, *Vita Martini* 13, in *Early Christian Lives*, trans. Carolinne White (New York: Penguin, 1998), 147.

84 Cyril of Jerusalem, *Catechesis* 13.36, in *The Works of Saint Cyril of Jerusalem*, trans. Leo P. McCauley and Anthony A. Stephenson, The Fathers of the Church 64 (Washington, D.C.: Catholic University of America Press, 1970), 28.

85 Gregory of Tours, *Lives of the Fathers*, trans. Edward James (Liverpool: Liverpool University Press, 1991), 72.

86 Theodoret, *Historia Ecclesiastica* 3.3, NPNF2 3:93.

87 *Recueil des inscriptions grecques-chrétiennes d'Asie Mineure*, ed. Henri Grégoire (Paris, 1922), 104, trans. Frank Trombley, *Hellenic Religion and Christianization* (New York: Brill, 1995), 1:102, and see 158.

88 *Acts of John* 38, in Ehrman, *Lost Scriptures*, 93–108.

89 *Acts of John* 42.

90 Interestingly, John the Deacon, who made the first Latin edition of Nicholas' life, sets this particular story during Nicholas' lifetime. Treharne, *Old English Life*, 111. Also see Iohannum Diaconum, *Vita sancti Nicolai* 19, in Falconi, *Acta Primigenia*, 118–19.

91 A revolting stench gave away the presence of a demon to St. Antony. While on board a boat with some fellow monks, he sniffed out a demon-possessed youth hidden in their midst. Athanasius, *Vita Antonii* 63, in White, 35.

92 J. R. Partington, *A History of Greek Fire and Gunpowder* (Cambridge: Heffer & Sons, 1960).

93 See Anrich, *Hagios Nikolaos*, 2:433–44.

94 Michael, *Vita per Michaelem* 44–48.

95 Theodoret, *Historia ecclesiastica* 5.21, NPNF2 3:147.

96 Callinicus, *De vita S. Hypatii* 45, in Philologisches Seminar of Bonn, *Callinici De vita S. Hypatii liber*, 68–72.

97 Severus, *Vita S. Martini* 11-12, in White, *Early Christian Lives*, 144–45.

98 Charles Jones, *Saint Nicholas of Myra, Bari, and Manhattan* (Chicago: University of Chicago Press, 1978), 24.

99 Michael, *Vita per Michaelem* 50–52; *Encomium Methodii*, in Falconi, *Acta Primigenia*, 56, 74; *Encomium Andreae Cretensis*, in Falconi, *Acta Primigenia*, 81.

100   J. V. Jarnik, *Zeitschrift für Volkskunde*, 2:348–49, cited in George McKnight, *St. Nicholas* (Williamstown, Mass.: Corner House, 1915, 1974), 144–45.

101   "Sadko," trans. James Bailey and Tatyana Ivanova, in *An Anthology of Russian Folk Epics* (New York: M. E. Sharpe, 1998), 304.

102   For a detailed study on this topic, see Phyllis Siefker, *Santa Claus, Last of the Wild Men: The Origins and Evolution of Saint Nicholas, Spanning 50,000 Years* (Jefferson, N.C.: McFarland, 1997).

Chapter 5

1   Zosimus confirms the existence of this tribe and testifies to the trouble it caused the Empire. Zosimus, *Historia nova* (London: Green & Chaplin, 1814), 2:31.3. *Zosimus: New History*, trans. Ronald Ridley (Melbourne: Byzantina Australiensia 2, 1982). See Gerardo Cioffari, *S. Nicola nella Critica Storica* (Bari: Centro Studi Nicolaiani, 1987), 179.

2   *Praxis de stratelatis* 3, in Gustav Anrich, *Hagios Nikolaos: Der heilige Nikolaus in der griechischen Kirche*, 2 vols. (Leipzig: Teubner, 1913–1917), 1:67–76, and Niccolò Carminio Falconi, *Sancti Confessoris Pontificis et Celeberrimi Thaumaturgi Nicolai Acta Primigenia* (Naples, 1751), 30.

3   *Sirmondiana* 1, in *Pagans and Christians in Late Antiquity: A Sourcebook*, ed. A. D. Lee (New York: Routledge, 2000), 218–20. The dating of this constitution and the discussions surrounding it help to establish the timeline for the events of the *praxis de stratelatis*, that is, between the years 330 and 335.

4   *Praxis de stratelatis* 8, in Anrich, *Hagios Nikolaos*, 1:70, and Falconi, *Acta Primigenia*, 31.

5   *Praxis de stratelatis* 8, in Anrich, *Hagios Nikolaos*, 1:70, and Falconi, *Acta Primigenia*, 31.

6   *Praxis de stratelatis* 9, in Anrich, *Hagios Nikolaos*, 1:71, and Falconi, *Acta Primigenia*, 31.

7   Charles Jones, *Saint Nicholas of Myra, Bari, and Manhattan* (Chicago: University of Chicago Press, 1978), 42.

8   Theodoret, *Historia ecclesiastica* 3.12–13, NPNF2 3:101–2.

9   Theodoret, *Historia ecclesiastica* 3.12–13, NPNF2 3:101–2.

10   *Praxis de stratelatis* 12, in Anrich, *Hagios Nikolaos*, 1:72, and Falconi, *Acta Primigenia*, 32.

11   *Praxis de stratelatis* 12, in Anrich, *Hagios Nikolaos*, 1:72, and Falconi, *Acta Primigenia*, 32.

12   Cioffari, *S. Nicola*, 183. This dating fits reasonably with the findings of Gustav Anrich, who observes that a certain Flavius Nepotianus served as consul in 336 and a certain Flavius Ursus did likewise in 338. He suggests that these are perhaps two of the men in our story. Anrich, *Hagios Nikolaos*, 2:371.

13   Socrates, *Historia ecclesiastica* 1.27, NPNF2 2:29. Theodoret, *Historia ecclesiastica* 1.25, NPNF2 3:61.

14   The precise allegations against Fausta and Crispus have been obscured and remain unclear. T. G. Elliot, *The Christianity of Constantine the Great* (Scranton, Pa.: University of Scranton Press, 1996), 232–34.

15   Sozomenus, *Historia ecclesiastica* 1.5, NPNF2 2:242–43.

16   Hugh Elton, "The Transformation of Government under Diocletian and Constantine," in *A Companion to the Roman Empire*, ed. David Potter (Malden: Blackwell, 2010), 199. Sara Parvis, *Marcellus of Ancyra and the Lost Years of the Arian Controversy 325–345* (New York: Oxford University Press, 2006), 138–40.

17   Cioffari, *S. Nicola*, 182–83.

18   Zosimus, *Historia nova*, 2:59.

19   *Praxis de stratelatis* 17, in Anrich, *Hagios Nikolaos*, 1:74, and Falconi, *Acta Primigenia*, 33.

20   *Praxis de stratelatis* 18, in Anrich, *Hagios Nikolaos*, 1:75, and Falconi, *Acta Primigenia*, 33.

21   *Praxis de stratelatis* 20, in Anrich, *Hagios Nikolaos*, 1:75, and Falconi, *Acta Primigenia*, 33.

22   *Praxis de stratelatis* 23, in Anrich, *Hagios Nikolaos*, 1:76, and Falconi, *Acta Primigenia*, 33.

23   Anrich, *Hagios Nikolaos*, 1:67–91.

24   Anrich, *Hagios Nikolaos*, 2:369–70; Cioffari, *S. Nicola*, 17–21, 37–45.

25   Scenes from this story occur in the earliest of all surviving artistic depictions of Nicholas' life: the eleventh-century icon in the Monastery of St. Catherine at Mt. Sinai. Nancy Ševčenko, *The Life of Saint Nicholas in Byzantine Art* (Torino: Bottega d'Erasmo, 1983), 29, 104–29.

26   *Martyrologium Romanum Greogorii XIII. Pont. Max. iussu editum* (Antwerp: Plantin, 1635), 426–27; Charles Jones, *The St. Nicholas Liturgy* (Berkeley: University of California Press, 1963), 45.

27   Karl Meisen, *Nikolauskult und Nikolausbrauch im Abendlande* (Düsseldorf: Schwann, 1931), 527–30.

28 Meisen, *Nikolauskult*, 452–55; Anrich, *Hagios Nikolaos*, 2:370–75.

29 Cioffari, *S. Nicola*, 43–45.

30 Most likely the word *Dioscorus* is a misspelling and represents a mistake in the text. The original author probably intended *Dioskouroi*, the Road of the Divine Twins.

31 Michael the Archimandrite, *Vita per Michaelem* 31; in Gustav Anrich, *Hagios Nikolaos: Der heilige Nikolaus in der griechischen Kirche*, 2 vols. (Leipzig: Teubner, 1913–1917), 1:129, and in Niccolò Carminio Falconi, ed., *Sancti Confessoris Pontificis et Celeberrimi Thaumaturgi Nicolai Acta Primigenia* (Naples, 1751), 50.

32 This message is reinforced in *Praxis de tributo* 17, in Falconi, *Acta Primigenia*, 37.

33 Socrates, *Historia ecclesiastica* 1.13, NPNF2 2:19; Sozomenus summarizes the same story, *Historia ecclesiastica* 1.14, NPNF2 2:251.

34 *Encomium Andreae Cretensis* 7, in Falconi, *Acta Primigenia*, 80; *Acta Sanctorum, Februarii, III* (Venice, 1736), 57–59; Cioffari, *S. Nicola*, 134.

35 For the regional protection afforded by saints, see Alba Maria Orselli, *L'idea e il culto del santo patrono cittadino nella letteratura latina Cristiana* (Bologna: Zanichelli, 1965).

36 It is with good reason that the author of the Old English *Life of St. Nicholas* prayed that "this precious saint" might think it fit to "intercede for us with the Lord, and that we will be able, through his holy merit, to withstand the deceit of the devil, and to receive eternal bliss after this life." E. M. Treharne, *The Old English Life of St Nicholas with the Old English Life of St Giles* (London: Leeds Texts and Monographs, 1997), 102.

37 *Praxis de stratelatis* 7, in Anrich, *Hagios Nikolaos*, 1:69, and Falconi, *Acta Primigenia*, 31.

38 *Encomium Methodii* 23, in Falconi, *Acta Primigenia*, 74.

39 *Encomium Methodii* 23, in Falconi, *Acta Primigenia*, 74.

40 Gregory of Tours, *The Miracles of the Bishop St. Martin*, 1.26, in *Saints and their Miracles in Late Antique Gaul*, trans. Raymond Van Dam (Princeton: Princeton University Press, 1993), 219–20. Also see Richard Fletcher, *The Barbarian Conversion from Paganism to Christianity* (New York: Holt, 1997), 55.

41 Gregory of Tours, *Miracles of the Bishop*, 220.

42 Fletcher, *Barbarian Conversion*, 55.

43 *Encomium Methodii* 23, in Falconi, *Acta Primigenia*, 74.

44   *Encomium Methodii* 23, in Falconi, *Acta Primigenia*, 13, 67.

45   *Encomium Methodii* 23, in Falconi, *Acta Primigenia*, 74.

46   Michael, *Vita per Michaelem* 2.

47   Charles Jones observes that the manuscript in question bears the inscription, *Lib. sci. Godehardi in Hild.*, which does not necessarily mean that the author was Godehard; it could simply indicate that they were from the Abbey of Saint Godehard. Jones, *Saint Nicholas of Myra, Bari, and Manhattan*, 128.

48   Reprinted in Jones, *Saint Nicholas of Myra, Bari, and Manhattan*, 132. Translation mine.

49   Jones, *Saint Nicholas of Myra, Bari, and Manhattan*, 132. The saint prayed these words:

> Have mercy on us, King of Glory;
> Grant us this pardon
> And by the power of your mighty strength
> Restore life to the clerks
> Who were so wickedly killed.

50   See Martin Ebon, *Saint Nicholas: Life and Legend* (New York: Harper & Row, 1975), 57.

51   James Henry Dixon, "Contributions from Foreign Ballad Literature: The Provençal Ballad of St. Nicholas and the Butcher," *Notes and Queries: A Medium of Inter-Communication for Literary Men, General Readers, Etc.*, 3rd ser. (January 15, 1866), 9:31–32. Also see Jones, *Saint Nicholas of Myra, Bari, and Manhattan*, 250.

52   Ševčenko, *Saint Nicholas in Byzantine Art*, 104–29.

53   Ševčenko, *Saint Nicholas in Byzantine Art*, 104–29.

54   This happens in Reginold's musical rendition of the story. Gerardo Cioffari, *Saint Nicholas* (Bari: Centro Studi Nicolaiani, 2008), 65; Jones, *Saint Nicholas of Myra, Bari, and Manhattan*, 128. For the semantic ambiguity of "children" in premodern literature, see John Boswell, *The Kindness of Strangers* (New York: Vintage, 1990), 26–35.

55   Michael, *Vita per Michaelem* 34.

56   Michael, *Vita per Michaelem* 34.

57   Michael, *Vita per Michaelem* 34.

58   Philostratus, *The Life of Apollonius of Tyana* 4.13, in *Philostratus: Apollonius of Tyana*, trans. Christopher P. Jones (Cambridge, Mass.: Harvard University Press, 2005), 345.

59   Hippolyte Delehaye, *The Legends of the Saints*, trans. Donald Attwater (New York: Fordham University Press, 1962), 166n81.

60 Washington Irving, *The Works of Washington Irving*, vol. 7, *Knickerbocker's History of New York* (New York: Putnam's Sons, 1881), 96.

61 Michael, *Vita per Michaelem* 37–39. "Saint Nicholas loaves" appear to have their origin in the story of the grain ships.

62 St. Benedict was likewise credited in this way by miraculously providing food for the monks of his monastery during a time of famine. Gregory the Great, *Life of Benedict* 21.1, in *Early Christian Lives*, trans. Carolinne White (New York: Penguin, 1998), 188.

63 Symeon Metaphrastes, *Bios kai Politeia* 20, in *Patrologia Graeca*, ed. J.-P. Migne (Paris, 1857–1866), 116:337C.

64 *Bios tou hagiou Nikolaou* 25, in *The Life of Saint Nicholas of Sion*, trans. Ihor Ševčenko and Nancy Patterson Ševčenko (Brookline, Mass.: Hellenic College Press, 1984), 49.

65 *Bios tou hagiou Nikolaou* 25, in Ševčenko and Ševčenko, *Life of Saint Nicholas*, 49.

66 *Bios tou hagiou Nikolaou* 25, in Ševčenko and Ševčenko, *Life of Saint Nicholas*, 49.

67 *Praxis de tributo* 1; the Greek text is reprinted in Maria Teresa Bruno, *S. Nicola nelle fonti narrative greche* (Bari: Centro Studi Nicolaiani, 1985), 65–71, and Anrich, *Hagios Nikolaos*, 1:97–110; for the Latin-Greek text see Falconi, *Acta Primigenia*, 34–38.

68 Anrich, *Hagios Nikolaos*, 2:402.

69 *Praxis de tributo* 2.

70 *Praxis de tributo* 4.

71 Constantius of Lyons, *The Life of St. Germanus of Auxerre*, in *Soldiers of Christ: Saints' Lives from Late Antiquity and the Early Middle Ages* (University Park: Pennsylvania State University Press, 1994), 75–106.

72 Fletcher, *Barbarian Conversion*, 51.

73 Canons of Nicaea, Canon 17, NPNF2 14:36.

74 Cioffari questions the historical veracity of this story based on a number of dubious details. For example, the temple in Blachernis was not constructed until half a century after Nicholas' death, sometime around the year 400. Cioffari, *S. Nicola*, 192.

75 *Praxis de tributo* 8.

76 *Praxis de tributo* 12.

77 *Praxis de tributo* 12–15.

78 *Praxis de tributo* 17.

79 Zosimus, *Historia nova*, 2:56.

80 Zosimus, *Historia nova*, 2:57.

81 Zosimus, *Historia nova*, 2:57.

82 Cioffari, *S. Nicola*, 190.

83 Arnold H. M. Jones, *Constantine and the Conversion of Europe*, rev. ed. (New York: Collier, 1962), 180.

84 It should be kept in mind that antique historians were quite comfortable outfitting historical events with fantastical flourishes and disregarding other facts for the sake of the story. To give one example, consider the best-read and best-educated man of his day, Jerome. J. N. D. Kelly evaluates his *Chronicle*, a serious attempt at history, with these words:

> It is clear that he devoted thought to its planning and to the technical problems of riveting his readers' attention, and was at pains to maintain his accustomed high stylistic standards. . . . Even so, his carelessness and haste are evident not only in his numerous errors (even of translation), but also in his apparent indifference to exact dating even where the material for it was provided by his sources and in his refusal to take the trouble to fill obvious gaps in these.

J. N. D. Kelly, *Jerome* (New York: Harper & Row, 1990), 74–75.

85 Richard Newhauser, *The Early History of Greed: The Sin of Avarice in Early Medieval Thought and Literature* (New York: Cambridge University Press, 2000).

86 Benedicta Ward, trans., *The Desert Fathers: Sayings of the Early Christian Monks* (New York: Penguin, 2003), 53–59.

87 Gregory of Tours, *Miracles of the Bishop*, 223.

88 Ward, *Desert Fathers*, 58.

Chapter 6

1 Michael the Archimandrite, *Vita per Michaelem* 41, in Gustav Anrich, *Hagios Nikolaos: Der heilige Nikolaus in der griechischen Kirche*, 2 vols. (Leipzig: Teubner, 1913–1917), 1:134, and Niccolò Carminio Falconi, *Sancti Confessoris Pontificis et Celeberrimi Thaumaturgi Nicolai Acta Primigenia* (Naples, 1751), 54.

2 Michael, *Vita per Michaelem* 41.

3 Michael, *Vita per Michaelem* 41.

4 Jacobus de Voragine, *Golden Legend*, trans. Granger Ryan and Helmut Ripperger (New York: Arno, 1969), 21.

5   de Voragine, *Golden Legend*, 21.

6   de Voragine, *Golden Legend*, 21.

7   Athanasius (c. 296–373), Alexander of Alexandria (d. 326/328), Eusebius of Caesarea (263–339), Arius (256–336), Constantine (272–337), Helena (c. 246–330), Lactantius (250–325), Antony of Egypt (251–356), and Pachomius (292–348).

8   Gerardo Cioffari, *S. Nicola nella Critica Storica* (Bari: Centro Studi Nicolaiani, 1987), 206–7.

9   Charles Jones, *Saint Nicholas of Myra, Bari, and Manhattan* (Chicago: University of Chicago Press, 1978), 12; Anrich, *Hagios Nikolaos*, 2:512; A. G. Gibson, "St. Nicholas of Myra," in *New Catholic Encyclopedia* (New York: McGraw-Hill, 1967), 454; Thomas Craughwell, *Saints Preserved: An Encyclopedia of Relics* (New York: Image Books, 2011), 220.

10 *The Oxford Dictionary of Saints*, ed. David Farmer, 3rd ed., s.v. "Nicholas."

11 Gregory of Nazianzus, "Oration 31," trans. Lionel Wickham, *On God and Christ: The Five Theological Orations* (Crestwood, N.Y.: St. Vladimir's Seminary Press, 2002), 136.

12 Gregory's letter to Augustine is reprinted by Bede, *Ecclesial History of England*, trans. A. M. Sellar (London: George Bell & Son, 1907), 1.30.

13 Gregory the Great, *Life of Benedict*, 8.11, in *Early Christian Lives*, trans. Carolinne White (New York: Penguin, 1998), 178.

14 Gregory of Tours, *Glory of the Confessors*, trans. Raymond Van Dam (Liverpool: Liverpool University Press, 1989), 3.

15 Gregory of Tours, *Glory of the Confessors*, 4.

16 Michael, *Vita per Michaelem* 41.

17 See Jones, *Saint Nicholas of Myra, Bari, and Manhattan*, 67.

18 Symeon Metaphrastes, *Bios kai Politeia* 32, in *Patrologia Graeca*, ed. J.-P. Migne (Paris, 1857–1866), 116:353C.

19 Iohannem Diaconum, *Vita S. Nicolai* 19, in Falconi, *Acta Primigenia*, 124.

20 Gregory of Tours, *Glory of the Martyrs*, trans. Raymond van Dam (Liverpool: Liverpool University Press, 1988), 47–49. For explanation, see nn. 31, 48. Also see Gregory of Tours, *Glory of the Confessors*, 9.

21 *Epistula II^a ad Aurelium diaconum*, qtd. in John Crook, *The Architectural Setting of the Cult of Saints in the Early Christian West* (Oxford: Clarendon, 2000), 17.

22 *Analecta Hymnica Graeca*, IV, qtd. in Cioffari, *S. Nicola*, 212.

221

23 Adam of St. Victor, *The Liturgical Sequences of Adam of St. Victor* (London: Kegan Paul, 1881), vol. 1, seq. 28.

> Ex ipsius tumba manat
> unctionis copia,
> quae infirmos omnes sanat
> per ejus suffragia.
> Ipsam nobis unctionem
> impetres ad Dominum,
> prece pia,
> quae sanavit laesionem
> multorum peccaminum
> in Maria.

24 Theofrid, *Flores Epitaphii Sanctorum* 3.5, in *Patrologia Latina*, ed. J.-P. Migne (Paris, 1844–1855), 157:379B–381A.

25 Gregory I reports a curious incident: there was an empty oil jar near to where St. Benedict of Nursia was praying. "As the holy man continued to pray, the lid of the jar was lifted up as the jar filled with oil: the lid moved and was lifted up as the increasing amount of oil spilled over the edge of the jar on the stone floor of the room where they had knelt to pray." Gregory the Great, *Life of Benedict* 29.1, in White, *Early Christian Lives*, 194.

26 Cited by Charles Jones, *The St. Nicholas Liturgy* (Berkeley: University of California Press, 1963), 45. Translation mine.

> There are four custodians
> To be found in the atrium
> Who extract with a sponge
> Liquid [*liquorem*] according to their customary method.

27 Procopius, *De aedificiis* 1.6, in *Procopius*, trans. H. B. Dewing, Loeb Classical Library 7 (Cambridge, Mass.: Harvard University Press, 1935), 62–63.

28 Jones, *Saint Nicholas of Myra, Bari, and Manhattan*, 12–13.

29 *Bios tou hagiou Nikolaou* 30, in *The Life of Saint Nicholas of Sion*, trans. Ihor Ševčenko and Nancy Patterson Ševčenko (Brookline, Mass.: Hellenic College Press, 1984), 55.

30 *Bios tou hagiou Nikolaou* 31, in Ševčenko and Ševčenko, *Life of Saint Nicholas*, 56.

31 *Bios tou hagiou Nikolaou* 31, in Ševčenko and Ševčenko, *Life of Saint Nicholas*, 56.

32 *Bios tou hagiou Nikolaou* 38, in Ševčenko and Ševčenko, *Life of Saint Nicholas*, 67.

33   *Bios tou hagiou Nikolaou* 36–38, in Ševčenko and Ševčenko, *Life of Saint Nicholas,* 63–67.

34   George McKnight, *St. Nicholas: His Legend and His Role in the Christmas Celebration and Other Popular Customs* (Williamstown, Mass.: Corner House, 1915, 1974), 122.

35   Iohannem Diaconum, *Vita* 21, in Falconi, *Acta Primigenia,* 124–25. Gayley ascribes the first theatrical version of this story to Hilarius, a twelfth-century Anglo-Norman. Gayley also transcribes the text of one medieval version of it. It is full of rowdy, humorous, and violent action. Charles M. Gayley, *Plays of Our Forefathers, and Some of the Traditions upon Which They Were Founded* (New York: Duffield, 1907), 63–65.

36   Iohannem Daiconum, *Vita* 22, in Falconi, *Acta Primigenia,* 125.

37   Jones, *Saint Nicholas of Myra, Bari, and Manhattan,* 173.

38   Patrick Geary, *Furta Sacra: Theft of Relics in the Central Middle Ages* (Princeton: Princeton University Press, 1991).

39   Plate XIV, *Nicolaus Studi Storici* 19.1–2 (Bari: Centro Studi Nicolaiani, 2008).

40   Nicephorus, *Historia translationis S. Nicolai* 2, in Falconi, *Acta Primigenia,* 132.

41   Nicephorus, *Historia translationis S. Nicolai* 4, in Falconi, *Acta Primigenia,* 133–34.

42   Gregory of Tours, *Glory of the Confessors,* 33, 65; also see Peter Brown, *The Cult of the Saints* (Chicago: University of Chicago Press, 1981), 92.

43   Nicephorus, *Historia Translationis S. Nicolai* 5, in Falconi, *Acta Primigenia,* 134.

44   Elisa Ottani, "San Nicola nelle Tradizioni Popolari" (academic thesis, Universita degli Studi di Genova, 1959).

45   Nicephorus, *Historia Translationis S. Nicolai* 12, in Falconi, *Acta Primigenia,* 137.

46   John the Archdeacon, cited in Jones, *Saint Nicholas of Myra, Bari, and Manhattan,* 195.

47   Nicephorus, *Historia Translationis S. Nicolai* 12, in Falconi, *Acta Primigenia,* 137.

48   Gerardo Cioffari, *Basilica of Saint Nicholas* (Bari: Centro Studi Nicolaiani, 1997), 46.

49   Richer de Senones, *Gesta Senoniensis Ecclesiae,* 283–84; cited in Jean-Luc Fray, *Villes et bourgs de Lorraine: réseaux urbains et centralité au Moyen Âge* (Clermont-Ferrand: Presses Universitates Blaise-Pascal, 2007), 216.

---

50 Fray, *Villes et bourgs*, 219.

51 In the same way, heartsick mothers trekked to Rome to light votive candles before the prison chains of St. Peter, housed in a humble basilica a few blocks from the Colosseum known as San Pietro in Vincoli ("Saint Peter in Chains").

52 Jones, *Saint Nicholas of Myra, Bari, and Manhattan*, 202.

53 Gerry Bowler, *Santa Claus: A Biography* (Toronto: McClelland & Stewart, 2005), 17.

54 Carol Myers, "Four Faces of Nicholas—Who Is He in His Hometown?" from St. Nicholas Center website, http://www.stnicholas center.org/pages/demre-statues/, accessed November 2, 2011.

55 Hugh Pope, "Moslem Turks Have a Bone to Pick Over the Lost Relics of St. Nicholas," *Wall Street Journal*, August 31, 1998, Eastern ed., B1.

56 William J. Bennett, *The True Saint Nicholas: Why He Matters to Christmas* (New York: Howard Books, 2009), 71.

57 Anna Jameson, *Sacred and Legendary Art*, 2 vols., 4th ed. (London: Longman, Green, Brown, & Longmans, 1863), 2:450.

58 Jameson, *Sacred and Legendary Art*, 450.

59 Karl Meisen, *Nikolauskult und Nikolausbrauch im Abendlande* (Düsseldorf: Schwann, 1931), 126–76.

Recommended Reading

The two most important twentieth-century contributions to the story of St. Nicholas came from Gustav Anrich and Gerardo Cioffari, respectively. Gustav Anrich's two-volume *Hagios Nikolaos: Der heilige Nikolaus in der griechischen Kirche* (Leipzig: Teubner, 1913, 1917) is an indispensable aid to Nicholas studies. The first volume reproduces all the relevant ancient Greek texts, and the second volume offers detailed appraisals, dates, commentaries, and comparisons. Since the publication of Anrich's collection, Gerardo Cioffari has enhanced, added to, and corrected the work where needed. The result—*San Nicola nella Critica Storica* (Bari: Centro Studi Nicolaiani, 1987)—is undoubtedly the most comprehensive treatment of the relevant source material to date. Furthermore, it establishes the definitive facts concerning Nicholas' life. For a short, English-language summary of Cioffari's findings, see his *Saint Nicholas: His Life, Miracles and Legends*, translated by Victoria Sportelli (Bari: Centro Studi Nicolaiani, 2008). Other significant works include Maria T. Bruno's reappraisal of the Greek sources in *San Nicola nella fonti narrative greche* (Bari: Centro Studi Nicolaiani, 1985) and Aart Blom's archaeological information in *Nikolaas van Myra en zijn tijd* (Hilversum: Verloren, 1998).

A number of good studies have been published regarding the long development of the cult of St. Nicholas, the history of his feast day, regional lore, and local customs throughout Europe and America. Most important among them: Karl Meisen, *Nikolauskult und Nikolausbrauch im Abendlande* (Mainz: Pädagogischer Verlag Schwann Düsseldorf, 1931, 1981); Charles W. Jones, *Saint Nicholas of Myra, Bari, and Manhattan* (Chicago: University of Chicago Press, 1978); and Phyllis Siefker, *Santa Claus, Last of the Wild Men: The Origins and Evolution of Saint Nicholas, Spanning 50,000 Years* (Jefferson, N.C.: McFarland, 1997).

For an informed reconstruction of the origins of Santa Claus in America, I would recommend three recent sources: Stephen Nissenbaum, *The Battle for Christmas: A Cultural History of America's Most Cherished Holiday* (New York: Vintage, 1997); Don Foster, "Yes, Virginia, There Was a Santa Claus," in his book titled *Author Unknown* (New York: Henry Holt, 2000), 221–75; and Gerry Bowler, *Santa Claus: A Biography* (Toronto: McClelland & Stewart, 2005). Some recently published and noteworthy books aimed at popular audiences include the entertaining travelogue by Jeremy Seal, *Nicholas: The Epic Journey from Saint to Santa Claus* (New York: Bloomsbury, 2005); Joe Wheeler and Jim Rosenthal's colorful *St. Nicholas: A Closer Look at Christmas* (Nashville: Nelson, 2006); and William J. Bennett's smartly written *The True Saint Nicholas: Why He Matters to Christmas* (New York: Howard Books, 2009). For a remarkable collection of Nicholas-related images, St. Nicholas churches, annual celebrations, and current customs, see the St. Nicholas Center website (www.stnicholascenter.org), professionally maintained and regularly updated by Carol Myers.

Index

Index

Index

Index

Proclus, 13–14, 142

Procopius, 13–14, 173

Reginold (bishop of Eichstätt),
50–51

Richer de Senones, 187

Sadko, 129–30

Saint-Nicolas-de-Port, 187

Santa Claus, 1–3, 5–6, 8–9, 11, 17,
63, 76, 141, 146, 188–90, 226

Seal, Jeremy, 226

Ševčenko, Nancy Patterson, 10

Severus, Sulpicius, 29–30, 171

Siefker, Phyllis, 226

sign of the cross, 85, 123–24, 175

Socrates (Scholasticus), 16, 107,
109, 137, 143

Sozomenus, 16, 138

St. Nicholas Day, 12, 28, 50, 149

Sundblom, Haddon, 6

Symeon (Metaphrastes), 9–10,
17, 38–40, 62–63, 80, 81, 121,
156, 170

Symeon (Stylites), 71

taxation, 40, 95, 113, 157–61

Tertullian, 56, 69

thaumaturge, 2, 81

Thecla, St., 90, 140

Theodore the Lector, 14, 16

Theodoret of Cyrrhus, 71, 107,
117, 123, 134–37

Theofrid (abbot of Echternach),
172

Theognis, 107–9

Thomas (Aquinas), 72–73

translation of relics, 180

veneration, 12, 23, 32, 36–38, 71,
112, 122, 127, 141, 173, 191

virginity, 28, 39, 46, 69

virtue, 27, 34, 39, 46, 55, 63–64,
66, 69, 73, 143, 162, 165,
168–69

Wheeler, Joe, 9–10, 226

Wilkinson, Caroline, 4–5

Wood, John Turtle, 19–20

Xanthaopoulos, Nicephorus
Kallistos, 92

Zelechy (Prince), 129

Zosimus, 58, 139, 161